THE MILLENNIUM POSTPONED

By the same author

THE MILLENNIUM POSTPONED

Edward Hyams

SECKER & WARBURG
LONDON

First published in England 1974 by
Martin Secker & Warburg Limited
14 Carlisle Street, London WIV 6NN

Copyright © Edward Hyams 1973

436 20996 9

Printed in Great Britain by
Northumberland Press Limited
Gateshead

Dedicated to the victims of bureaucracy past and present, wherever they have been, are and will be.

Contents

Preface

As I am not an historian but a polemicist making use of history
I can quote a witticism of the philosopher Dean Inge who once
said that events in the past could be roughly divided into those
that probably never happened and those which do not matter.
The lesser historians have been obliged to pretend that what
doesn't matter does; the rare great ones distil from the events
which probably never happened the essence of what men once
felt and thought the myth implicit in the tradition that those
events did happen. This is valuable work: for, despite the
vulgar meaning of the word, myths are true; nothing truer.

To write this book which I had long had at heart I did all in
my power to rid my mind of cant—in this case the dense fog of
painstaking scholasticism which has accumulated round the
noble story of men's attempt to get the exploiter/exploited society
off our backs and give us a just society. Their splendid purpose
is not advanced nor better understood as a result of discussions,
however long and however erudite, of the exact meaning of a
phrase used by Marx or of the number of anarchists who could
dance on a needle's point.

To accomplish my purpose of getting back and down through
the murk to the essence of one of the noblest myths we have
lived by, I had to read a great deal of history and to intrude into
areas where I was as a child; and to impose on myself the duty
of being the sort of child who can see that the emperor is naked.
This made it advisable to have the book read in manuscript by a
number of specialists and each found fault: one objected to the
spelling of Russian names; another found that I was sometimes
out by a year or even two in the dates of publication attributed
to source books; a third disagreed about the number of Mao
Tse-tung's children. I was grateful for their corrections, meekly

accepted their rebukes, and went painstakingly through my work again and again in an effort to eliminate cause for complaint; and all the time I had in my mind the story of T. E. Lawrence correcting the proofs of *The Seven Pillars of Wisdom* and answering a proof-reader's reproach that he had spelt his camel's name in seven different ways with the words, *She was a splendid beast.*

If such errors have slipped through the net I am sorry for it; but also point out that this book is not meant to be a work of reference but a polemical pamphlet. If one treads on a man's toes and he happens to suffer from corns, he may slap your face: I am braced.

EDWARD HYAMS

Part One

THE THEORISTS

ONE

From the Golden Age
to the Millennium

'The earth is the Lord's and
the fulness thereof.'

Socialism is the name we give to a rational attempt to give
expression, in the social life of mankind, to an irrational belief in
immanent justice. That this belief is irrational by no means
invalidates the attempt, nor does it necessarily reduce its chances
of success. The greatest invention of mankind and one of the
most powerful prime movers of mankind's acts, love(*agape* : *eros*
is another matter), has no foundation in the rational observation
of nature. So human, that is so humane, so alien to nature is the
idea 'justice' that the mere observation of nature has led great
and good men to the conclusion that if God exists he must be
an insane sadist, whereas they should have concluded that He
has no moral qualities at all.*

The Greeks, looking clear-eyed and with their minds free from
cant at their own nature and that of their institutions, concluded
that the Millennium, when immanent justice was manifest in the
social institutions of mankind and which they called the Golden

---

* Spinoza argued that since God has the power to create everything,
He could not refrain from creating the whole range from imperfection
to total perfection. This is tantamount to saying that He could not *not*
create a universe which, from the human point of view, is necessarily
unjust. In other words, justice cannot possibly be a Divine concept, for
it would, as it were, disturb the balanced ecology of the universe. In
a comment (*Carnets*) Camus points out: ' ... cet univers ne tend à
rien et ne vient de rien ...' a view which has the support of at least
one important school of physicists ' ... parce qu'il est déjà accompli *et
l'a toujours été* ... Il n'a pas de tragédie parce qu'il n'a pas d'histoire.
Il est *inhumain à souhait.*' (My italics). If this be accepted, the notion of
immanent justice, or of any other moral attribute including love, is
merely absurd: and I find it impossible not to accept it, for the argument has the simple elegance which distinguishes truth. The more
credit, then, to mankind, conceiver of the notions love and justice: the
creature accomplishes what the Creator cannot. I am aware of the flaw in
this argument but accept the imperfection.

Age, must have been somewhere in the limbo of the past.* Justice was a condition which man had fallen from, not a condition he was rising to. Plato, in *The Republic*, produced a plan for restoring it, but made a shocking mess of the job in practice as adviser to the government of Syracuse.

Two things made possible the 18th- and 19th-century shift of the Millennium into the future: awareness, driven into the hearts and minds of one part of the human race by Christ's teaching,† of the sufferings of the poor which became, with Christianity, a reproach to the rich; and the evolution of an industrial technology which made the elimination of those sufferings an attainable goal.

The origin of belief in immanent justice is curious. Justice, I repeat, is not a concept to be found in nature; indeed, the rational justification of, for example, the capitalist system, is that it truly reflects the natural condition, that is, injustice, which must be accepted as man's, because nature's, rule. And because justice is not in nature it will not be found as a concern of any of the myriad gods invented by man to give nature a persona or a creator (the existence of a watch implies the existence of a watchmaker), until man, having conceived the idea 'justice', attributed it to his gods and, in his humility, made them the fount of justice; just as the Essenes, followed by the Christians, defied the evidence of their senses to make God the fount of love.

But since the gods had to be used to sanction the law by which society came to be ordered; and since the grossest inequities

---

* Dr A. R. Burn in his Pelican *History of Greece* suggests a literal derivation of the term 'Golden Age'. The Greeks of the Iron Age, he says, knew that it had been preceded by a Bronze Age and knew something of the grandeur of Minoan and Mycenaean. They deduced a still earlier Silver Age, and before that a Gold Age. Thus, there is a decline in the nobility of the principal metal used and, by extension, of human conduct and institutions.

† Camus went so far as to describe the preoccupation with social justice and immanent justice as a 'Christian perversion' and as 'absurd'. 'Dans le drame antique celui qui paie c'est toujours celui qui a raison, Prométhée, Oedipe, Oreste etc. Mais cela n'a pas d'importance. De toute façon ils finissent tous aux enfers, raison ou tort. Il n'y a ni récompense, ni châtiment. D'où, à nos yeux assombris par des siècles de perversion chrétienne, le caractère gratuit de ces drames ...'

(*Carnets*)

were necessarily defended by that very law which was concerned
to establish and institutionalize property rights, it became necessary to conceive of divine justice as mysterious, to account for
God's ways not only to man but to all living creatures by supposing that only God could know all the conditions in the universe
on which his conduct was based, so that what seemed to man
unjust was, *sub specie aeternitatis* and given God's all-knowledge,
perfect justice. In short, the attribution of man's own invention,
justice, to God produced the idea of immanent justice and, by
extension, of natural law. And this I call irrational because it
certainly cannot be deduced from the observed facts of nature.

As to how justice was conceived, that is not quite so clear.
Ideas, ideals, do not come out of the blue, thereafter to be acted
on; necessity is their mother, as it is of all inventions. They are
as much the outcome of need as are material tools, although
their evolution and refinement in the course of time often masks
this truth. Hammers and saws were invented because man needed
them: so was justice. The most probable ancestor of justice is
jealous resentment: the numerous weak, resenting the greater
wealth and happiness of the few strong, combined to prevent
them from appropriating more of their mathematically equitable
share of the good things—land, for instance—than they would
otherwise have done. So justice becomes equal shares, an arrangement which is not in nature, where all living creatures take and
use in proportion to their strength and cunning. Equal shares
becomes the social aim. What is expedient for the weak majority
becomes 'justice', becomes 'right' and 'fair'.

Socialism began as an attempt to revert from the institution of
private property in goods thought of as naturally 'common', back
to what was supposed to have been the natural and uncorrupted
respect for immanent justice implicit in, among other things,
common ownership, that is to say, communism.

By no means all the suppositions of the earliest 'socialists' (the
condition long antedates the name for it) touching the primitive
past of mankind were fairy-stories. Take the case of private
property in land: it was believed that land was originally owned
in common. In so far as it was 'owned' at all, this was true. The
fact is that the earth was indeed the Lord's and the fulness

thereof, and the animal called man, like the animal called tiger or the animal called earthworm, lived off its produce, his fellow living creatures, vegetable and animal, or the carrion of their dead.

In common with some animal species, man claimed for himself a particular piece of territory during the time of his residence in any given place. His title to it was the threat of force: on the whole 'territorial' species respect that threat. There can have been, in the hunting and gathering communities of the Palæolithic, no question of (and no point in) private property in land within the territory appropriated by a group: nor can the question have arisen in early (Neolithic) farming communities. As for the pastoral communities, pastoralism, developing into stock farming, had its origin in the parasitism of small groups of men on moving herds of game animals and thus grew into a nomadic way of life whose very condition was 'the land is free to all', though that concept might be limited by tacit agreement on boundaries separating one from another group of nomads and made necessary by expedient 'territorialism' backed by the implicit threat of force.

So that, in the case of land, it would seem that communism was indeed the rule. Once universal, it survived in some communities into historical time, even into our own time, and was the economic basis of great empires, like that of the Inca in Peru, Chile, Bolivia and Ecuador.

There is some evidence that in the very earliest industrial enterprises, enterprises in which men, instead of hunting, gathering or growing their food, manufactured tools or utensils and traded them for food, were also collective. It is inconceivable that the flint in the Grimes Graves flint mine in Cambridgeshire was thought of as 'belonging' to anyone. It was mined and manufactured into tools for exchange (sale) by a community of equals; and probably any man who tried to assert title to it—which he could have done, of course, only by force—would have been dealt with by means of a flint-headed club. But in that case, how did the institution of property in land and minerals come into existence? The insight of a great comic novelist will be useful here. It is the holy man Maël, evangelist of the Penguins, speaking:

'Behold, Bulloch my son, look towards the Surelle. There in that sweet, cool valley, I see a dozen Penguin men busy knocking each other down with their spades and mattocks with which they would be better occupied cultivating the land. Meanwhile, even more cruel than their menfolk, the women are tearing at each other's faces with their nails. Alas! Bulloch, my son, why are they thus massacring each other?'

'Out of the spirit of association, Father, and foresight for the future,' Bulloch replied, 'for man is by nature sociable and endowed with foresight. Such is his character ... those Penguins there, O master, are appropriating land.'

'Could they not appropriate it with less violence?' the old man enquired; 'even as they fight they are exchanging abuse and menaces. I cannot hear the actual words, but they appear, from the tone, to be irritated.'

'They are mutually accusing each other of theft and usurpation,' Bulloch replied. 'Such is the general sense of their exchanges.'

Thereupon the holy man Maël, clasping his hands, gave vent to a deep sigh and cried,

'Do you not see, my son, that enraged madman there, biting off the nose of his prostrate adversary, and that other bashing in a woman's head with a huge stone?'

'I see them,' Bulloch replied. 'They are engaged in founding the Law and creating the institution of property. They are establishing the principles of civilization ... by enclosing their fields ... their work will be consecrated throughout the centuries by lawyers, protected and confirmed by magistrates ...'

(Anatole France: *Penguin Island*)

But force was not the sole early title to land. When the leader in hunting and war turned into the King, and the magician who placated the gods on behalf of his fellows turned into the High Priest, they, severally or as one, became, as incorporations of the community's soul, the living depositories of its 'property'. The land was the people's, but the King was the incarnation of their collective. The land which he allowed a man for his sustenance was held from him, that is from the collective, in a sort of trust. By a corruption of that institution, the King came to regard what he, on his side, held in trust from the people as his own alienable property, and as such he could sell it or give it away. As Proudhon was to say: property is theft.

If, despite its origin in theft,* private property in land, the 'means of production' *par excellence*, and in the minerals under the land survived and flourished as an institution against all attempts, both pacific and violent, to put an end to it, it was partly because ownership conferred on the owner the economic strength to defend what he had and partly because his ownership was defended by philosophers both secular and religious. Aristotle, for example, argued that private property in land was economically superior to collective ownership because a man takes better care of things he owns than of things the community owns; and nearly two thousand years later, St Thomas Aquinas was of a like opinion. Yet both Greek philosophers and Christian teachers did hark back nostalgically to a happier age, an uncorrupted time, the Golden Age of primitive communism, that is to say of manifest justice in tune with immanent justice; and looked forward to a Millennium when that Golden Age would begin anew and common men be happy, while men like themselves would be relieved of the burden of guilt loaded upon them by the intolerable spectacle of the injustices entailed by the institution of private property.

The first great teacher to advocate a return to communism as an essential condition of a just society did so with fortuitous irony, just at a moment in time when, in England, the common land was being taken from the people by the Enclosures: Sir Thomas More's *Utopia* (it means 'Nowhere') was published in 1516, and the land of Utopia is what we should now call a Socialist country. But perhaps the irony was not fortuitous: More was aware of the distress of the poor majority of Englishmen. His book may also have been intended as a counterblast to Machiavelli's *The Prince*. It was written in Latin and is an imaginary conversation with a traveller called Ralph Hythlodaye who has discovered the island of Utopia. The inhabitants of the

---

* Since the act in question antedated the concept 'justice', the word 'theft' in this context is really an anachronism; but let it pass.

island despise gold, have no private property but hold all goods in common, reject war as a political means and tolerate all religious persuasions whatsoever. The book was widely translated and was still having an influence on socialist thought as late as the 19th century.

But Utopia was premature—it was not until the 18th century that men began to think seriously of applying the very successful monastic practice of running great estates co-operatively to whole nations and vast territories. The pioneers of socialist thought were French and English: Morelly (*Code de la Nature*, 1755); Jean Meslier (*Testament*, written in the 1730s but published in 1764); Thomas Spence (*The Mode of Adminstering the Landed Estate of the Nation*, 1775); Mably, who, in *De la législation* (1778) made a thorough examination of the basis of social justice in economic equality; and William Ogilvie (*The Right of Property in Land*, 1782) all adopted communism in at least one respect, the nationalization of the land. They were all Marxists *avant la lettre* in that they saw the State as the only possible trustee and administrator of the people's property. Here the next of the great pioneers parted company with them: William Godwin (1756-1836) was, like Mably, concerned in his *Enquiry Concerning Political Justice* (1793) to discover the true basis for social justice. He found it in economic equality; but he concluded that this was not possible without the complete abolition of private property and, moreover, without getting rid of the State, since it was in the State that injustice was necessarily incorporate.

> 'With what delight,' he wrote, 'must every well-informed friend of mankind look forward to the dissolution of political government, of that brute engine which has been the only perennial cause of the vices of mankind, and which has mischiefs of various sorts incorporated with its substance and no otherwise to be removed than by its utter annihilation.'

Godwin, like so many English socialists to come, began as a radical Nonconformist. His father was a Nonconformist minister, his grandfather had been a famous Dissenting preacher and he himself was for five years, until 1783 when he faced the fact that he had no vocation, a pastor and preacher. Indeed, even as a schoolboy, he had tried out his powers of moving his fellows by religious eloquence. Like so many of his spiritual heirs he lacked only one quality, but it was a very important one for dealing with the realities: a sense of humour, for which a synonym might be a sense of the real. He belonged to the great and noble and slightly ridiculous race so superlatively depicted by George Eliot in *Felix Holt*.

Godwin believed that human societies originated in man's realization of the need for mutual aid; their ideology was Justice, that immanent justice which like all primitive socialists he could not but believe in. Although all government was necessarily evil —here we have the one absolutely manifest truth in his works— since a measure of government might be, temporarily and provisionally, necessary, we had better choose the least evil of the several regimes which were offered: democracy, even though social justice is clearly incompatible with any kind of authority. Democracy, then, but decentralized down to parish level. As for the economy, co-operation is the only possible answer, and it must not be carried too far lest the co-operative harden into an institution wielding authority in which, necessarily, injustice would become embodied.

The problem posed by the human need for differentials in rewards is not shirked: the man who contributes more than the average to the common wealth and wellbeing will want to be more highly rewarded than less gifted men. But—again that simple-mindedness—in a truly egalitarian society outstanding contributors to the common wealth will find their satisfaction in the distinction which the superior value of their contribution confers.

Like other socialists after him, Godwin made the mistake of arguing that the technological progress which he foresaw, a progress which would reduce the average working week to three hours* of labour, would confer a greater and greater freedom from the need for association and collaboration, thus completely freeing the individual not only from political and social institutions but even from the need for economic co-operation. It was always institutions of all kinds which he saw as evil, for they necessarily entail the injustice of a discipline imposed upon the individual despite his own will, instead of leaving him to impose

*Literally, half-an-hour per day.

upon himself that self-discipline in regard to the feelings and wellbeing of others which would arise from his own moral nature, part of the moral nature of the universe, a version, here, of Fournier's universal harmony, in short, of that chimera, immanent justice or 'natural law'.

So much for the father of anarchism. Like his predecessors and contemporaries, English or French, he was a mere theorist. But there was one man at least who tried to put socialism into practice before it had been—one cannot say 'invented', so I shall say 'identified'. His name was François Noël (Gracchus) Babeuf and he was a French revolutionary. His attempt had no consequences and is not important but is worth a brief notice.

Socialism was never an aim of the French Revolution as a whole: even the Ultra-Democrats, the Left-wing extremists of the Paris Commune, the, as it were, *soviet* of that revolution, in which the voice of the working class (as against that of the middle class and the peasant in the various Assemblies) made demands which were purely political and never dreamed of advocating any kind of collectivization, or organizing the working class with a view to seizing from the middle class the power which they were snatching from the aristocracy. Babeuf and his friends were, therefore, exceptional. Calling themselves the Society of Equals, they mounted a conspiracy to seize power and not only grant the most extreme demands of the Commune's Left wing, but impose collectivization of all property whatsoever and absolute equality of incomes. The conspiracy was discovered and Babeuf guillotined (1797) and that, for the time being, was the end of practical socialism. The conditions in which it would become acceptable to a sufficiently large number of people and, indeed, necessary, did not yet exist: they were to be created by the phenomenon miscalled the Industrial Revolution.

If Babeuf's was the only practical socialist conspiracy produced by the French Revolution, he was not the only man to think in terms of economic revolution in the context of a revolution which was primarily political and dominated by the bourgeoisie. The *Enragés* movement, centred on Jacques Roux and Jean Varlet, reacting against bourgeois domination like the Bolsheviks and Social Revolutionaries to the Kadets of Kerensky's government in 1917, and against the unrelieved grinding poverty of the working class, saw what we now call 'industrial action', amounting to economic revolution, as a better way to re-order society than political action. In this they anticipated the syndicalists. Roux, the ablest of the *Enragés*, was curé of a country parish and preached to his congregation that the land belonged to all, equally. An ascetic, living in strictest Christian poverty, he was one of the men who led Louis XVI out to the guillotine. His ferocity towards kings and the rich and mighty was the product of his compassion for the way poor shoemakers and carpenters of the Paris district where he lived. He was condemned to death by the Jacobins—Robespierre could no more stomach a real revolutionary than Stalin could—cheated the gallows by suicide, and before he died declared that he did not blame the Tribunal. It had acted according to law; he, for his part, had acted according to liberty. Varlet, Roux's friend and associate and last of the *Enragés*, made an even more significant statement before he died:

> For any reasoning being, government and revolution are incompatible, at least unless the people wish to constitute the organs of power in permanent insurrection against themselves.

Trotskyism *avant la lettre*: but, I repeat, the conditions for socialist revolution did not exist at the end of the 18th century. It took the process miscalled the Industrial Revolution to create them.

TWO

Hope out of Misery

Before that abrupt acceleration of industrial development which
followed the invention of steam-driven machinery and which
was called the Industrial Revolution, the conditions in which a
political and economic revolution might be made and socialism
installed did not, then, exist. This is by no means to say that
there was no call for 'socialism', no economic injustice embodied
in society in those pre-steam-power conditions: had that been
so, there would have been nothing to inspire, or maybe 'provoke'
is the right word, the writings of those philosophers who were
proto-socialists, men like Mably and Hall. Inequity in the distribution of wealth and power was, of course, gross: but since,
as we shall presently see, it was to be shown that socialism could
only be installed by the class which created wealth, that is to
say the workers, that class had to be strong before a socialist
revolution, peaceful or otherwise, could be made. Yet it could
not, in the nature of things, be politically or economically strong
until *after* a measure of socialist-inspired legislation had made
it so. But it could be numerically by far the strongest in the
world; and it was the growth of machine industry which made
it so.

In the process, industrial development did something else to
bring about the precondition (see Chapters Three and Four) for
socialist revolution: it transferred economic and political power
from the aristocracy of landowners, to the industrial and commercial middle class, the 'bourgeoisie', and it was the growth of the
bourgeoisie's wealth and might which generated that huge class
of industrial workers, the 'proletariat', strong enough in numbers
to seize economic and political power for the only class which,
in equity, had a right to it (again, see Chapters Three and Four).

The reason why the term Industrial Revolution is objection-
able is that there never was any such phenomenon: the growth
of industry was evolutionary, an accelerating and continuous
process from such beginnings as the prehistoric Grimes Graves

flint-tool factory until our own time, and it is, of course, still continuing and still accelerating.* At times progress was so slow as to be scarcely noticeable. There may have been fallings-off and fallings-back but at other times there were great forward surges, in the 14th century for example, again in the 16th and 17th, in the late 18th, and in the mid-20th. By way of example, take a brief look at the process in England where, as a result of Henry VIII's confiscation of monastic lands, capital for industrial investment became available earlier than in most European countries.

When the wealth in land possessed by the monasteries was seized and redistributed to the King's friends in the 16th century, it created a class of capitalists, men with money to invest. This generated a boom in house-building, in ship-building and the carrying trades and, at the same time, stimulated improvement in agricultural technology which, in their turn, produced more wealth for investment which stimulated the founding of new industries, while the agricultural improvements and enclosures created a class of dispossessed and unemployed peasants, that is to say a pool of labour available to capital. At the beginning of the 16th century there was not a single paper-mill in England; by the end of it paper-mills driven by water were established on a great many English rivers. In the same century were founded the heavy armaments, gunpowder, saltpetre and sugar-refining industries. The discovery by prospectors of zinc in Somerset and new sources of copper in the West Country, where copper-mining had in any case been a prehistoric industry, attracted capital which was looking, as it were, for work, and generated a new metallurgical industry.

Here, as early as 1619, is an early case of bad industrial relations of the kind we are painfully familiar with. George Lowe, a leading capitalist in the Yorkshire alum industry centred on Whitby, writes of this industry:

> ... a distracted worke in severall places and sundry partes, not possible to be performed by anie one man nor by a fewe. But by a multitude of the baser sort of whom the most parte are idle, careless and false in their labour.†

* See my *The Changing Face of Britain*, Longmans Young Books, 1974.

† Landsdowne *MSS* quoted by J. U. Nef, *Essays in Economic History*, London, 1961.

The alum industry was not the only one employing 'a multitude' in each factory, cannon-founders employed as many as two hundred men, and at least one paper-mill had six hundred on its payroll. By the mid-16th century steel-mills and coal-mines were adding their quota to the growing class of exploited workers, that is workers who were paid the barest minimum wage out of the new wealth they were creating. Opencast coal-mining had started at least as early as the 12th century and by 1400 there were Tyne Valley pits yielding upwards of one hundred tons of coal a year, and coal exports to Europe had reached seven thousand tons a year. A century-and-a-half later the figure was half a million tons, and this tale of growth was much the same in other coalfields—Durham, Northumberland, South Wales, the Midlands and Cumberland. The availability of cheap coal for evaporating sea water led to swift growth in the salt industry to supply the rapidly growing demand for salted meat for the provision of ocean-going ships. It was also in the 17th century that the factory replaced the farmhouse in the soap-boiling industry, and brewing, too, began to be shifted from the farmhouse to the brewery employing specialized labour. Weaving and spinning might still be cottage industries—the dark, satanic mills were a by-product of steam-power—but the processes of dyeing, calendering, fulling and so forth, that is of finishing the cloth, were industrialized.

Where did the labour for these industries come from? The capital was self-generating as the volume of trade grew, but what of the hands? Not until the mid-16th century did the population of England recover to its pre-Black Death level and for the next two hundred years it increased only slowly. But also, during those two hundred years, land enclosures were dispossessing the peasantry, creating a labour pool. Then, from the beginning of the 19th century a much faster growth-rate is apparent: from about 1550 to 1800, two-and-a-half centuries, the population doubled to reach just under nine million. *The next doubling took only sixty years* (and the next doubling fewer than forty years, to just under forty million before World War One).

All the factors which contributed to industrial growth worked upon each other to increase the impetus of that growth and force up the rate of acceleration. The spirit of enquiry into nature born of the Renaissance led to physical and chemical inventions which were seized upon by capital seeking investment; population growth and the transformation of agriculture from a labour-intensive industry into one which employed fewer and fewer men per acre put more and more labour at the disposal of urban industry. The search for foreign markets led to the importing of more and of new raw materials and so to the founding of yet more industries, and both these factors stimulated more and faster ship-building and the growth of service industries.

The mastery of steam-power between 1663 when the Marquis of Worcester built a workable steam-engine and 1781 when James Watt found a means of imparting rotary motion to a wheel, resulted in a great surge forward in industrial growth. The new engine both drove the mill machinery and carried its product to market. Steam-engines demanded more coal and more and more iron; demand for coal stimulated deeper and more intensive mining and the steam-engine now did the pumping and lifting. More coal available meant more pig-iron possible, but the more iron was used, the more coal was wanted. From this interaction of coal and iron came the stimulus which created still more industries.

There was, however, under capitalism—the means by which this continuous and accelerating process was brought about—one special condition for success: the class which was piling up all this new wealth had to be denied the fruits of its labour. We tend to look back on the atrocious suffering in poverty and hopeless misery for the workers which industrialization entailed as an avoidable evil: but was it? The surplus value of the product of the worker's labour, had it been fairly distributed (that is, left to its rightful owner, the worker) would not have been available, or would have been so to a much smaller extent, for industrial investment. It was that continuous and continuously growing re-investment which created the whole body of industrial plant; incidentally, it created a class of richer and richer, mightier and mightier capitalists and pointed up the injustice of the whole system. But the system was unjust in much the same way as nature is unjust; it would be possible to argue that Darwin's *Origin of Species* is a justification of capitalism and it is not without significance that Kropotkin, gentlest of the anarchist-socialists, was driven to interpret nature as a system of mutual aid and to deny that it was a competitive system. In a sense we have seen in our own time a speeded-up version of European industrialization: Stalin was faced with the choice between allowing the Russians, the workers, to enjoy a greater and greater share of the surplus value of their labour and slowing the pace of industrialization, or achieving rapid and massive industrialization by 'misappropriating' the fruits of that labour. He chose the latter course and thus became the greatest and most ruthless capitalist of all time.

What, now, has all this to do with socialism? The answer, of course, is 'everything'.

The proto-socialism of the early social philosophers glanced at in Chapter One sought to find a just means of raising the condition of the majority, the peasants chiefly, since there were few industrial workers and the artisan was not badly off, and lowering the unjustly high condition of their exploiters, the landowners, by either the 'nationalization' or the radical re-distribution of land; either the abolition of rent, or its application to the public service. But the process we have just briefly examined, the evolution of industry, generated an industrial working class whose relationship with the capitalist who owned the plant was very much the same as that of the land-worker with the landowner, a relationship of exploited with exploiter. Class-war animus has falsified our view of industrial history in more ways than one: it was not the capitalist who was cruel, it was capitalism—like nature. And this reveals an important truth: capitalism is a primitive economic system which has very little to do with science but relies on much the same exploitation of chance, of the 'random', as does for example, natural selection.

And therefore it had the merit of necessarily generating its destroyer. The urban, industrial working class, the proletariat, was soon by far the largest class in the Western world; and it was also and manifestly unjustly exploited. The *only* source of increase in wealth is labour—the labour of the mind which invents, which penetrates to the workings of nature, which improves technique—the labour of the hand which digs out or grows the raw material of industry, which processes that material into workable form, which manufactures goods from the processed raw material. The social philosophers had made it perfectly clear that there could, in justice, be only one title to the wealth produced by labour: labour.

As I have said above, that gross injustice which had set the social philosophers to work was a mere by-product of capitalism, just as the injustice suffered by the gazelle under the claws of the lion is a by-product of nature. The 'capitalist' was not, originally, wicked; he was as shrewd, as crafty, as 'natural' and therefore as stupid, as the tiger. But men are not lions or gazelles, for they have the means, given the will, to override the 'natural'.

An immense difficulty was an almost universal misunderstanding of the nature of money arising out of the fact that money-tokens originally had intrinsic value. They were as much a 'commodity' as gold, silver or copper. Probably very few things have so hampered the smooth and rapid growth of industry to becoming the servant rather than the cruel master of the majority as the misunderstanding which arose and still arises from this circumstance. Consider this example: the only things which go into the making of a house are timber, bricks, mortar, metals, architectural and trade skills, and labour, labour being also the principal component in the value of the elements listed. I can see no gold coins, no banknotes incorporated in the fabric of any house. I perceive then, that money is, in fact, simply a medium of exchange of goods and services between men. It is clearly monstrous that the hoarding of such tokens should confer on the proprietor economic power, that he, by lending to the architect, the bricklayers, the carpenters, plasterers and paperhangers the means of procuring the materials of their trades and of their subsistence, should be rewarded with the lion's share of the surplus value of the house. In short, as Proudhon was to write: 'What is the capitalist? Everything. What should he be? Nothing.'

The growth of the proletariat to the overwhelming numerical majority made the simple and ugly truth more and more obvious, more and more disgraceful to the thoughtful and feeling members of the society which protected and perpetuated so monstrous an evil. The charitable practised charity; the liberal sought means of reforming society which would avoid unpleasantness for the rich while improving the lot of the poor. But the socialists—the men who were as hard-minded as they were soft-hearted, dreamed of revolution. But if the power conferred by capitalism on the capitalist was a mere by-product of its functioning, it had, in course of time, corrupted the capitalist. Unable or unwilling to see clearly the disgraceful role in which the operation of the system had cast him, he was now ready and willing to defend his privilege, if necessary by force. The proto-socialists had assumed, as I have said, that once the truths they had discovered were clearly demonstrated, all men of goodwill would see that they were the stuff of righteousness and would join in correcting the errors and eliminating the moral flaws embodied in society. But, as Marx was to show, a dominant social class does not voluntarily relinquish power. It must be made to do so.

It was, however, one thing to show that the economic and political system was profoundly unjust, and that only political and economic democracy carried to the point at which all men and women really were equal in terms of both wealth and political power could put society on just lines; it was quite another to work out practical means of installing socialism and, ultimately, communism—that is, economic justice. It was not very difficult, given sufficient research, to define the problem in emotional terms; or to present it in terms proper to ethics; or to present it aesthetically as, for example, Godwin did in *The Adventures of Caleb Williams*, Mrs Gaskell in *North and South* and Gorky in a dozen works. It was very much more difficult to deal with it, as it were, mathematically, to expose the fraud in the story of a Rothschild handing two francs to the man who protested that the millionaire capitalist's wealth should be redistributed to all, as his fair one-thirty-millionth part of the Rothschild fortune owing to the people of France.

What mankind needed was a science of socialism: it is perhaps needless to say, given that we are talking about the 19th century, that it came from Germany. But if the scientific socialism we call Marxism came out of the brains of a genius who had thoroughly digested the material which the proto-socialists had left him, it was generated in the mind or, rather, in the heart of Engels, his warm-hearted and nobly emotional collaborator, by the misery of the majority of the world's people.

THREE

The Social Scientists

Claude de Saint-Simon was a *comte* by birth, born in 1760, into the same family as the ducal memorialist. Like Lafayette, he served against England in the American War of Independence. He escaped the guillotine in the French Revolution by lying low and by renouncing his title: he even made money out of it by speculating in confiscated estates. This, and all the rest of his money, was invested in scientific experiments, and when these had left him a ruined man—he was in serious financial difficulties for the rest of his life—he tried to marry Madame de Staël, the financier Necker's millionaire daughter, on the grounds that they were, respectively, the most remarkable man and the most remarkable woman in the world.

In 1802 Saint-Simon published a pamphlet, *Letters from a Resident of Geneva to his Contemporaries*, in which he proposed a thoroughgoing re-organization of society with the object of speeding up material progress in order to improve the lot of the poorest and most numerous class of the people as quickly as possible. These *Letters* were followed by other works, notably *The Industrial System* published between 1820 and 1823. In all of them he shows himself to have been the first real social scientist and, at the same time, the first scientific socialist. But his was a socialism with a difference: for what Saint-Simon envisaged was an élitism of the kind bitterly condemned by the latter-day socialists of the New Left, and which amounts to a repudiation of democracy.

A troublesome flaw in all perfectionist political-economic philosophies, with the exception of anarchism, is that they imply the attainment of a state of political-economic stasis. Once you have established your Utopia you cannot reasonably alter it, for almost by definition it can only be changed for the worse:* that

* In Butler's *Erewhon* technological progress was sternly suppressed.

is the trouble with paradise.

In any natural mixed community composed of certain species of plants and animals in which the 'balance of nature' is preserved there is, in fact, a state which might, without stretching the meaning of the word too far, be called stasis: the interdependent species hold each other in check—the herbivorous animals controlling the herbs, the carnivores the herbivores, etc., producing a condition, in biological terms, rather like that in a field of mutually neutralizing forces in physics. Such changes as there may be to the advantage of one species at the expense of another are not only so slow as not to be noticed in a single or even in several generations, but will not disturb the overall balance since all the species will make minor adjustments to accommodate them. But trees, shrubs, tigers and butterflies are not trying to alter their condition; man is. They have only to live their lives, man has to try to live it more fully. Consciousness has afflicted him with divine discontent. In aspiring to paradise (which, if one ignores the hideous sufferings of individuals and thinks only of species, is the natural condition), man aspires to a condition in which he would either have to modify his own nature or die of boredom. The condition of Adam and Eve was the condition of animals in a land without predators, like Australia, and original sin is the assertion of human consciousness. All makers of Utopias are, usually unwittingly, trying to lead mankind to what may, indeed, be his final condition: the anthill, the hive, immutable because, within expedient limitations, perfect.

The real strength, the strong appeal of capitalism,* is that it is a gamble. The Saint-Simonian new order would have produced a comfortable and just stasis. Only the anarchists, among all the varieties of socialists, escapes from this trap. From which we may conclude that since capitalism is, in the last analysis, intolerable because it offends against our sense of justice and against the common sense of any reasoning man, the choice before us is between anarchism and the Hive.

What Saint-Simon proposed to do was to rid the nation of

---

* Here, I mean, of course, *Realkapital*. For the modification of both Leninist 'Imperialism' and Stalinist 'Socialism' towards a common goal in the Hive, see Chapter Nineteen.

the incubus of the merely ambitious and grasping adventurer
in politics and the economy, and hand over to professionals:
that is, to recruit the most brilliant men in science, the arts and
industry and entrust them with the organization and administration of the national economy. Capitalism, governed in its operation by incalculable 'market' forces, would thus (but without
revolutionary animus and quite incidentally, as one sweeps up
so much old rubbish) be eliminated and the nation's business
would be run by means of planning followed by scientific management. The State, at least as a political entity, would disappear.
In the place of its organs would appear a board of business
and technological directors. In short, Saint-Simon was foreshadowing the managerial society, but again with a difference:
for his managers would be the servants of the community serving
its needs, not the servants of capitalist companies whose business
is to make profits for their shareholders and only incidentally to
serve the community.

There would be some division of this labour of government.
Thus, the men of science and the artists would be responsible
for the intellectual and spiritual business of the nation, while
the industrialists—and it is important to note that among them
Saint-Simon included the workers themselves—would wield the
temporal power. The very first business of this meritocracy must
be to raise the standard of living of the poor workers in agriculture and industry to a decent human level.

Every new order needs an ideology. Whether Saint-Simon
realized this coldly, or whether he personally felt the need, is
not clear: at all events, he adopted the Christian Moral Law
(in *The New Christianity*, 1825) as the ideology of his new order.

How was this new order to be established? Saint-Simon was
certainly a kind of socialist but he was never a revolutionary.
None of the early social scientists was; it seems not to have
crossed their minds that their rational arguments would be resis-
ted, that interest and privilege would fight ferociously in their
own defence. Proudhon was, perhaps, the first of them to realize
clearly that the great landlord, the industrial and commercial
capitalist, is necessarily a *méchant animal* who, when attacked,
defends himself. Saint-Simon, in his innocence, that debilitating innocence of the man of good will, did not for a moment

entertain the notion of using force to establish the new order; he probably believed that it would not be necessary to do more than use persuasion and propaganda. In this respect, this brilliant and compassionate Frenchman was the first of a long line of liberal socialists who have supposed, or acted as if they supposed, that a majority of men were as rational, reasonable and inspired by goodwill as themselves and that cogent argument inspired by good sense and generous feeling has the power to change habits, overcome prejudices and neutralize self-interest. Nothing has done more to ensure the failure of the socialist Millennium to materialize than the simple-minded goodness of heart of those who, had they not been simple-minded and good-hearted, would never have conceived the Millennium in the first place.

Intellectually more brilliant even than Saint-Simon among the pioneers striving for the Millennium was another Frenchman, François Fourier, born at Besançon in 1772.

Fourier's first work was his *Théorie des quatres mouvements et des destinées générales*, published in 1808. It was based on a notion of immanent justice in that he predicted a principle of universal harmony which entailed an anticipation of Sigmund Freud in the argument that crime and vice are due not to evil, which Fourier simply did not believe in, but to mental sickness caused by the repression of strong passions into the subconscious (although he did not, of course, use that word). What Fourier urged was a re-organization of society to bring it into tune with his universal harmony, and he offered a detailed plan for accomplishing this end. It was socialist in so far as it was based on planning and the rational service of real needs; on the other hand, it did not promote the abolition of capitalism although the managers of the new order would be chosen not because they controlled capital, but for their talent. Fourier also concerned himself with the distribution of the surplus product of industry. He was no egalitarian: five-twelfths were to go to labour, three-twelfths to the planning and directing intellectuals, and four-twelfths to capital. This Fourieresque new order was to be installed by the establishment of small model communities—pilot socialist communes—which he conceived of as expanding to absorb the whole economic activity of the nation.

Although, then, Saint-Simonian socialism eliminated capitalism it did so quite incidentally and without revolutionary feeling, while Fourier gave it a very well-remunerated place in his new order. The first of the pioneers to repudiate it, indeed to indict it as a positive evil, was an Englishman, Thomas Paine, who has some claim to be considered co-father, with Godwin, of anarchism.* He accepted government as a necessary evil (only the democratic form being even barely tolerable) but argued that whereas society is a product of our wants, government is a by-product of our wickedness:

> Government, like dress, is a badge of lost innocence; the palaces of kings are built on the ruins of bowers of paradise.

That sorrowful evocation of the Golden Age is from his *Common Sense.* For Paine, government, like capitalism, was a wicked interference with that 'mutual dependence and reciprocal interest which man has upon man and all parts of the civilized community upon each other ... common interest regulates their concerns and forms their law.'

These ideas were put forward in *The Rights of Man*, written as an answer to Burke's *Reflections on the Revolution in France*, a work which (despite its pompous tediousness so well worthy of the man whose oratory, even more tiresome than the *Philippics*, earned him the title of the 'the dinner-bell' among his fellow MPs because it always cleared the House) made an enormous impression on the class whose privileges seemed threatened by the Revolution. *The Rights of Man* was an illegal publication (a 'seditious libel') but circulated underground in enormous numbers, especially in the industrial regions. Of its arguments the Prime Minister, William Pitt, said, 'Tom Paine is quite in the right but what am I to do? As things are, if I were to encourage his opinions we should have a bloody revolution'—a magnificent example of the separation between rational man and economic man in the late 18th and early 19th centuries. Pitt then did his duty as a servant of the aristocracy and bourgeoisie, and Paine

* It should perhaps be said that George Woodcock (*Anarchism*, 1962) points out that only hindsight establishes these claims: there is no traceable line connecting either Godwin or Paine with the later European anarchists and it was with surprise that, Kropotkin, for example, discovered his own ideas in Godwin.

had to take refuge in France from a capital charge of treason.

Another Englishman, Dr Charles Hall, a physician, moved far beyond Paine towards communism in his *Effects of Civilization on the Peoples of European States*. He seems to have been the first socialist to indict capitalism as the *exploiter* of the workers, that is to introduce, willy-nilly the idea of capitalism as not merely inexpedient but wicked.* Briefly, his conclusions were that the worker, by his labour, produces all the wealth; the capitalist then takes the greater part away from him in profit, rent and interest. The first part of the remedy Hall proposed was nationalization of the land, and then its division into farmers' holdings for cultivation in the common interest. This was looking backwards to an idealized feudalism with the Nation as sole lord; there is no suggestion of collectivization. But in any case Hall's chief importance is that he influenced the thinking of the first practical British socialist, Robert Owen.

Owen (1771-1858) was a self-made millowner whose exceptional ability to see history with unclouded eyes led him to believe that organized religion lay at the root of all evil. Son of a shopkeeper in Montgomeryshire, he had only the simplest primary education and was working for his living at nine years of age. By his early twenties he had become manager of a big cotton-mill in Manchester, master of 500 workers; from there he went on to become a partner in a group of Manchester mills. He fell in love with the daughter of a millionaire millowner of New Lanark near Glasgow, persuaded his partners that they should buy a mill there, and married the girl.

His experience as an employer of labour convinced Owen that character is formed by environment: free will is an illusion and the Church's teaching that man is free to save himself by obeying a certain moral law, or to damn himself by defying it, is fraudulent nonsense. Give men decent conditions of work, a fair wage, a respectable standard of living, and they would do right. Deny them these things and the consequences would be crime and vice. It follows that a means is required to accomplish the minimum conditions for decent human behaviour. This Owen

---

* It never occurred to most early socialists that the capitalists were anything worse than ill-informed or just plain stupid: only show them the light and they would see it as clearly as other men.

found in a theory of industrial co-operatives. In a memorandum presented to the Parliamentary Commission on the Poor Law in 1817 he suggested the establishment of co-operative socialist communes on a voluntary basis. The suggestion was well received and widely discussed but, of course, nothing was done about it.

But, in his own cotton mills at New Lanark where Owen had two thousand hands, five hundred of them sent there as Poor Law apprentices at the age of five, he introduced startling reforms: he refused to employ children under ten years of age; he reduced the working day to ten-and-a-half hours; he set on foot a number of welfare schemes; he infuriated the shopkeeping fraternity by opening a shop for his workers in which goods of quality were sold at a price which just covered the running costs; he set up infant schools in which the beating of the little pupils was, in Godless defiance of proverbial wisdom, forbidden; and, when the Americans put an embargo on the export of cotton to Britain so that the cotton-mills had to close down, he continued to pay all his workers at full wages.

One imagines the consternation, developing into hatred, of the real capitalists : but this dangerous revolutionary who had some-how managed to get a footing in their world had, happily for their case, already shown the cloven hoof by his fierce attacks on religion. Only the devil or one of his disciples could have conceived of such wickedness as refusing to put to work in the mills and mines those five-year-old children whom divine Providence had obviously destined for that lot. And think of the downright wickedness of pandering to the notorious idleness of the labouring classes, whose condition was ordained, as any good Church of England parson could tell you, by God, by cutting to ten hours a working day which was clearly intended to last fifteen. Owen's partners were among those who objected strongly to this thoroughly un-capitalist and, indeed, un-Protestant behaviour. Owen, with the help of contributions from sympathizers as diabolical as himself such as the Utilitarian, Jeremy Bentham, and men who had been impressed less by the humanity than by the plain common sense of Owen's pamphlet *A New View of Society*, bought out his partners. He then reconstituted the business so that all its profits could be channelled into improvement of workers' conditions and workers' education.

The mills, and the model village, of New Lanark became world-famous. With the help of the aristocracy who aimed to break the already uneasy alliance between the alarmingly self-assertive industrial magnates and the workers, he pushed the first Factory Act (1819), limiting the working hours for children, through Parliament. He set up his first socialist commune near Glasgow.

In 1824 Owen went to Indiana where he bought a village which had been built by German immigrants with co-operative ideas, and twenty thousand acres of land around it. There he started another communist settlement. But there was, by his own theories, a serious flaw in this foundation. A great many of the settlers, victims of their early environment in Europe, that is of having been economically and politically maltreated, had had their characters malformed accordingly. They did not pull their weight in the commune. The rest, who did, objected to sharing the profits of their labour with the idle; the Saint-Simonian 'to each according to his work' rather than Louis Blanc's 'to each according to his needs' was their motto. The commune failed and Owen lost the forty thousand pounds he had used to finance it. He received little sympathy: for one thing, his increasingly fierce attacks on the evil of organized religion had alienated many of his former allies. He gave up the Lanark mills, withdrew to London, and devoted the rest of his life to work for trades unions and Co-operative Societies.

In 1824 the London Co-operative Society began to publish a monthly magazine, *The Co-operative Magazine*, chiefly for the discussion and development of Owen's writings and works. It was in this magazine that, in 1827, the word 'socialist' appeared in print for the first time. It had probably been coined by a speaker in some discussion and was then adopted by the writer. The same number (November) of the magazine explains it: 'Those who think that capital should be common are the Communists and Socialists.' Did the French socialist Pierre Leroux, writing in the Saint-Simonian daily newspaper *Le Globe*, borrow the word from the English, or was it coined in France at the same time? At all events, *socialisme* and *socialiste* were in common use by the early 1830s.

* * *

Trade unionism had been legalized in Britain (but not in France where it remained illegal) following the recommendation of the 1824 Parliamentary Committee that the notorious Combination Laws should be repealed. With trades unions thus promoted to a measure of respectability, Owen put forward a plan whereby the workers might 'in a short time emancipate themselves from the thraldom of their present condition ... I now give you a short outline of the great changes which are in contemplation and which shall come suddenly upon society like a thief in the night,* but without violence or injustice ...' His plan was to bring the trades unions, indeed the entire working class, into a single great Union for the carrying on of all industrial production by national corporations of which every man of the trade in question was to be a member. Members would include 'all producers of wealth and whatever contributes to knowledge or happiness'. There would, henceforth, be no more masters and no more servants, and the workers in each industry would themselves own that industry.

The Grand National Consolidated Trade Union was formed in 1834 to realize this plan for the socialization of Britain, and soon had over half-a-million members of both sexes. The Grand National then set about urging its component unions in each major industry to turn themselves into producer co-operatives which would soon engross their whole industry, thus peacefully eliminating capitalism. But since capitalist resistance was to be expected—by this time the practical leaders who followed the socialist intellectuals had got rid of the element of astonishment that capital should be so lost to all good sense and decent feeling as to defend itself—there must also be a policy for militancy. The means to be used to crush the capitalist was the general strike, as explained by Owen's disciple Benbow:

> There will be no insurrection: it will simply be passive resistance. The men may remain at leisure: there is and can be no law to compel them to work against their will. They may walk the streets and fields with their arms folded, they will wear no swords, carry no muskets; they will present no multitude for the Riot Act to disperse. They merely abstain,

* Echo: 'A spectre is haunting Europe ...'

while their funds are sufficient, from going to work for one week or one month; and what happens in consequence? Bills are dishonoured, the *Gazette* teems with bankruptcies, capital is destroyed, the revenue fails, the system of government falls into confusion, and every link in the chain which binds society together is broken in a moment by this inert conspiracy of the poor against the rich.

The strike was never called. The British working class was to show, again and again, that it was too gentle (some would say too cowardly in its own cause) to adopt extreme measures, even short of violence. Besides, Benbow's reasoning was all very well: what such a strike must come to was a case of the capitalist sitting down on the belly of the worker's baby, and then waiting to see which tired first, the capitalist's broad arse, or the baby's empty tummy. While the Grand National and the component unions squandered their energies in negotiating regional and sectional wages and hours agreements, the Dorset magistrates were deporting the Tolpuddle Martyrs for the crime of 'administering an oath' and so contriving, despite Parliament, to smash the trade union movement for the time being. The real difficulty was that the workers' leaders could simply not, not yet, match the implacable ferocity of the bourgeoisie faced with the prospect of dispossession, expropriation.

Meanwhile in France the Saint-Simonian movement, in the hands of men like Pierre Leroux to whom is due the slogan 'from each according to his capacities, to each according to his work', was proposing, in *Le Globe*, to abolish inheritance and so to get rid of unearned incomes and put the means of production into the hands of the workers' co-operative State. Under the influence of such preaching and teaching the workers of Lyons combined— which was illegal—to demand a minimum living wage; this was refused, whereupon the workers flew to 'arms', poured into the streets, and forced the local government authorities to fly for their lives. Stendhal, in *Lucien Leuwen*, symbolizes the wretchedness of the workers' weapons by calling the strife between capital, supplied by the Orléanist monarchy with troops including cavalry, and labour as 'cabbage-stalk' warfare. Cabbage stalks are tough, but hardly a match for sabres and artillery. It was in analysing this brave but hopeless rebellion that Pierre Leroux concluded that society was divided into two mutually hostile classes, the 'bourgeoisie' and the 'proletariat'.

The miserable condition of the workers everywhere, aggravated by a long depression of trade and industry, and the manifest truth of the discovery that wealth was created only by labour (see the Labour Theory of Value below), together made it inevitable that theorists should increasingly attack the capitalist system as inadequate, the leaving of production to private enterprise as inequitable, and should seek to invent something better and more just to replace it. Opposed to each other, then, were, on the one hand a rationally attained assertion that the economy could and should be scientifically planned and managed for the service of all men equally; on the other an irrational belief, sustained by observation of nature, that private enterprise was the only possible viable economic system because it automatically obeyed the categorical imperatives of what were, absurdly, believed to be 'natural' economic laws which, like those of the Medes and Persians, 'alter not'. This was tantamount to saying that production and distribution were, like birth and death, subject to natural laws which man could not change: in other words, the capitalist bourgeoisie had not only money but God on its side, a faith which the Churches strongly encouraged and supported. Socialist ideas were not only foolish; they were downright ungodly.

And yet the Labour Theory of Value did make a very strong appeal to the sense of justice which not even the bourgeoisie could, despite its 'realism', escape. And since justice was, as I have said, conceived of as immanent, there might be an uneasy feeling that God was, after all, on the side of the Anglo-Jewish economist David Ricardo who had published his *Principles of Political Economy and Taxation* in 1817. What, in a line, Ricardo had said was that since natural resources were given by Providence, the value of manufactured articles must be directly proportional to the quantity of labour required to make them. That seemed fair. Yet an objection soon occurred to critics: if it took, say, one hundred man-hours to make a plough and two hundred to make a fashionable dress for an idle rich woman, must we conclude that the dress was twice as valuable to the

community as the plough? How Marx overcame that difficulty
will appear in due course. Meanwhile a Swiss economist,
Sismondi, developed Ricardo's theory of Labour Value in *New
Principles of Political Economy*, in which he argued as a pure
rationalist (he was not a socialist and was not making propaganda
for the Left), just as Dr Charles Hall had long since done in
England, that since profit, rent and interest represented the surplus value created by labour, they should belong to labour;
whereas, as things were, they were appropriated by others, to
wit, by capitalists. Misappropriated, said the socialists, was the
correct word, notably William Thompson in his *Inquiry into the
Principles of the Distribution of Wealth* (1824). Thompson was
concerned less with the production of wealth than with its just
division. Its unjust division was, he argued, due to the fact that
whereas Leroux's 'bourgeoisie' had all the capital, his 'proletariat'
had all the labour Obviously, capital and labour should be in
the same hands, that is all the workers should be capitalists: that
state of affairs could be brought about by means of the Owenite
producer and distribution co-operatives, and best of all by co-
operative communes. In short, by socialism, to use the word
three years before its coinage.

In France Saint-Simon was not the only prophet of a new
economic order, though his disciples and their active groups
were more numerous and energetic than the Fourierist socialists,
who were also numerous. Louis Blanc, a Saint-Simonian, advanced the theory of socialism nearer to the Millennium by revising
the Saint-Simonian slogan. In *The Organization of Labour*
(1840) he changed it to 'From each according to his capacity, to
each according to his needs'—in other words, the aim must be
absolute equality of wealth, or communism. Blanc was also a
pioneer of syndicalism: each industry should be owned and managed by its own workers, the State to provide capital in the shape
of plant. But, although he became the first socialist to be a Minister in a bourgeois government, the 'revolutionary' government of
1848, he was in no position to do very much in practice and could
or would not even help his fellow legislator, Proudhon (see below),
to get a practical trial for some of his theories.

In the great French Revolution the middle class made use of
the working class to help seize power from the aristocracy, and

then used Bonaparte to send the worker-allies back to their dirty kennels. Much the same thing happened in Britain, but without the use of so much violence. The middle class had working-class support for getting the Reform Bill onto the Statute Book and repealing the Corn Laws. (The aristocracy got its revenge in 1847 by going over, briefly, to the workers' side and forcing the Ten Hour [Factory] Act onto the Statute Book, thereby limiting the bourgeoisie's exploitation of the workers.) But, their object achieved, that is, a measure of power transferred into their hands, the middle class at once betrayed their allies. The reform was to go no further, there could be no question of enfranchising the working class. As Lord John Russell, a Whig leader, put it, they were 'determined to go no further but to use their best endeavours to preserve the renovated constitution entire and unimpaired'. The workers responded with the Charter. Here is what Francis Place said of it in 1838:

> This [Chartism] is a new feature in society produced by the increased intelligence of the working people. This is the first time that the desire for reform has been moved by them and carried upwards. Until now it has always proceeded downwards, and expired when abandoned, as it has always been, by its gentleman leaders. It will not again expire, but will go on continually, sometimes with more, sometimes with less, rapidity, but on it will go.

And so, of course, it did. It would have been difficult entirely to ignore Chartism here, yet the truth is that it had very little to do with the progress of socialism excepting in that it taught the workers to combine and organize, to speak for themselves. The Charter called for universal manhood suffrage, equal electoral districts, voting by secret ballot, annual parliaments and payment of Members. None of these demands is socialist, they are simply democratic. Perhaps that may explain why Chartism expired with a whimper, extinguished by a shower of rain at what was to have been its great demonstration in 1848, and by fear of the bourgeoisie's one hundred and seventy thousand special constables, including a Mr W. E. Gladstone and Prince Louis Napoleon Bonaparte, ready and willing to club the life out of the working class's aspiration to full political rights. Few things have contributed more to the stability and persistence of British capitalism than the restraint—some might say pusillanimity—of the British worker when faced with middle-class threat of violence: probably the meagre diet of the working class was less productive of the necessary ferocity in class war than the pounds of beef, mutton and pudding in middle-class bellies.

We come now to one of socialism's very great men, Pierre Joseph Proudhon, the anarchist. No man was ever more convinced of the existence of immanent justice than this son of a bankrupt tavern-keeper and a cook, who was earning his living as a mountain cowherd at the age of nine, and of whom it was to be said that he wrote like one of the great French classicists and should, no less than Molière, have belonged to the Académie Française. He was born in 1809, suffered in the famine which afflicted the Franche-Comté following Bonaparte's wars, won a scholarship to Besançon College but was forced to cut short his education when pig-headed litigation had reduced his parents to destitution, and became a compositor. Many years later he wrote that his composing-stick became 'the symbol and instrument of my freedom'. He won the Besançon Academy's award for young scholars with an essay on grammar, went to Paris and was there deeply moved by the wretched condition of the workers. Drawn towards the socialist and other revolutionary clubs and groups trying to do something about this mass misery, he used the opportunity suggested by another prize offered by the Besançon Academy for an essay on *La Célébration du Dimanche*, to raise Moses to the status of a social reformer, retranslate the Eighth Commandment to read *Thou shalt not put aside anything for thyself*, and thereby to launch his first attack on the institution of private property which he stigmatized as 'the last of the false gods'. Those who possessed 'accumulated property' (capital) were 'exploiters of the proletariat', and that proletariat would soon call on them to be ready to defend themselves.

Two years later, in 1840, came one of the seminal works of the socialist complex of movements, *What is Property?* It made him famous; and in some quarters, infamous, for his short answer was, 'Theft'. As usually happened, the author's meaning, intention, purpose were judged and a certain kind of reputation fixed on him for ever not by critics who had read the book, but by those who had merely glanced at it. For, by 'Theft', what, as he explained, Proudhon meant was, 'the sum of its [Property's] abuses'. Far from utterly condemning property, he believed that possession of a house to live in, a plot of land to grow food on and the tools of his trade, were the minimum requirement for man's liberty. What, on the other hand, no man had a shadow of right to was the accumulated capital which enabled him to exploit other men. His philosophy of property can be summed up in two lines of his own: 'The right to products is exclusive: *jus in re*; the right to means is common: *jus ad rem*.' In other words, the worker has absolute right to own what his own labour produces; and no man any right to own the means of production excepting his own tools to be used with his own hands. In a passage of characteristically shining clarity he explains why the means of production must, in common justice, be common property:

> Now this reproductive leaven—this eternal germ of life, this preparation of the land and manufacture of implements for production—constitutes the debt of the capitalist to the producer, which he never pays; and it is this fraudulent denial which causes the poverty of the labourer, the luxury of idleness, and the inequality of conditions. This it is, above all things, which has been fitly named the exploitation of man by man.

Because I shall be returning to a consideration of Proudhon and his works in Chapter Ten I shall say no more about him at this point. From the passage quoted above it should be clear of what his major contribution to the advance of socialism consisted.

Two other Frenchmen should be mentioned briefly here. In 1842 Constantin Pecqueur published a book which had a great deal of influence on Russian and other revolutionary movements in the next half-century, *A New Theory of Social and Political Economy*. In it he argued the case for the suppression of all property as an intolerable abuse, the public ownership of all capital goods and credit institutions and the running of all industry by the State. Seven years earlier, Etienne Cabet had published a novel in which he used More's method in *Utopia*:

in his *Travels in Icaria* (1840) he depicts a socialist commune in being. The novel had a wide and international circulation and since it was on the bookshelf of most revolutionaries for the next several decades, it presumably, albeit a fiction, had some influence.

Until this point in time the socialist initiative had been with the English and French. It was now to pass into German hands.

FOUR

Philosophers and Socialists

Modern socialism is more or less synonymous with Marxism, or Marxism-Leninism. There are, it is true, some politicians who call themselves socialists but who are obviously not Marxists. That is because journalistic abuse has tended to foist upon the word socialism a meaning which it should not be used to convey —using it to describe any political creed which is slightly and vaguely left of centre; that, for example, of the British Labour Party which when in office is hardly socialist. Moreover, 'socialist' is used as a term of mild abuse by the bourgeois-capitalist press to imply that such harmless liberals as Mr Harold Wilson or Mr James Callaghan, Senator McCarthy, Chancellor Willy Brandt or MM. Monnet or Mendès-France are irresponsible revolutionary firebrands to whom political power must by no means be entrusted. It would, clearly, be very ridiculous to regard men of that moderately liberal persuasion as socialists if, as we must, we derive the meaning of the word from the contents of the last chapter: for there is one thing a socialist must be convinced of —that capitalism is a dispensable evil.

We have, then, now to examine the origins of modern socialism, that is to say post-Saint-Simonian and Owenist socialism, before we come to Marx and Engels, its creators. For Marxism is not Marx's work alone, far from it. Apart altogether from the fact that he drew upon all the writers glanced at in the last chapter, and many more, in the elaboration of his theories, his friend Engels contributed at least as much as Marx did himself to the making of socialism. And it is from Engels that I take a guide to the philosophical antecedents of Marxism. In the foreword to the first German edition of Marx's and Engels' *Utopian Socialism and Scientific Socialism* (1880), Engels wrote:

We German Socialists are proud to trace our descent not

only from Saint-Simon, Fourier and Owen, but moreover from Kant, Fichte and Hegel.

He might, had he not been making the patriotic point that Germans, too, had contributed to the making of socialism in the primitive period, have added 'David Hume'. But it is a fact that the socialism of Marx, or rather the philosophy of History by which he justified it, was based upon his study of Hegel although, as will appear in its place, he rejected Hegelian idealism. It is also a fact that, at a critical point in the formation of his own philosophy, Lenin went back to a thorough re-reading of Hegel. What they, and other important German socialists of the epoch, found in Hegel is briefly summarized below. Meanwhile, there are the other two philosophers named by Engels in his foreword.

There is no need to say much about Immanuel Kant: his importance in the intellectual ascent of socialism is simply that his writings, his doctrine concerning the basis of our knowledge of the physical universe, expounded in *The Critique of Pure Reason* (1781), *The Critique of Practical Reason* (1788) and *The Critique of Judgement* (1790), were the origin of both Fichte's and Hegel's philosophical thought; ultimately, therefore, of their respective systems.

There are, to the layman at least, striking similarities in the systems of Fichte and Hegel, and since Fichte was the older man by eight years we will take him first although, for Marxists, he is the less important. He was born and christened Johann Gottlieb in 1762, made his name as a theologian and scholar after a long and bitter struggle with poverty and, by 1810, had made such a reputation that he was asked to write the constitution of Berlin University which was then being founded and was thereafter elected its first Rector. In the philosophical system he constructed, the Universe begins when Ego posits itself and in the process of so doing generates its opposite, all that is non-Ego. In short, the creator is Absolute Ego, and the world of nature is a by-product of Its self-creation, existing only through, for and in that Ego. Here would seem to be the origin of Hegel's Absolute (see below). But when Engels invoked Fichte as a spiritual ancestor of German socialism, I believe that he had in mind another aspect of Fichte's teaching. Although Fichte was not as bold and downright in asserting that the Germans must be the master-race of the 19th century as Hegel was to be, he was an arch-patriot with a strong sense of the superiority of German thought in his time (an opinion then shared by many non-Germans). Now the German socialists of the second half of the 19th century might try to be internationalists, or perhaps one should say supra-nationalists; but their philosophical teachers and their own observation of the paramount importance of German philosophy in their time, as well as ordinary patriotism reacting from the humiliations of German defeats at Bonaparte's hands, taught them to believe fervently in a German mission to take the lead in mankind's advancement of Mind. The growing point of Mind was in Germany, at least for the time being, and the progress which Reason could accomplish for all the human race would be made there and not elsewhere. This patriotic aberration, the elevation of one community of men over all others, a sort of intellectual and high-minded version of Pan-German arrogance in politics, was to have appalling consequences for socialism and, much worse for mankind in general, in 1914 and again in 1939. But of the two great thinkers who cannot be cleared of responsibility for this disaster, Fichte is the less blameworthy; the unwitting villain of this tragi-comedy was Hegel.

Georg William Friedrich Hegel was born at Stuttgart in 1770 and read theology at Tübingen University. He became a teacher and was more or less obscure until, at the age of forty-eight, he was given the chair of Philosophy at Berlin University where Fichte was Rector. In his lectures and in two books, *The Philosophy of History* (1821) and *The Philosophy of Law* (1821), he expounded the philosophy which he had elaborated on Kantian foundations which became, after his death and as a consequence of its influence on Marx, Engels, and Lenin, by far the most powerful system of thought, at least in its practical effects on mankind, since Aristotle's. For while a philosopher whose thought only impresses other philosophers may be of the utmost importance in the history of thought—Kant, for example, or Hume—he may well remain quite without influence on the history of action, that is to say, on History. It is the philosopher who happens to impress men of action with his ideas whose life-work may change the whole course of human events. *His* pen may indeed be mightier than the sword.

The assumption which Hegel began with he called the Absolute: it might fairly safely be compared to the sophisticated religious intellectual's notion of God. Everything whatsoever in nature is a manifestation, or perhaps one should say an expression, of this Absolute. The highest of these perhaps infinitely numerous expressions is to be found in the operation of Man's mind; for in mind, in reason, the Absolute, otherwise unwitting, at last becomes conscious of Itself. (One might interpret this, although with reservations, by saying that God's love of man derives from the fact that only in the mind of Man does He come to know Himself and His works.) Thus in Mind, the Absolute and its numerous manifestations (Nature) become aware of each other and are reconciled. And this process of reconciliation occurs by means of the synthesis of thesis and antithesis, Hegelian terms which require some explanation.

Thesis is the given, it is the datum. It has an opposite, generated by its mere existence, which Hegel called *antithesis.** But since, by its nature, Mind cannot tolerate the state of contradiction, it has to reconcile these opposites: this it does by *synthesis* and in synthesis the highest manifestation of the expression or manifestation in question is attained.

Plato had coined the word *dialectic* to signify the process of carrying an idea, or an argument, to the ultimate conclusion which a strict use of logic could lead to, with the object of detecting error or inconsistency, thus enabling the thinker to correct his idea or argument. Hegel borrowed this word, extending its meaning greatly, to describe his process of reconciling thesis and antithesis in synthesis.

His own dialectic lies at the root of his explanation of man's role in the universe: matter is thesis, mind is antithesis. They are synthesized in man who is both matter and mind. The dialectic is necessarily applicable to every expression of the Absolute—that is, to both nature and History (see below). But the unavoidable implication is that all the laws of both nature and History are derived from the laws of thought, from

* There are obvious parallels in modern nuclear physics, e.g. particles and antiparticles.

Mind: in other words, the idea comes before the thing, and mind alone interprets the universe, cannot but do so because of the operation between mind and matter, the tension between thesis and antithesis resolved in synthesis.

The aim of philosophy is to discover a system within whose terms the whole universe, all its manifestations whatsoever, can be satisfactorily explained, or at least fitted. It can fairly be described as a search for the order which is felt to be fundamental and a unity. The philosopher will not, therefore, be satisfied unless he can apply the rules of the system he has constructed out of his human need for law and order (but he would probably say 'discovered by inductive reasoning', rather than 'constructed') to every manifestation of the universe including the history of mankind. Not, I suppose, until the post-Kierkegaard Existentialists was this gallant if desperate attempt abandoned, excepting in so far as we are forced back to it by discoveries of the physicists. Hegel, in his two major works, applied his dialectic to the study of both Christianity and the political State. Thus, taking the Christian Trinity, the Father becomes thesis, the Son antithesis; and the Holy Spirit is their synthesis in which Father and Son are reconciled. Now shift to his consideration of politics: the individual is thesis, man in the mass, 'the people', or rather the problem of the opposition between the individual and the mass of other individuals, is antithesis: they are reconciled in a synthesis—the State. In other words, what the Holy Spirit is in religion the State is in politics, *the highest manifestation of that expression of the Absolute here in question.* Probably no philosophical conclusion ever resulted in such a volume of suffering for the human race.

For consider the implications of Hegel's reasoning: his deification—it is by no means too strong a word—of the State would have been as merely entertaining, as harmless, as Plato's *Republic* (which despite its dangerous arguments, as far as I know never hurt anyone barring, perhaps, a few citizens of Syracuse in the reign of Dionysius the younger), had it not made an immediate and strong appeal to the Prussian *étatisme* reinforced by Jewish love of authoritative Law (and need for a Jehovah substitute) of Karl Marx; to Stalin's lust for absolute power; to Engels' yearning for a benevolent master-and-father to replace the harsh

Protestant God he had given up after such an agonizing struggle,* and the bitter-tempered father he had been unable to love; and to those theorists, also, whom Adolf Hitler conjured into existence to justify the horrors of the Nazi State.† If I have left Lenin out of this list of men of action who found justification for crimes against humanity in the deification of the Hegelian State, it is for good reasons which will appear: it seems to me that in his later writings, notably on the cultural revolution, he was having serious doubts about the godhead of the Hegelian State.

Hegel's application of the dialectic to history has, because the growing-point of socialism after 1840 shifted from France (and England) to Germany and because Hegel was by far the most persuasive philosopher of the 1840s, bound socialism to the State in a way which ensured that the socialist Millennium did not happen when it was expected to do so. And it created a new and very formidable kind of imperialism. It is as a consequence of this that the New Left has had to take socialism back to the drawing-board; but of that hereafter.

Since the individual was *thesis* and the State *synthesis*, it followed that the State was perfectly entitled to tyrannize over the individual, in fact bound to do so, for it was the higher manifestation of the two Moreover there was, in any given historical epoch, a particular State in which synthesis had been accomplished with near perfection, much more nearly so than in any other State. That State was entitled—no, was in duty to mankind, bound—to assert its authority over other States, less perfect *syntheses*. In other words, not only did war have a positive part to play in history, it was a glorious part, a morally admirable part. For the most nearly perfect Synthesis-State had, during the time of its zenith, responsibility for forwarding the work of Mind—continuous reconciliation, that is to say, the growth of the Absolute's consciousness of Itself. Prussia clearly was that State, and was, in Hegel's lifetime, about to become the party responsible for that supremely important work of enlarging God's awareness.

In fairness to Hegel it should be made clear there was no such

* See Chapter Five.
† Cf., e.g. Alfred Rosenberg's *Der Mythus des 20. Jahrhunderts*.

stupid nonsense as a Thousand-Year Reich in his mind: he already had a successor in mind who would, in due course, probably in the 20th century, take from Germany's hand the torch of responsibility for winning the race of Mind's advance in awareness—the United States of America.

A President of that republic, were he well read in Hegel, would no doubt find justification for the wheeling and dealing that elected him, for the war in Vietnam, the operations of the CIA in Latin America, and for the criminal proceedings by which his re-election was ensured, in the works of Karl Marx's favourite philosopher.

FIVE

Scientific Socialism (1)

It was upon the foundation of work done by the pioneers we have referred to, and on the works of the three philosophers glanced at in Chapter Four, chiefly that of Hegel, that scientific socialism was built by Karl Marx and Friedrich Engels. Of course, there were other contributors to the basic work on which they constructed their system: philosophers like Ludwig Feuerbach and Bruno Bauer and leaders of working-class socialist organizations such as the Communist League in Germany, the Fraternal-Democrats and the Chartists in Britain, the Saint-Simonians and Fourierists in France and many more. But here we shall concern ourselves only with principals, not with secondary characters, however important, whose work was that of either practical application or theoretical refinement and, too often, of a refinement reduced to hair-splitting.

Karl Marx was born at Trier in the Rhineland in 1818 three years after the fall of Bonaparte, which Prussia had helped England and Spain to accomplish. His father was a prosperous and broadminded Jewish lawyer who had been converted to Christianity more, one imagines, for the sake of convenience than faith, so that Karl was brought up in a formally Protestant household. His secular schooling was the best to be had and he completed his education at the Universities of Bonn and Berlin, both of which were under the influence of the teachings of Fichte and Hegel. Marx read Law; but he also followed other courses, being particularly interested in the history of art and in Greek mythology.

The social life of Bonn university students was centred on *Kneipvereinen*, drinking clubs which met in particular taverns. Marx joined one of them and occasionally got drunk. He ran up debts which his father paid and he fought a duel in which he was wounded. He also joined the Poet's Club whose members were the revolutionaries among the students, those who rejected the authoritarian Establishment and excitedly discussed radical policies for overthrowing it. He wrote a great deal of verse, most of it romantic rather than didactic, and none of it of much merit.

If I include these details it is because it is desirable to correct the solemn, indeed grim, image of the great socialist revolutionary, the one most commonly received. The truth is more interesting: as a young man he was high-spirited, romantic, passionate, with a tremendous capacity for play as well as work. As a scholar he was among the most brilliant; yet he seemed to have no particular vocation. And throughout his life, although his attitude to the work he set himself was indeed deadly serious and his principal tool was cold logic, he was driven by warm and passionate feeling.

The summer vacation of 1837 intervened between his residence at Bonn and his shift to Berlin. During the holidays he fell deeply in love with the girl next door, daughter of his father's aristocratic German-Scottish friend von Westphalen. There was every excuse for him: Jenny vón Westphalen had a beauty which enchanted all the men who met her, and which survived even the hardships which were to be her lot. She loved Karl as passionately as he loved her, and they became secretly engaged: secretly because they knew that the consent of their parents was unlikely and that Jenny's brother, a humourless and ultra-Right State Councillor, whose attitude to his sister's marriage to Karl Marx was to be rather like that of the younger Baron Thunder den Tronkh to that of Cunégonde and Candide, would oppose their engagement as offensively as possible. Their engagement was still a secret when Marx departed for Berlin, but Jenny then confided in her father and in him discovered an ally.

Marx was to read Law and History. His tutor in those subjects was Hegel's most brilliant pupil and professional successor, Eduard Gans. Gans persuaded the young man to add some reading of philosophy to his formal studies. He did so, found he had a keen taste for it and wrote a 300-page *Philosophy of Law* which was not published. At the same time he was studying Italian and English which led him to the literary love of his life, Shakespeare Only in the last years of his life, when he was sick, exhausted and broken by Jenny's death, did his pleasure in

Shakespearean play-going desert him. Since he was also still trying to be a poet by writing verse, he worked such long hours that he began to injure his originally robust health by doing without sleep, an abuse which had consequences which lasted all his life.

Gans had, of course, introduced his pupil to the works of his own revered master, Hegel. But Marx the romantic reacted strongly against the Hegelian philosophy; it offended his heart and he mistook this feeling for a rational rejection. He set out to refute it in a long essay written in dialogue (*Cleanthus: the Point of Departure and Development Necessary to Philosophy*). At the end of it he discovered that the last sentences which the logic of the work had led him to write concluded in the very philosophy he had set out to refute. Thus his '. . . dearest child, fostered by moonlight, had, like a perfidious siren, led him straight into the enemy's arms'.* The words are light enough, but in fact he had received a severe shock which, combined with overwork, resulted in his falling ill. His doctor sent him to live in a suburb where he would have better air and access to the country. It was there that he met the men who introduced him to the *Doktorklub* of liberal-revolutionaries, and into the salon of Bettina von Arnim where he met people of consequence, both conservative and radical. In both these circles he was in touch with the movement known as the Young Hegelians. He very soon became, by reason of his brilliance, their leader.

As Boris Nicolaevsky and Otto Maenchen-Helfen pointed out in their admirable *Life of Karl Marx*,† German political aspirations to freedom in mid-19th century had to be disguised as mere philosophical opinions of no practical application. The Hegelians were divided into a Right and a Left, ostensibly over the question of what should be retained, what rejected, in the master's works. By insisting on retaining the entire Hegelian system, the men of the Right demonstrated their support for Prussian authoritarianism, since they accepted, with the rest,

* Letter from Marx to his father 10 November 1837, quoted by Nicolaevsky, 1937.

† *Karl Marx*, 1937; *Vie de Marx*, 1970. Surely one of the greatest biographies of our time.

Hegel's pan-Germanism and glorification of patriotic war.* They, therefore, were safe from the authorities.

Very different was the Leftists' case: they, led by Marx, rejected Hegel's 'idealism' and with it his political attitude; but they retained the dialectic because it 'fluidified' everything, it eliminated all quesion of stability and permanence, it shifted the emphasis from Being onto Becoming, it provided students of history with the equivalent of the differential calculus in mathematics. In rejecting Hegelian Idealism, guided by Feuerbach (see below), they turned his system upside down, putting the Thing before the Idea. In retaining the Hegelian dialectic as a method, however, they acquired what one of the *Doktorklub* intellectuals, Rutenberg or Köppen perhaps, or Bruno Bauer, or maybe Marx himself, called 'an algebra for Revolution'. The use of the mathematical analogy is significant; German socialism was to be nothing if not scientific.

In the *Doktorklub* and in Bettina von Arnim's salon Marx became famous as an aggressive and original thinker, quick and perspicacious, 'a young lion, a magazine of thoughts, a hive of ideas' (Nicolaevsky). That, of course, did him nothing but harm with the authorities, and with the advent of Frederick William IV and a thoroughly reactionary government he lost that hope of a lectureship at Berlin, or at least in Bonn, which he had envisaged for the immediate future. All he received from the university was a certificate of studies. The University of Jena was more generous and gave him his doctorate. But he would certainly not get a teaching appointment. He therefore decided to turn journalist for the time being, went to Bonn (1842) and began to write revolutionary articles for the *Rheinische Zeitung* and give ostentatious expression to his contempt for the Establishment by

---

* Pure Hegelianism of the Right has best been summarized in the words in which the narrator Ratcliff reports the ideas put into Gavin Stevens' mind by William Faulkner (*The Mansion*) 'German culture ... never had no concern with and if anything a little contempt for, anything that happened to man on the outside, or through the eyes and touch ... but jest with what happened to him through the ears like music and philosophy and what was wrong inside his mind ...' For the orthodox Hegelian it was the Idealism, the mystical aspect, *der Mythus*, which counted.

driving, in the burgesses' Sunday carriage-parade, behind a team of donkeys.

How did he, in this epoch of his life, become a dedicated revolutionary socialist? Intellectually, by following where his use of the Hegelian dialectic applied to history led him; emotionally, by reacting, with thousands of other young men and not a few old ones, against the already anachronistic, heavy-handed absolutist *Urdummheit* of Frederick William's government. I do not include the motive which was the prime mover in Engels' case—compassion for the labouring poor and indignation at their terrible condition: I find no evidence for it.

While Marx made a characteristically thorough study of French communism and English Chartism and, to provide the powerful mill of his mind with concrete raw material, devoured the works of English and French political economists, he and a group of his friends took over the *Cologne Gazette*—he was already editing or helping to edit the *Rheinische Zeitung*—to use it to attack the 'romantic-absolutist' nature of the Prussian State. They made it into a socialist organ with international influence. Yet, for some time still, it was tolerated by the Prussian government for two reasons: it provided them with an ally against an enemy as dangerous, or seeming to be, as the new socialism—the strong Roman Catholic clericalism of the Rhineland; and it was not yet quite daring to rouse into fury that pride of half-awakened lions, the German intellectuals.

It was while he was part-editing and writing for these two newspapers that Marx first met Engels who, two years younger than himself, passed through Cologne on his way to a job in his father's English factory at Manchester: their meeting was cool, for Marx did not trust the, as he thought, flighty radicalism of the latest generation of Berlin *Freigelassenen* (see below).

There was a potentate more certain even than Frederick William of Prussia that the only way to deal with revolutionary thinkers and agitators was to stamp on them and who, unlike the King of Prussia, had the confidence to do it: the Tsar Nicholas I of Russia, to whom the Prussian government was expediently subservient. Nicholas, furious at Marx's sustained and high-spirited attack on absolutism, angrily demanded the suppression of the *Cologne Gazette*: there was no question of not complying, and

Marx lost his paper. He responded by attending to his private life, by marrying Jenny von Westphalen and moving, with his bride, to Paris, there to edit and write for a new revolutionary review, *The Franco-German Annals,* inspired by Ludwig Feuerbach's dictum that a philosopher who wished to play a full part in life and identify with mankind, should be of Franco-German moral stock, i.e. French heart, German head—the head of a Calvinist and the heart of a Revolutionary. Marx, writing to Feuerbach, expressed it thus: 'We Germans are the contemporaries of the present in philosophy, without being its contemporaries in history.' It was the French who were the contemporaries in history, so that Paris was 'the new capital of the world'. Thus, the review should be an intellectual alliance in which the most advanced theory (German) should be combined with the most advanced practice (French).

Such was the tone of the new review's first number that the Prussian government immediately issued warrants for the arrest of Marx, Heine and other Prussian citizens who wrote for it, the moment they crossed the frontier, for treason. At this their backer lost his nerve and withdrew his support, and not even a second number of the *Annals* appeared. During all this time Marx was making a thorough study of political economy in the authors we have already noticed, and half a dozen more modern French ones, and familiarizing himself with the various revolutionary movements among the Paris workers. He met and talked with Louis Blanc and with Proudhon and he received a second visit from Friedrich Engels. He was, as will soon appear, ready to give his younger contemporary and earnest admirer a much better reception than he had done in Cologne.

It would have been difficult to find anywhere in all the Germanies two family backgrounds, two family histories more different from each other than those of Marx and Engels. Engels was born in 1820 at Barmen in the industrial valley of the Wupper whose water, before the use of steam was introduced from England, had driven the wheels of cotton-mills. His father was a textile manufacturer with factories in Barmen and at Manchester (England), and a stern, narrow-minded, gloomy Calvinist. Unlike Marx, Engels had been in close touch with the abject poverty and grinding misery of the workers—his father's millhands—since childhood. It would never have crossed the withered mind of Engels Senior that anything could or should be done about the vile conditions and lifelong suffering of his workers. They were what they were and must bear it because God had so ordained; in this world as in the next you were saved and justified or eternally damned and there was nothing you could do about it. (Not for nothing were the leading industrial capitalist countries all Protestant.) But young Friedrich, warm-hearted, gentle, sympathetic with others to the point of empathy, and with twice the normal endowment of generosity, reacted very strongly against the narrow obscurantism of his family's religious, economic and political opinions.*

This reaction led him to read the young revolutionary poets, notably Heine and Börne, to try his own hand at poetry, and to make up his mind to escape from Barmen into a broader, sweeter world. He had a remarkable gift for learning languages which opened all the great literatures of the West to his seeking mind and heart. His father, sensing a revolt which would also be a blasphemy, cut short his schooling, put him to work in the factory, and then sent him to learn another part of the business with a Bremen cloth-merchant and to lodge with an austere Calvinist minister. It is curious to reflect that by doing his duty as he saw it, and so ensuring that his son would hate everything he was and stood for but would, also, be a competent cotton-goods businessman and his heir, this narrow-minded and bitter-hearted capitalist made a considerable contribution to the creation of the USSR and the Chinese People's Republic.

In Heine and Börne the young Engels had found justification, if not doctrine, for his rebelliously generous feelings. Now, reading Strauss' *Life of Jesus*, he moved further along the road to freedom. The book did for him what it did for its English translator, George Elliot, flung him into an agonizing struggle with the life-hating faith of his fundamentalist upbringing: the struggle was won by his own better feelings, his rejection of the

---

* For insight into what Calvinism means in philosophical terms of social behaviour, I suggest a reading of James Hogg's (the Ettrick Shepherd) great parable novel *Memoirs and Confessions of a Justified Sinner*.

grim bondage to a God it was impossible for any youth with
decent, natural feelings not to hate. He rid himself of the harmful
burden of his father's religion, went on to read Hegel, became a
Hegelian, and perhaps even a Young Hegelian before he had
ever heard of those high-spirited young philosophers. Hegel led
him to Feuerbach, and he emerged from this intellectual ordeal
a potential if not an actual socialist, or maybe communist is the
right word.

Feuerbach's importance in this story is to be found in his
formalization of the Young Hegelians' inversion of Hegel's
system. Like Marx, he turned poor Hegel upside down and
thus, with Marx, produced 'an algebra for revolution'.

> ... the being is subject, thought an attribute. Thought
> emanates from the being, not the being from thought. All
> speculation made outside and beyond man, concerning law,*
> will, personality is no better than speculation devoid of unity,
> arising from no necessity, without substance, foundation or
> reality. The human being is himself the very condition for
> the existence of personality, liberty and law ...

That is from Feuerbach's *Provisional Theses for the Reform of
Philosophy* (1842). One of its accomplishments was to free
socialists from the bondage of its pioneers to the notion of
immanent justice, and as such is the origin, or at least justification
for, Marx's detestation of 'sentimental' socialism (or, rather,
communism). It means, of course, that the Thing engenders the
Idea, and never the Idea the Thing. In history, it means that it
is *never* the Idea of the State, being then realized in a State,
that creates and directs society. On the contrary, it is the nature of
a society which determines that of the State; ideology is
secondary.†

But how could this argument lead Engels, or anyone else, to
socialism? This is where Marx's further arguments from Feuerbach come in: although Feuerbach recognized in man the creator
of ideas, whereas Hegel had treated Idea itself as creative, he

* *Recht*: not simply jurisprudence but the political organization of
States.

† There is a beautiful demonstration of the truth of this proposition
in the *Islam et Capitalisme* of that no longer very orthodox Marxist
historian, Maxime Rodinson.

still left Man as a generic and generalized concept, an abstraction virtually 'outside nature' (vestige of the pernicious influence of the Old Testament?). Marx carried Feuerbach's arguments a stage further by 'realizing' the Feuerbachian abstraction 'Man'. For 'Man', he was to write in his *Introduction to a Critique of Hegel's Philosophy of Law*, 'is the world of men, is the State, is Society.' So that any critique of the State necessarily becomes a critique of Society, and must get down to the very basis and foundation of Society. What is that basis? It is productive labour. Whose is that labour? Obviously, the mass of the world's workers, i.e. the proletariat (plus, but this was Lenin's interpolation, the creative intellectuals: the Cultural Revolution will be dealt with in its place). This being so very clearly so, then:

> The work which was to deliver man from barbarism could be accomplished only by the proletariat ...
>
> > (Nicolaevsky)

and

> Revolutions require a material base. Theory is realized in practice among any people only to the extent that it represents a realization of that people's needs. It is not enough for thought to tend towards that realization; the realization must tend towards the thought ...
>
> > (Marx)*

By volunteering for military service before the date of his conscription, Engels could achieve two things: he could escape from his father's clutches, and he could win the privilege of having his term reduced to only one year. He volunteered and had the good fortune to be posted to Berlin (1841). There he soon discovered and joined the circle of Young Hegelians, and *Freigelassenen*. He contributed articles to the radical press, wrote some anti-'Idealists' pamphlets, and very quickly won a literary reputation. Nothing could have annoyed and alarmed his father more: the moment that Engels was free of the service, he was ordered (1842) to Manchester; and it was in Cologne, on his way (or, rather, out of it—he wanted to see Marx),—that that first, cool meeting with Karl Marx occurred. Marx, however, overcame his

* 'Zur Kritik der Hegelschen Rechtsphilosophie', *Deutsch-französische Jahrbucher*, 1-11 Feb. 1844.

prejudices against the *Freigelassenen* sufficiently to enable him
to commission some articles from England where, since it was
the most advanced industrial country, the problem of the workers'
misery was most acute. He had not received many before he
recognized their brilliance and was converted to that admiration
for Engels' talent which lasted the rest of his life.*

If Engels senior had expected that the discipline of the work
in Manchester would cure Friedrich of all that silly and blasphe-
mous socialist nonsense, he received a nasty shock. The young
man did not neglect the work he had been sent to learn, but he
certainly did not concentrate on the business of his life as
ordained by the Calvinist God—making money. He had to be
allowed some leisure and he used it to join forces with the
Chartist leaders. Instead of cultivating the society of the rich
Manchester burgesses he made friends among the millhands and
accomplished the remarkable feat of studying their conditions
objectively without losing their affection. I call the feat remarkable because, in those days to be 'a chiel amang us takin' notes'
without having a brick flung at your head was an achievement
indeed; today we are more used to being spied on.

Then came, in 1844, Engels' second meeting with Karl Marx,
in Paris. It was an unqualified success: they spent ten days
together, fell into total, confiding and enduring friendship with
each other, easily and enthusiastically agreed to work together.†

Back in England, Engels was writing articles for Robert Owen's
The New Moral World, while Marx, no longer tolerated by the
French government, moved to Brussels where he had already
sent Jenny and the children. There he perfected that theory of
Historical Materialism on which he had been working and, at
the same time, busied himself forming 'correspondence committees' designed to link Belgian, French, German and English
socialists—they were the seed of the International to come.

In a letter written to Paul Annenkov at a later date (28 Decem-

---

* When Engels' first major work, *Umrisse zu einer Kritik der
Nationalökonomie*, appeared in Paris (1844) Marx hailed it as a work
of genius.

† Their first joint work was *German Ideology*, a critique of romantic
revolutionary notions—i.e. unscientific radicalism—which was not published until 1932.

ber 1846, quoted by Nicolaevsky) Marx, conveniently for us, summarized the essence of his historical materialism, his point of departure being that Ludwig Feuerbach was, from the political-economic point of view, the only philosopher worthy of respect:

What, in whatever form it may take, is society? The product of man's reciprocal activities. Is man free to choose this or that social formation? By no means. At any given point in the evolution of man's productive forces, there will be a corresponding form of trade and consumption, there will be a corresponding form of social constitution, a particular organization of the family, trades, classes, in other words, a corresponding civil society. Given such a civil society, there will be a corresponding political situation which will be only the official expression of that civil society.

It is important to add that men do not direct their productive forces—basis of their entire history—just as they please; for any productive force is a heritage, produced by some anterior activity. Thus, productive forces are the result of men's practical energy, but that practical energy is itself determined by the circumstances in which the men in question find themselves as a consequence of their inherited productive forces, of the social form existing among them, a form not of their making but produced by the preceding generation. By reason simply of the fact that each generation finds itself endowed with the productive forces acquired by the preceding generation, forces which serve as raw material for new production, a continuity in humanity's history is created, a history of humanity is created ...

Perfecting his theory and forging international socialist links was not the sum of Marx's work in Brussels. He wrote and, on occasion, spoke against the romantic or sentimental 'communism' of the kind he had come to see as a danger to the whole movement, a squandering of revolutionary energy in efforts which could never lead to the radical re-organization of society which he now had in mind. And he joined the revolutionary secret society, then known as the League of the Just but to become better known by its later name, the Communist League. If this

seems inconsistent with his anti-romantic attitude, it is much less
so than appears: he disapproved strongly of clandestine revolutionary groups, but approved of the people who formed the
League. He joined with the intention of giving the League a
hard-line and definite socialist policy (his own, of course) and
of bringing its activities out into the open.

Engels, meanwhile, had been travelling in Germany, joining
enthusiastically in the socialist (they were called communist)
movements which he found spreading there among the workers,
especially in his own Wupper valley. Out of his experience among
the Manchester cotton-spinning and weaving operatives he had
written *Die Lage der Arbeitenlumenden Klassen in England*
(1845)—*The State of the Working Class in England,* an important contribution to understanding the problems facing political
economists and therefore the new scientific socialism since, like
all science, it relied on sufficient objective data. Now, responding
to pressing letters from Marx, Engels joined his friend in
Brussels where Marx had just coined, for the Communist
League, the slogan *'Proletarians of all countries, unite!'* and was
continuing, in the *Brussels German Gazette,* his campaign
against both the bourgeoisie and the sentimental-intellectual
'communists' with equal wit and ferocity.

Marx introduced Engels into the League; they already had a
joint work to their credit, *Die heilige Familie, oder Kritik der
kritschen Kritik* (1845), a satirical pamphlet. They began to
work regularly together.

Marx and his family were poor and he again ran into debt.
His father had died and left him some money, but his mother,
executrix of the will, and unable to forgive her son for disgrac-
ing the family by becoming a socialist, refused to hand over
Karl's share. At long last she was persuaded to let him have six
thousand marks (£300 gold) which he then spent on revolutionary
causes, leaving himself and his family as poor as ever.*

In 1847 both men went to London, Marx as Belgian delegate
of the (Continental) Democratic Association to the English movement known as the Fraternal Democrats who had called an
international congress of the Left, and Engels as the delegate of

---

* According to Nicholaevsky some evidence exists that Marx's mother
let him have more than his fair share of the estate.

the Paris Communists, most of whom were German exiles. It was during this Congress, held at the White Hart Inn in Drury Lane, that Marx's *'Proletarians of all countries, unite!'* was adopted as the international movement's order of the day. Marx and Engels used it, modified by the additional statement, *'You have nothing to lose but your chains'*, as the conclusion to the Manifesto which they were commissioned to draft for the forthcoming Congress of the Communist League, a Congress which was never held because the year chosen for it, 1848, turned out to be an *annus mirabilis* of revolution all over Europe, and socialists were too busy fighting in the streets to bother with congresses.

Marx took an active part in the Belgian manifestation of the revolution, was accused of using the long-spent 6000 marks of his legacy to buy arms for Belgian workers and, when the government regained control of the situation, was expelled from the country. He went to Paris, tried to prevent the crazy scheme of the German *émigrés* who were raising and arming a legion to invade Germany, and was elected Chairman of the Anglo-French-German Communist League, whose strength was growing daily. Engels was fighting in Baden. The Legion of German revolutionaries was, as Marx had foretold, wiped out as soon as it crossed the Rhine. Marx slipped quietly into Germany and met Engels in the most revolutionary of the German cities, Cologne. The Communist League, with a large following of the workers whose leaders had founded it in the first place, demanded the immediate introduction of radical reforms and in Prussia won the concession of a parliamentary, and moderately democratic, constitution. But this did not satisfy the extreme Left Workers' Association, the *Enragés* of this revolution, which had armed its members. Fighting in the streets broke out. Marx fought hard to mitigate the violence and to prevent the Workers' Association from carrying out their threat to boycott the elections which had been conceded: when the enemy was an absolute aristocracy, wisdom lay in collaborating, for the time being, with the revolutionary bourgeoisie fighting for a parliamentary democracy. He founded and led a Democratic Association to realize this alliance and edited his new journal, the *New Rhenish Gazette*. When the Prussian government, regaining its nerve, went over to the attack and besieged Cologne with troops, Marx at first changed his tune and called for a refusal to pay taxes and for an armed rising *en masse*. But he soon had second thoughts : Germany was not ready for proletarian revolution. He called on the Cologne workers to lay down their arms and refrain from a violence which could accomplish nothing and would cost them their lives.

While living in France and Belgium, Marx had renounced his Prussian citizenship. The Prussian government could thus treat him as an undesirable alien. Once they regained the upper hand, they ordered him to leave the country at once. Engels, meanwhile, had returned to Manchester—Britain, in those days, was much more nearly a free country than it is now and offered the right of asylum to all revolutionaries; but in any case because of his father Engels would not have been challenged.

Marx published one more number of the new *Gazette*, defiantly printing it in red, and took Jenny, pregnant with their fourth child, and the three children, to Paris where he plunged into the fight against the reaction to the revolution. But he could not accomplish much. He was penniless and various projects for making a living came to nothing. Then the French government ordered him to leave within twenty-four hours.

SIX

Scientific Socialism (2)

Expelled from France, Marx sought and was refused permission to go first to Belgium and then to Switzerland. No middle-class or aristocratic government was willing to give living room to this meddlesome rouser of the working-class dog which, for want of the bone they had been too mean to give him, might turn savage and start biting. There were two exceptions: the United States, still too empty and loosely organized to care much about the antecedents of the immigrants it needed as cheap labour and still under the illusion, which was to last nearly another century, that its founders had made the last revolution needed to establish the rules for life, liberty and the pursuit of happiness; and Britain, too proud of and confident in its parliamentary system (though 'democracy' was still a pejorative word) and in the ability of its ruling class to keep the working class cowed, to be afraid of such wild men as Karl Marx. Let him come: a German Jew could be no danger to Britons. True, the working classes, to whose cause he was, one heard, devoted, might heave bricks at him on the sufficient grounds that he was a foreigner; that was his own look-out.

For Marx, although he was employed to write articles on Europe for an American newspaper, America would have been exile to Barbary; he chose Britain. He and his family landed as penniless exiles; Engels, up north in Manchester, was their only friend. They found lodgings in London and Engels sent them, and continued to send them, what money he could spare or, rather, ill spare. For not only did his father keep him on short commons, but Messrs Ermen and Engels expected him to keep up a good appearance and he had, also, the expenses of maintaining his adored mistress, Mary Burns, an Irish working-class girl who loved him dearly and made no demands on him but had, after all, to be housed and fed. The real expense of living with Mary—Engels was far too consistent in his rejection of 'bourgeois'

institutions to marry—was the maintenance of her parents; not
that they asked for help, but he could not bear their poverty.

Engels' future was, in fact, settled by the arrival of the Marx
family in England. Marx had no intention of remaining longer
than necessary, a few months at most; in the event, he remained
until his death thirty-four years later. And for thirty-four years—
no, forty-four, for his devotion continued for a decade after
Marx's death—Engels was to devote attention, which he grudged,
to the business of his firm; to neglect his own work in social
research; and in general to put his own real interests second in
order to help Marx with his work and ensure that he had at
least a measure of freedom to get on with the task which Engels
regarded as far more important than anything he could himself
contribute to the cause: the gathering of material for, and the
writing of that great critique of the economic system, *Das Kapital*.

Marx had other work, the earning of a part of his living at
least, which he was obliged to do as well. As I have said, he was
European correspondent of the *New York Tribune* and he did
such journalistic freelance jobs as friends could find for him.
But so little did he earn that, despite subsidies from Engels, the
Marx family were reduced to the most grinding poverty, were
often close to starvation, lived in two wretched rooms in various
slum quarters, and had their few sticks of furniture seized for
small debts to tradesmen. At least it was experience of what
capitalism meant to the poor and none of this could distract Marx
from the task he had set himself: he spent every moment he
could afford in the British Museum Reading Room, accumulat-
ing and ordering material for his great book. He took some
part in the chief radical movements in England, even though
he did not go beyond following their progress and criticizing
their policies and methods. He joined the principal associations
of working men.

There were some brief times of happiness for the family whenever a little money came in: Marx adored his children—who
called him 'Old Nick' or 'The Moor' and mocked his bad
English—and he liked to take them for long summer days on
Hampstead Heath where they picnicked and sang German songs;
to play with them, read to them, and take them, with Jenny, to
concerts or Shakespeare's plays; at the theatre they always had

to be satisfied with standing-room, since they could not afford to pay for seats. And he liked sometimes, when there were a few shillings in hand, to sit up half the night with friends, drinking beer and talking, talking about every aspect of the revolution to come but not of what must follow it; Marx alone among the great revolutionary socialists did not believe in a millennium.

To dispose, once and for all, of the matter of Marx's subsistence problem during the rest of his life: his own earning-power did not improve and he lost his American earnings when the *New York Tribune* decided to dispense with a European correspondent. But in 1860 Engels Senior took his son into partnership so that Engels was better able to afford the subsidies he paid to Marx. Even so they did not solve the family's problems, and Marx quite often had to write for more help. On one occasion (1863) he gave his request for money precedence over his casual and offhand condolences on the death of Mary Burns. Engels was very deeply wounded and wrote him a reproachful letter; the reply was so graceful and so contrite, and so moving on the subject of the Marx family's condition, that Engels forgave him at once; but then Engels forgave everyone their trespasses. At last, in 1870, Engels inherited the English side of Ermen and Engels when his father died, and became a comparatively rich man. From that moment he made Marx a substantial and regular allowance. Later, when Marx's mother died, he received a legacy which enabled him to buy a small house where he lived for the rest of his life.

In 1863 the Poles rose in arms against the Russian imperial tyranny. For liberals and socialists all over the world Tsarism was the arch-enemy and they enthusiastically supported the Polish rising against the domination of Alexander II, later to be assassinated by the Russian Populists. The French workers, through their political associations, petitioned the Emperor Napoleon III to intervene on behalf of Poland. They were told that while the French government sympathized with the Poles, it could not help them for fear of irritating the British government. Meanwhile, associations of British workers had petitioned Palmerston's government to intervene to help the rebellious Poles against their oppressor. Her Majesty's government, they were told, while sympathetic to the cause of freedom in Poland as elsewhere, could not intervene without alarming the French. Unfortunately for the cynics at the head of the two greatest powers on earth at the time there were many links, some of them originally forged by Marx, between British and French workers. The farcical fraud was exposed, and there followed a Franco-British workers' demonstration in support of the Polish rebels (July 1863). The demonstration was more or less socialist and was attended by delegations from Belgium and Italy. It could not help the Poles materially, but it had one positive and very important outcome: the various national delegations agreed to form an International Working Men's Association with the object of acquiring for Labour, regardless of frontiers, as the sole creator under God, of all wealth, economic power and, therefore, political power. In short, there would now exist a powerful international organization to put socialist theory into practice; the workers of the world were responding to Marx's call to unite and it seemed that Saint-Simon and Fourier, Owen, Hall, Thompson, Ricardo and a score of other theorists and, above all, Karl Marx and Friedrich Engels, were to be vindicated in practice.

On a French initiative Marx was invited to sit on the platform at the inaugural meeting of the Association as representative of the absent German workers. This he would not do; he would never commit himself to support any movement until he knew exactly what it proposed to do and how it proposed to set about it. But he nominated his friend Eccarius to represent the Germans, and himself agreed to sit on the platform as an observer. The meeting (28 September 1864 in St Martin's Hall, Longacre), formally founded the Association with a London HQ and elected a committee to draft rules and a programme of action. The Committee co-opted Marx as a member. He was too heavily committed to his work on *Das Kapital* and to various pamphlets to take much part in its work; in any case, he was never able to work with a committee, only to dictate to it. But when first a British and then an Italian draft were rejected as unsatisfactory, he responded to an appeal to come to the rescue. He and Engels then produced a Constitution for the International, as it came to be called (later, First International to distinguish it from the

Second). It was based on two principal propositions:

(i) The emancipation of the working class must be accomplished by the workers themselves.
(ii) The conquest of political power has become the principal task of the working class.

The use of the word 'political' was the seed of the International's ultimate decay. A very large number of European socialists, for example the followers of Proudhon, did not see their task in those terms: the thing was to conquer economic, that is industrial, power and to get rid altogether of the political State. But this division did not at once appear although Proudhon, for instance, refused to be co-opted into the International despite its initial and astonishing success. For, successful it almost immediately was. Working-class, consciously socialist political parties were being formed in most European countries, linked internationally and with the Trade Union movement in Britain and the United States. But, paradoxically, the International was too successful, for its striking success generated two Hegelian antitheses: it tempted socialists whose doctrines were very different from the 'Marxism' which Marx's and Engels' writings were bringing into being, and who saw in it a means to immediate revolution which Marx, of course, never did. And it alerted the bourgeoisie to a threat to capitalism which had to be taken seriously, and prepared it to fight for its dominion.

As to the first danger, even at the International's Second Congress, in Lausanne in 1867,* Marx was only just able to retain control for himself and scientific socialism, that is for realism, against Proudhon-inspired 'Collectivists' and Anarchist 'Mutualists'. Thus the mutual hostility between anarchists and communists, which was to have its terrible dénouement seventy years later in Spain, began with the very beginning of the organized international socialist movement. Marx considered the anarchist plan to get rid of the State not only heretical, but chimerical. Even had it been possible, he postponed that possibility into the very remote future; but it was also undesirable. Marx remained a Hegelian, whatever tricks he had played with the Hegelian system, and as such regarded the State as paramount.

* The first was in Geneva in 1866.

But so strong was the opposition within the International, that he only kept control of that Second Congress by keeping all matters of controversy—all the most important business—off the agenda.

As for the second danger, the year 1867 was one of savage industrial strife all over Western Europe and the United States. There were huge and prolonged strikes in every industrial country and the International was unexpectedly successful in arranging for working-class co-operation across national frontiers, so that capitalists were unable to bring in foreign strike-breakers. The middle-class capitalist press alarmed its readers everywhere with enormously exaggerated tales of the International's power: its strength was put at seven million members, a figure it never approached, and the coherence of its organization was also grossly exaggerated. This propaganda, in which the propagandists may themselves have believed, for Marx and his friends were not backward in making threatening noises, united the enemies of socialism: the tyrannies of Russia and Prussia looked much less offensive to British parliamentarians than they had done, and West European liberalism more like a bulwark against the socialist landslide to the absolutists of Eastern Europe. It was a case of capitalists of the world, unite!

In fact, however, they need not have worried. Two men were at hand who would do their work of wrecking the International for them: the arch-anarchist, Mikhail Bakunin and, it must be said, Marx himself, who had none of the arts of the politician, no skill in getting his own policies adopted while seeming to make concessions to the other side; and no ability so to bamboozle the 'don't knows' as to get them on his side without offending against their belief in their own judgement. Marx was one of nature's dictators, adept at manipulation but never one of nature's committee men. He, of course, thought that he was saving the International by being implacably anti-anarchist; and Bakunin thought that he alone knew how to make proper and effective use of it. Between them, they broke it. Marx so clearly realized what would be the outcome of Bakunin's tactics that he once accused the Russian of being in the pay of the Tsarist political police, though later he retracted that accusation. It was indeed unjust, and it might have been said of Bakunin, as it was of

Marshal Bazaine at his trial—'*cet homme n'est pas un traitre; c'est un imbécile!*' We shall come to him in due course; for the time being we are concerned only with his attempt to win control of the International for the policy of his half-open, half-clandestine and conspiratorial Social-Democratic Alliance—immediate revolution by armed insurrection; abolition of all national States; abolition of all existing economic institutions; management of society by co-operation without compulsion.

Marx, leading the scientific socialists, and with a much more realistic view of what was possible for the advance towards socialism, was implacable in his hostility to the anarchists. It was not only that he would concede nothing to their opinions, he would not even appear to concede the smallest point. He retained control and he succeeded in having Bakunin and his party expelled from the International (1872). But not before Bakunin had made it possible for the European ruling class to denounce the organization as one which was committed to a continent-wide civil war, and only at the cost of working-class solidarity in the socialist movement and of many thousands of members who did not necessarily agree with the anarchists but disliked Marx's dictatorial, or at best unyielding and obstinate, management of the International. As will appear, it was Bakunin's antics, in the name of the International in Lyons during the Paris Commune, that did most of the damage. The internecine strife at and between Congresses so wasted the strength, fractured the integrity and confused the purpose of the International that it was fatally weakened. An effort was made to restore its strength by shifting its HQ from the disturbed atmosphere of London to the calmer and cooler atmosphere of New York: but Marx himself could not inspire and guide the New York office from London and he could not go to New York, for the British Museum library was essential for his work. The International, cut off from its roots in working-class political consciousness, which was much livelier in Europe than in America, withered slowly away.

Meanwhile the first volume of *Das Kapital* had been published and Marx was busy working on the second. But not with the drive and steadiness of his past years of labour: the struggle was proving too exhausting to a man who was stricken by blow after blow. As a result of hardships and want of proper medical care, two of his beloved children had died; Jenny's health had broken down and she was never again perfectly well; Marx himself was frequently a sick man, suffering repeated returns of pleurisy, and he had lost, in the wrecking of the International, what had seemed to be the means of steady and well-founded progress towards the realization of the theories which had been his life's work. The freedom from want and from the distraction of trying to earn money conferred by Engels' allowance and the legacy from his mother came too late.

From 1870 Engels devoted himself to working with and for Marx, and when, after another bout of sickness in 1873, Marx seemed to lose the will for sustained and coherent work, and became bogged down in the sheer mass and volume of the material he had accumulated but no longer had the power to organize, Engels did his best to take the task upon himself.

SEVEN

From the Paris Commune
to Marxism

When, in 1871, Second Empire France was swiftly defeated by Bismarck's Prussia and Napoleon III fled from Sedan, the workers of Paris, Lyons, Marseilles, Brest and other great cities saw dazzling visions of the Millennium brought close. One of their class enemies had destroyed another and out of the resultant chaos would emerge the new proletarian order. Inspired, excited by dedicated socialist leaders from their own ranks, by the hotheads of the French branch of the International, and above all by the call to arms of Mikhail Bakunin, they would raise such a violent hurricane of revolutionary passion as would sweep Bismarck's armies out of France, crush the bourgeois 'vermin' and transform society into a socialist paradise.

Bakunin, to whom we shall return in a later chapter, was the Grand Old Man of revolutionary socialism, communism, and anarchism, the only man ever to have been received by a Congress of the International with a standing ovation. He was in Switzerland when he received news that the Second Empire had fallen and that the people of Lyons had proclaimed a Republic. Now it was above all in Lyons that he had his most devoted French followers, where his anarchist preaching had made more impression than the 'Internationalist' socialism of Karl Marx. He was forced to spare precious days raising a fighting fund, but then set off for the city to persuade the Lyonnais, or at least the spinning and weaving operatives and other workers and small artisans, that their new bourgeois Republic was not enough, was the wrong solution to their political problem. Sufficient numbers of workers and workers' leaders rallied to him to enable him to act: on the night of 27/28 September 1870 they 'arrested' the new Republic's officers, or such of them as they could be bothered to find, and on 28 September they seized and occupied the Hotel de Ville. From that seat of the provisional Third Republic, Bakunin declared the Republic at an end and the Revolutionary Commune in being. Europe had its first government of socialist (to use the word in its broadest sense) workers and its first act was to 'abolish the administrative and governmental machinery of State'.

All this Bakunin did in the name of the International. Marx, when he heard the news was furiously angry, but we shall come to his part presently. Meanwhile, Bakuninists in the other principal cities had made attempts, but very feeble ones amounting to nothing much more than street demonstrations which merely bored the citizens and attracted no real working-class support, to follow their friends' example in Lyons; they were not yet aware that Bakunin's anarchist Commune had only lasted about ten hours. It was not really crushed by force, although the Republicans, rallying, did sweep away its debris: it faded away of its own unrealism. Not even the excited men who made the Commune, always excepting Bakunin, were convinced by it, and with Republican authority reasserted, Bakunin was forced to fly for his life, and, a few days later to write:

> Farewell liberty, farewell Socialism, farewell Justice for the People and the triumph of humanity!*

and two months later he was to conclude from the tragi-comical Lyons *débâcle*:

> I no longer believe in the revolution in France: that country is no longer in the least revolutionary. Even the common people have become doctrinaire, as logic-chopping as the most bourgeois of bourgeois. Social revolution could have saved them and only social revolution can save them. But this people has shown itself incapable of ensuring its own salvation. Farewell all our dreams of emancipation soon. The reaction will be overwhelming and terrible ...†

When the Parisians, following the Lyons example, proclaimed the Republic in being, there seemed, at first, to be no question of surrender to the Prussians. The French *francs-tireurs*, partisans

* In a letter to Louis Palix, *Oeuvres*, IV, p. 78.
† In a letter to Gaspard Sentinon, *ibid*, II p. 275.

on the model of the Spanish *guerrilleros* of the First Empire wars, at least were carrying on the war; surely the Republic would support them, especially as the Prussians were retaliating by seizing and shooting villagers as hostages. Moreover, all was not as well with the Prussian armies in France as might seem on the surface; they were facing serious difficulties. As it happened, Karl Marx had received from an old Communist League comrade, now a high official in the Prussian service and close to Bismarck, Johannes Miquel by name, reliable information of those difficulties; and he at once passed it on to the French Government of National Defence.

For Marx, and almost all the Internationalists, had no doubt whatever that it was the duty of all socialists to support the new Third Republic by all the means in their power. Let Bismarck remember that when his king-puppet went to war, he swore in God's name that he was not waging war on the French people but solely on the French Emperor. In an open letter to Bismarck, published in *The Daily News* (19 January 1871) Marx informed the Prussian that France was now fighting 'not only for her own independence, but also for the liberty of Germany and all Europe'. It was a threat of the same order as the famous opening phrase of the *Communist Manifesto*. And, under Marx's guidance, it was the General Council of the International which organized the monster demonstration, in Trafalgar Square, of workers and their middle-class allies, all carrying tricolour flags in support of the French Republic.

It was not, of course, that Marx had any illusions about the social nature of that Republic: it was whole-heartedly bourgeois and anti-socialist at heart, however it might seem to welcome socialist support and hint vaguely at concessions to socialist demands. When Engels, as ever warm and active in the cause and passionately anti-Prussian, proposed to set out at once for France to urge upon Gambetta his own carefully worked-out plan for breaking the Prussian blockade of Paris whose people were being starved to death, Marx discouraged him with, 'Never trust those bourgeois republicans; at the first sign of a hitch, they'll shoot you as a spy.' But unlike the anarchist Bakunin, Marx did not believe that installing the Third Republic was a case of driving out Satan with Beelzebub: the Republic was an improvement on, offered more hope of social progress than, the Empire. It was not as if any realist, any good judge of the political situation, could possibly believe that there was any hope of establishing a proletarian government immediately. Therefore the proper course for socialists was to win from the Republic as much as possible for the workers in return for working-class support. This reasoning is, of course, the origin of such more recent historical events as Stalin's insistence on supporting the Kuomintang revolution of Chiang Kai-shek in the 1920s, of the massacre of half-a-million communists by the Nationalists in Indonesia, and of the refusal of orthodox communist parties in Latin America to support the guerrilla actions of the Marxist-Leninist New Left.

But other socialists thought differently. Bakunin had shot his bolt in Lyons and, as we have seen, lost heart when he failed to install the Millennium at once. But he was far from being the only *imbécile* on the Left. The extremist leaders in Paris were causing the very greatest alarm to the Republic's government in Versailles. On 28 January 1871 that government asked for, and was granted on monstrously extortionate terms, an Armistice from Bismarck. That request, and the acceptance of the terms, were not unconnected with the socialist threat from Paris.

The government had already been accused, by the Bakuninists and the 'Jacobins' of the socialist Left, of feebleness in its attitude to Prussia, and of a cowardice which amounted to a betrayal of the French people. There was something in this accusation. True, Paris was starving, true all French armies had suffered defeat, but it is also true that the government had the means, the Parisians the will, to defend Paris and, by prolonging the defence, force Bismarck to strike an easier and less humiliating bargain in the peace talks. The workers and the middle-class liberals of all Europe were demanding intervention by their governments in support of Republican France against the Prussian tyrant. Help might perhaps come from outside France; already Garibaldi had come with an Italian Legion, to fight shoulder to shoulder with the French. Yes, Paris, at least, should be fought for.

What none definitely knew but many suspected was that the provisional government in Versailles was much more afraid of an armed rising by the Paris workers, of social revolution, than of anything Bismarck could do. There is a remarkable consistency in the behaviour of the French bourgeoisie: the first government, like the last, of the Third Republic, when forced to choose between fighting the national enemy and fighting the class enemy, chose to fight the class enemy. Politically, from their point of view as bourgeois determined to maintain bourgeois power, they were perfectly right. They were setting, to the workers, an example of international class solidarity which the workers would have done well to follow in the cause of socialism. The provisional government came secretly to terms with Bismarck: he would release enough French prisoners of war to form an 'Army of Order', provided the French government would use that army to 'restore order', that is to say, crush the incipient social revolution in Paris. Rumours of this agreement circulated. (Later Marx was able to supply the Commune's leaders with details, provided, again, by Johannes Miquel.) The 'Jacobins' and Bakuninists seized upon those rumours to support their claim that the Republic was betraying the French people into the hands of their ferocious German enemy.

Four days after the Armistice, the Commune was proclaimed in Paris.

The last great struggle which Marx and Engels waged for socialism in the field (as distinct from their work as theorists creating a body of doctrine) was their attempt to save the Paris Commune from foundering in futile chaos and total defeat. They had not wanted it proclaimed at all, but since it was in being it must not be allowed to fail to accomplish anything whatever, and above all, since some of its leaders were Internationalists, everything possible must be done to prevent it from behaving in a way which could be used to discredit the International to which Marx and Engels had imparted a sense of responsibility and order —which was precisely what made it so terrifying to bourgeois governments. Not very long before his death, Marx summarized what his attitude to the Commune had been:

> With a small dose of common sense the Commune could have obtained a compromise useful to the whole mass of the people

—the only thing it would have been possible to obtain at that time.*

What, in the name of the General Council of the International, Marx urged on the Commune was loyal support of the new Third Republic in return for concessions to working-class demands for economic improvement of their lot and a share of political power. The Commune had some fairly strong cards in its hand: it controlled Paris, thus forcing the Prussians to maintain a siege which they wanted over and done with; it had in its hands a number of compromising secret treaties—one, as we have seen, provided by Marx—and could use the threat of publication to obtain better terms for the workers of Paris from the men trying to rule France from Versailles. Under Marx's influence the French representative on the General Council wrote to the leaders of the French branch of the International, who had gone to Paris to commit, as Marx very much feared, 'stupidities in the International's name', advising them:

> Power is still in the hands of the bourgeoisie. In these circumstances the workers' role, or rather duty, is to let the bourgeois vermin make peace with the Prussians (for they will never rid themselves of the shame of that act), not to strengthen them by insurrection but to profit from the measure of freedom which the circumstances will entail to organize the forces of the working class.

Marx had approved the Lyons proclamation of the Republic, but even then was insisting that the workers must on no account try to seize power from the bourgeois Republicans until after a peace with Prussia had been signed. Engels was of the same mind, writing to his friend and leader, '... if the workers conquer now, in the service of the national defence, they will have to accept the legacy of Bonaparte and of the existing worm-eaten Republic; they will be crushed by the Prussian armies and our movement will be set back twenty years.'

Compromise, compromise, was urged on the leaders of the Commune in letter after letter from the General Council, that is to say from Marx, and through their agent, the shoemaker

* Letter to Domela Nieuwenhuis, 22 February 1881, quoted by Nicolaevsky.

Auguste Serrailer. They were successful in discouraging a mad project to form an 'international brigade' in Switzerland to march on and relieve Paris.* Marx knew that any such legion would be butchered by the combined French and Prussian forces, as Herwegh's legion of German *émigré* socialists had been butchered in 1848. And, as I have said above, he provided the Commune with details of the secret treaty between Jules Favre and Bismarck which, if published, would have outraged the patriotism even of the Republican bourgeoisie.

But many of the General Council's letters from London never reached their destination in a Paris besieged and starving, and those which did were not attended to, while Serrailer proved inadequate to the task of making the French 'Internationalists' listen to, much less act upon, advice from London HQ.

As Marx had foreseen, 'the wolves, the swine, and the vile curs' of the old society flung themselves, snarling, on the revolutionary Paris workers. The Capitalist Beast, that *méchant animal*, feeling itself attacked, defended itself. And most effectively it did so: the communard Jacobins had responded to government terrorism, by terrorism; the two generals commanding the troops sent in from Versailles to disarm the Parisians and 'restore order' were captured and executed; the archbishop of Paris, seized as a hostage for the lives of communard prisoners in government hands, was put to death when those prisoners were shot. The liberal and reactionary press all over Europe not only used those truths but an astonishing farrago of lies, inventions and calumnies to present the communards as a gang of rootless, heartless, mindless, ferociously sadistic monsters—the same treatment was to be given to the Bolsheviks less than half a century later. The chance to discredit the dreaded International by presenting the acts of the Commune, true and false, as typical of what might be expected of the workers in power, was much too good to miss. This propaganda was widely credited—even some of the people who wrote and published it believed it.

At a critical moment when the General Council of the International was in frequent session and doing all it could to counter

---

* Switzerland had, at the time, very strong socialist and even stronger anarchist movements, the latter of Bakuninist inspiration; it was, in fact, one of the white hopes of socialism.

this attack, Marx, its best head and strongest will, fell gravely ill and was unable to attend meetings. Sick though he was, he accepted the task of drafting an Address to the Paris workers which, it was hoped, would not only make some impression on the French hotheads, but make clear where the International stood with regard to the revolution. Before he could finish it Thiers had come to terms with Bismarck and obtained the Prussian's permission to send an army into Paris to smash the revolution. After some days of savage street-fighting, during which the thousands of prisoners taken by the government forces, many hundreds of them pacific bystanders who had taken no part in the revolution, were systematically massacred in the pens into which they had been herded. The government triumphed, the Commune was crushed, its leaders and a great part of its rank and file murdered—for this action was one of mass-murder and Thiers had, as Cassivelaunus said of the Romans in Britain 'made a desert and called it a peace'.

Marx's *Address* thus became an obituary on the Revolution and the Commune, a 'hymn to the martyrs of the fight for the liberation of the working class', as Nicolaevsky calls it. It was more than that, however; it was a copious source of lessons for the socialist revolutionary of the future.

The Commune, Marx wrote, although it had been but 'an imperfect sketch of a national organization' had nevertheless been '... in essence a government of the working class, resultant of the struggle of the producing classes against the owning classes'. It sketched 'the political form, thus discovered at last under which the task of emancipating Labour could be carried on ...'

The Commune, moreover, had 'incorporated political power in the society of which it was the life-force, instead of being the instrument which controlled and dominated society'. Embodied in the masses, political power became their strength, instead of being as it had been, the organized means of their suppression; it became the political form of their emancipation, whereas it had been the artificial means belonging to their oppressors, of their oppression by their enemies.

The workers have no ideal to realize, no Utopia ready to be

established by decree of the people. Their task is to liberate
the elements of that new order by which the old bourgeois
order, now falling into ruin, is surrounded.

Marx's *Address* concluded:

The Party of the workers, with its Commune, will for ever be
famous as the glorious forerunner of the new order. Its martyrs
have their place in the mighty heart of the working class. As
for their exterminators, history has already nailed them to an
eternal pillory from which all the prayers of their priests will
be powerless to deliver them ...

The Commune had been defeated; a battle had been lost. The
struggle of the working class continued.

During all but the final years of his last decade Karl Marx
enjoyed, at long last, a small measure of peace. With age, his
view lengthened—the great socialist revolution was not for today
or even tomorrow; but it would certainly come and when it did
his life-work had ensured, surely, that it would be on sound,
logical lines and would succeed. His view also broadened: for
the first time in his life he took an interest in Russian social
politics, studied the struggle of the various Populist movements,
and forecast a communist revolution in that country. Three
decades of work with the British working class and its leaders,
and with British radical thinkers, had given him insight into the
character of the British worker and his institutions and he had
come to believe that Britain was the one country in the whole
world which might attain to socialism, and at last to communism,
without having to pass through the ordeal of a bloody revolution.

For a year or two, also, his private life was pleasanter. He now
had the means to ensure that Jenny need not drudge her life away
and might conserve her little remaining strength. He loved and
took a great interest in his grandchildren, Jenny Longuet's children, and from time to time went to Paris to see them. When,
foreseeing as he did as much as a century of wars and revolutions
before the world-wide establishment of a rational international
socialist State, he deplored that Jenny's children were girls, he
was only half joking: for would not the cause need men, need
fighters? Still a good German bourgeois in his attitude to such

matters as marriage and the place of women (he disapproved of Engels' refusal to marry Mary Burns), he would have been very shocked at the notion of such female partisans as fought social-ism's war in, for example, Yugoslavia.

But his very last years were wretched: Jenny had cancer and he was repeatedly bed-ridden with pneumonia or pleurisy. In 1881 Jenny Marx died and Marx never recovered from his grief. His health declined even further. He was sent by his doctors to the Isle of Wight to recover from another bout of pleurisy and while he was there he received the news that Jenny Longuet had died suddenly in Paris. He rose from his sick-bed, went back to his house in Highgate, went to bed, refused to eat or speak. And in March 1883 he died.

Engels had already taken over much of the work of *Das Kapital*. On his friend's death he found a vast mass of notebooks, of chapters started but never finished, of cryptic annotations, vague drafts and scrappy sketches, terrible evidence of the effects of sheer exhaustion. Out of this chaos he produced order: first, volume two; and then, after ten years' more labour, much of it research which Marx had barely initiated, volume three. That was published in 1894, and having finished his work Engels died. Among the socialist giants of the 19th century, he had the greatest and kindest heart and the sweetest nature.

Such, then, were the makers of scientific socialism. What was it that they made? One might call it a technology for attaining the Millennium were it not for the fact that Marx himself can never have believed that there would be a Millennium. He never dealt in Utopias: his business was to discover social and political 'laws' and ensure that the proletariat understood and acted upon the responsibilities to which, he believed, it was called by those 'laws'. And one recalls that very uncharacteristic vagueness on the subject of the final withering away of the State as full com-munism is accomplished. What I mean is that Marx and Engels, using the tools which the pioneer socialists had forged for them, surveyed the road-of-the-head to socialism, seeing clearly that the road-of-the-heart was no road at all, but a footpath into a quagmire.

The basis of philosophical Marxism is the dialectical materialism developed out of the Hegelian dialectic. It has become obscured and overlaid by Marxist scholasticism, an ugly and immensely complex parasitic growth on an analysis as simple as all great and true analyses are. Marx himself, who was never, of course, a Marxist, summarized his method as 'inclusion in the understanding of existing things, understanding of the negative implications of their necessary termination'. Apply this to history: in Historical Materialism, event is thesis, anti-event (think, here, in the terms used in modern physics), antithesis provoked by the event. What we are seeking is order and pattern: once we have it, extrapolation becomes a useful tool—one of the names for our species is *homo faber* (man is an artist, a maker, or he is nothing). Put it in other words: all historical forces generate their opposites. Now, in practice: a feudal society generates a bourgeoisie ultimately hostile to it and bound to overthrow it. The capitalist society arising out of that bourgeoisie generates a proletariat to serve its ends and, again, bound to overthrow and destroy it.

Marx did not see the process as going beyond that point, not out of any emotional prejudice in favour of the working class but for logical reasons. At that point you are down to real brass tacks, down to the foundations, for the only foundation of any society is productive labour so that when it is the class responsible for that labour which wields the power of the State, one can go no further excepting that, taking advantage of the (in Marx's day) unlimited productiveness of industrial technology (Owen made the same miscalculation), it is possible to pass from socialism to communism. At this point, the State withers away as unnecessary and society is composed of men voluntarily cooperating in production and all other activities proper to civilization.

These things being so, Marxism calls on the proletariat to recognize its 'historical necessity' and to work deliberately towards taking the power of the State out of the hands of the bourgeoisie and into their own; in short to establish the dictatorship of the proletariat through direct or representative assemblies conveying decisions to an executive. The workers would, of course, have their own political party for this purpose—a social-democratic party. Marx did not envisage more than one such party; there could be no need for that since the workers could have only one policy—socialism developing into communism.

But this revolution must be accomplished in a rational and sensible way, with a proper regard for the facts of political life. Before discussing the Marxist policy in this part of the matter, it will be necessary to take a look at the conditions in which it was evolved. First, Marx gave only marginal attention to the two great parliamentary oligarchies, the British Empire and the United States. That this was so is quite clear from the nature of his thought which was chiefly concerned with the Continental European countries. The German kingdoms and principalities were absolute monarchies increasingly dominated by Prussia, the most absolute and disciplined of them all despite the slow gains of a more or less liberal constitutionalism. Russia was an absolute monarchy unmodified by a constitution, with a vast empire run on semi-Oriental lines. Beyond lay the absolute imperial monarchies, again, of China and Japan, but Marx never showed any interest in the non-European world or in North America. The rest of Europe, excepting Italy, was dominated by France and the ancient and ramshackle Austrian Empire which was less an empire than the family estate of the Hapsburgs. Italy had recently won independence and union as a constitutional monarchy on more or less English lines. Spain was another theoretically absolute monarchy in which, from time to time, the Cortes made a determined effort to establish parliamentary rule. All of which comes to this: that, in a great part of Europe, the bourgeoisie had still to take power from an aristocracy, or from a plutocracy disguised as an Empire. Marx's thinking was conditioned by this rather than by conditions in Britain or America, where the power was in the hands of the bourgeoisie.

His advice to the working class was, therefore, that they must

> march forward with the great democratic army as the extreme point of its left wing, but being careful always to maintain its connections with the main body of the army ... the Proletariat has no right to isolate itself.

So the good Marxist will help the bourgeoisie to overthrow the older pre-bourgeois establishments, then work with the bourgeois Left against the bourgeois Right, and so continue until the moment comes to seize power, either by revolution including armed rising *en masse*—but then only when victory is made certain by the revolutionary situation in the country in question —or, perhaps, for example in the case of Britain, by getting control of the parliamentary system and using it for Socialist ends.

In economics Marx adopted and then refined the systems of several predecessors, notably Ricardo. He overcame the chief objection to the theory of Labour Value by applying it only to socially useful production with the implication that there should, in any case, be no other kind, at least until society was so rich and all men whatsoever so well provided for that there would be no harm in fantasy. In other respects he was at one with the earlier socialist economists but his study of capital led him to conclusions which they had not yet drawn—chiefly to the conclusion that capital tends to become concentrated in fewer and fewer hands since by the very nature of the system the richer capitalists would tend to absorb the less rich. This, as far as it goes, has turned out to be true. But he argued from it that as the rich grew richer and fewer, the poor must grow poorer and more numerous—in other words, that the condition of the working class would grow steadily worse as the increasingly great capitalists acquired the power, by the elimination of competition for labour, to depress wages. This was the innate contradiction which would lead capitalism to perish of its own accord. Follow such logic to the necessary conclusion, using the Platonic rather than the Hegelian dialectic, and it is obvious that the system was self-destructive. So many socialists were completely convinced by this that some of the coming social democratic thinkers were to argue that revolution would be quite unnecessary since, if Marx was right, there was no need to take the pains to kill a system which was in any case dying of its own internal contradiction.

It is not sufficient to dismiss as faulty, by hindsight, Marx's reasoning in this area. The researches of the Drummonds have shown that in the first decade of the 19th century the nutrition of the working class as a whole was *at its lowest ebb since 1760*. In the third decade of the same century from fifteen to twenty-five per cent of the workers in all industrial countries were unemployed and either starving or near starving and living in atrocious conditions. What Marx did not foresee was that a man of genius would be born capable of seeing that the advance of technology could go some way to so changing the conditions in which production was carried on that the premises of Marx's argument were no longer true and, in the second place, that capitalists, and the governments which represented their interests and controlled the most powerful States on their behalf, were capable of learning from him, Marx, when shown how to do so by another man of genius who saw that socialist planning could be used by capitalists.

Not all Marx's disciples by any means agreed that since capitalism was dying of its inner contradictions, socialists had only to sit and wait for it to die ('Socialist Revisionism'). A majority saw things differently: the moment that the bourgeois system had been so weakened by its own debility that it was clearly possible to give it the *coup de grâce* by an armed revolution, then that revolution should be made.

Bearing in mind, once again, the dates between which Marxism was created by Marx and Engels (it has since been as much modified as Christianity since it left the creative hands of Saint Paul), here are the principal economic changes which it called for: expropriation of all land and application of rent to State expenditure; expropriation of the means of production, distribution and exchange, and their management, for the people—their creators and therefore their only owners, under justice—by the State; abolition of the right to inherit property (here, as in the case of Proudhon's policy, is meant accumulated capital, not personal chattels); nationalization of all credit institutions with the object of centralizing control of credit by the State and abolishing usury, interest to cover no more than service charges; State education for all; abolition of child labour; the duty of all, without exception, to work.

None of these demands was new: all will be found in pre-Marxist socialists and even in the works of political economists who cannot properly be described as socialists. But one thing at least was quite new in Marxism: the proposition, based on the reasoning which the use of the Hegelian dialectic in the manner of the young Hegelians had led to, that only the working class, the basic producers, should wield the power of the State; and only the working class could bring about the revolution which would ensure that result. And the implication of these propositions—class war. With the possible exception of Proudhon, none of the pre-Marxist socialists thought in those terms. Their work might be and usually was inspired by the obvious need to do something to raise the deprived majority of the human race to the conditions of decency and comfort, and the opportunities for a fuller enjoyment of life which were the privileges of a minority. But they saw the change being wrought by men of their own kind out of the goodness of their hearts and the soundness of their reasoning. Marx's study of history led him to the conclusion that this was nonsense. The class in power, serving its own interests, not only held onto power until forced to leave go, but found plausible ideologies to justify what was, in fact, brutal selfishness, the blind and unconscious selfishness of all living species.

A number of phenomena have made modern revision of Marxist socialism necessary, have, indeed, made of it, excepting in doctrinaire government circles in 'communist' countries, a concept which is always becoming, always growing. Its philosophical basis is recognized as valid beyond Marxist circles and the historical dialectic is used as a tool by non-Marxist writers. But what Marx and Engels did not foresee were:

(*i*) The mass-production techniques invented by the greatest industrial genius of the century, Henry Ford, and the amount of surplus value which technologically sophisticated industry can produce, with the consequent need for capitalists to pay higher and higher wages in order to create a market for their product. In other words, they did not and could not foresee that scientific progress plus the steady pressure of his own economic thinking on both workers' organizations and capitalism, would ensure that after a certain trough in the curve of decline workers' wages would begin to rise.

(*ii*) The flexibility and enormous growth following on the above, of the ancient device of usury, in the expansion of credit commerce to enable the workers to become the largest consumers of durable consumer goods—owners of houses, cars, etc., on credit, a credit which furthermore had the advantage for the capitalists of keeping the worker bound by legal obligations to the capitalist system. He no longer had nothing to lose but his chains.

(*iii*) The advent, in John Maynard Keynes, of a genius capable of adapting socialist economists' ideas for controlling the economy and its growth, to capitalist ends. After Keynes it was no longer necessary for capitalism to be governed simply by uncontrollable market fluctuations; it could be controlled and steered, though only within certain limits.

(*iv*) The growth of very large industrial and commercial corporations to the point at which they could be managed, like the State, only by a bureaucracy; and the scale of State interference in capitalist business, together resulting, under trade-union pressure, in partial adoption into capitalist enterprise of socialist planning and a measure of socialist welfare.

(*v*) The extent and pace of the expansion of world trade.

(*vi*) Finally, the threat of exhaustion of certain natural resources. A socialist, like an expanding capitalist, assumption was that these would be virtually inexhaustible. As a result of the deliberate fostering of demand for consumer goods by capitalism and, of course, of excessive population growth, supplying demand on a fair-share basis must result in exhaustive consumption of natural resources on such a scale that certain commodities essential for the continuance of a high-consumption economy will soon become scarce.

Are we therefore to conclude that these six and other developments have taken the wind out of socialism's sails and that they promise a capitalist Millennium to make the socialist one unnecessary to fulfil our aspirations? No, of course. The reasons for that downright negative will be advanced in due course; but, for one thing, the coming scarcity of certain raw materials and the food shortages which are already almost upon us, are two new and, by Marx and Engels, unexpected reasons for the only system which would make possible the management and sharing of what there is a basis sufficiently equitable to avoid a hideous struggle for supplies, probably taking the form of wars of extermination.

EIGHT

Libertarian Socialism

I now devote a single chapter to brief lives and works of four men who were giants in the libertarian socialist movement—anarchists, in short whose vision was of a Millennium in which freedom would be a reality, would be all. The history of anarchism considered as a manifestation of socialism cannot, because of its bulk and importance, be adequately treated in a work of this kind. (For my part I believe that the hideous and degrading character of the Nation-State as revealed to us during the past half-century across the whole political spectrum from parliamentary oligarchy as we have it in Britain and America to Moscow-style communist tyrannies, makes re-examination of anarchist theory as a possible means of ridding ourselves of this foul parasite on human life a matter of urgency.*)

Two roads seemed to lead to the Millennium: the Marx-Engels road by way of the Hegelian State, and the road sketched by such men as Godwin and Tom Paine, and firmly inked-in and corrected by Pierre Joseph Proudhon, which entailed the demolition of the State and elimination of formal government. For Marx the State could, and should, by socialization, be made the source of all good, composed as it would be of the whole people—the Hegelian synthesis of man and nation and ultimately of man and mankind. For Proudhon and the anarchists in general the State could not but be the embodiment of injustice, so that the very first step to the Millennium must be to get rid of that incubus.

Anarchism (from the Greek *anarkia*, non-rule) is the doctrine which starts from the proposition that formal, institutionalized government is not only not necessary to mankind, but is necessarily oppressive however composed, and as such, an evil to be

* For those readers who are moved to study it I recommend, for a start, Franco Venturi's great *Roots of Revolution* (Weidenfeld & Nicolson, London, 1960) although its chief concern is with the Russian movement, and George Woodcock's *Anarchism* (Pelican, London, 1963).

avoided. We have already noted that its first great exponent was an English industrialist of genius, William Godwin, and its first great literary work his *Political Justice* (1793). Its first poet of genius was Percy Bysshe Shelley. And its first scientific exponent was a Frenchman who is among the half-dozen most brilliant and feeling men of talent produced by the socialist dream of the Millennium.

PROUDHON

Pierre Joseph Proudhon was born in the Franche-Comté in 1809, son of a feckless and bankrupt taverner and cooper. The man was unable to provide his son with an education and Pierre Joseph was working for his living at nine years of age; he was also educating himself and in due course he apprenticed himself to a printer. Meanwhile he had been reading and writing. His essay, written for a prize offered by a benevolent association of local gentry interested in culture, not only revealed a literary talent of the highest order, but took the young man to Paris where, moved by compassion for the miserable condition of the poor in the industrial suburbs, he undertook a study of political economy. From it he emerged with what was to be the guiding principle of his life: it can be stated in fourteen words:

> All political parties without exception, insofar as they seek power, are varieties of abolutism.

All liberals and, of course, all socialists, regarded absolutism as an intolerable evil, whether the autocrat was the Russian Tsar, the Turkish Sultan, or the Hapsburg Emperor. The liberals, because it withheld power from the capitalist bourgeoisie; the socialists because its law was the protection of privilege and an intolerably oppressive status quo. Now Proudhon was saying that even such liberal institutions as, for example, the British Parliament were also intolerable tyrants. The evil of tyranny was necessarily embodied in the State; therefore the State must be replaced by something less oppressive. This could be a complex of voluntary contracts between free individuals, which Proudhon called 'Association'. And Association, as he expounded it in *On the Creation of Order in Humanity* (1843)—he was never afraid to tackle big themes—would not become merely a political-economic device, but a reservoir and source of collective consciousness, and therefore of strength, transcending those of the free individuals composing it.

From the beginning Proudhon took as his premise the existence of immanent justice: in *On Justice in the Revolution and the Church* (1858) he calls it 'the central star which governs society ... the principle and regulator of all transactions'. Since we now know that immanent justice is not in nature,* is, in short, an imaginary condition, it might be supposed that Proudhon's arguments must be invalid from the start. But as nearly all mankind has, from the remote past when man, having invented Justice, cautiously attributed the invention to God, a great part of the human race had been behaving *as if* immanent justice were a fact: consequently, since it was the human race and not the cosmos which Proudhon was concerned with, the imaginary nature of his premise does not invalidate his arguments.

The two books mentioned above were widely read and attended to because before he published either he had published his conclusions following an examination of the nature of property, in a work entitled *What is Property?* (1840). It had caused a sensation and also caused many men in and outside France to regard the author as an infamous and dangerous revolutionary; for he had answered his own question with 'Property is Theft'. It was a direct and audacious attack on the institution which was the very foundation of aristocratic and bourgeois society protected by a vast body of law in every country in the world and which was regarded, moreover, as the only possible basis for a stable society.

What is Property? is not a sensational work but a carefully reasoned exposure of facts revealing irrefutable truths touching the basis of society. It is not Proudhon himself who argues that injustice is built into the system of private property, but rather the truths he revealed which expose this fact. Even Karl Marx, who came, after a brief initial flirtation between the two of them, to detest Proudhon and his anti-State doctrine, described the book as 'the first decisive, vigorous and scientific examination of property ...'

* Its apparent and occasional manifestations are one of the countless products of random combinations, i.e. of chance.

It is important to look at Proudhon's answer to his titular question: he was not concerned with chattels, or rather he approved of chattel-property, holding it to be essential to every man if that man was to be free. Every man should own a house, enough land about it on which to raise food for himself and family, an adequacy of furniture and clothing, and the tools of his trade. The property which Proudhon stigmatized as 'Theft' was that property which enables the proprietor to exploit the labour of other men: in other words, capital. Every man had the right to own and sell the product of his labour; no man had any right to own the means of production—land or plant—other than the tools of his trade which he used with his own hands. Cultivable land, industrial plant and technical skill composed the accumulated wealth of all mankind, to the making and accumulation of which all men had contributed their labour; it should therefore belong to everybody. Moreover, private ownership of the means of production demonstrably led to injustice—to degrading poverty on one side, demoralizing riches on the other. And if, with the advances of technology, the tools of a trade were becoming too big and complex—an iron-foundry, for example, or a papermill—for one man to own and operate unaided, and in any case too dear, for one workman to afford, then such plant must be owned in common by the group of workmen who operated it.

Like Marx, Proudhon saw the salvation of man from the degrading and demoralizing scourge of capitalism only in the working class: he did not, like the proto-socialists, expect the upper and middle classes tamely to give up their privileges simply because his argument was sound. His first revolutionary call to the workers came in his *Warning to the Proprietors*. He summoned the workers to seize the initiative in the reformation of society; and he warned all 'proprietors and magistrates' not to provoke the peaceful working-class revolutionaries or reformers by using police or magisterial violence against them, or it would go very hard with them indeed.

The action to which Proudhon summoned the workers of France and, by implication, of the world—he was a strong and consistent anti-Nationalist and anti-Patriot—was neither violent, nor was it political. It was one of the deep differences which alienated Marx and Proudhon from each other that Proudhon would have nothing to do with political revolutionary action. It was undesirable and, indeed, dangerous in that the only outcome of political revolution must be another tyrant State. In his *Economic Contradictions* (1846) he foresaw that communism, however libertarian and benevolent its intentions, must end by establishing a tyrannical monopoly of power, a foresight which, as we know to our cost, has turned out to be true. Therefore, revolutionary action must be on the economic, the industrial level and its aim to bypass the State and make no use of institutional politics in the future. The workers everywhere must simply walk out of capitalist undertakings, and freely associate together in industrial co-operatives. In due course, first the nation's and then the world's trade system would come to consist in exchanges of goods between voluntary Associations of workers controlling their own industries as trustees for mankind at large : the Millennium.

Proudhon was far too able a thinker and far too honest a man to put forward this proposition without considering how, in practice, the great change was to be accomplished. It had to be achieved within the context of a capitalist and bourgeois society and he did not envisage a violent solution unless government terrorism forced it on the workers. An instrument was required which would at once connect the first Associations with capitalism in so far as that was necessary and until capitalism had withered away for want of labour; and yet insulate the Associations from the capitalist taint. He found the instrument for this complex operation in the idea of a People's Bank. This was to be a co-operative of 'Mutualists' as Proudhonian workers came to be called, which would operate as a clearing-house for exchange transactions between workers, using labour-value certificates in place of money and, at the same time, it would manage the sale of goods and purchase of materials, dealing with the capitalist world in that world's own money.

Although this chapter is concerned with theory, in the case of Proudhon thought and action were so closely integrated that it will be necessary to glance briefly at what he did in his attempts to implement his ideas. I have said that he repudiated political action but, seeing a chance to have some of his notions tested in practice when in 1848 revolution seemed about to overthrow thrones and bourgeois parliaments all over Europe and deal a hard blow to unrestricted capitalism, he stood for and was elected Deputy to the Constituent Assembly of the revolution in Paris. He was not able to accomplish anything and was confirmed in his contemptuous opinion of parliaments. In the same year he founded a newspaper, *Le Représentant du Peuple*. By the time it attained the then staggering net sale of forty thousand, a bourgeois government was firmly back in power, and the paper was suppressed. Not so Proudhon: he immediately founded another paper, *Le Peuple*, and, at the same time, his People's Bank. Response to that foundation was gratifying: the Bank soon had twenty-seven thousand 'Mutualists' drawn from the classes of skilled industrial workers and of small artisans. What might have come of this is an unanswerable question. The fact is that Proudhon was, above all, a didactic, polemical and revolutionary writer and one of his leaders for *Le Peuple* ruined his chances of making a success of the Bank and the first Associations which it was to serve. He wrote that France's President (later Emperor) Louis Napoleon Bonaparte, Gladstone's old comrade in the agreeable task of bashing Chartists on the head, was 'conspiring to enslave the people of France'. Warned that a warrant was out for his arrest, he took refuge in Belgium. He realized that, as a wanted man, he could not run the People's Bank, and, not wanting it to fall into the wrong hands, he returned secretly to France to liquidate it. This he accomplished but was caught by the police, tried and sent to prison for three years.

The prison regime was mild and Proudhon spent the three years writing two of socialism's great books, *Confessions of a Revolutionary* (1850), in which he again exposed capitalism as the great degrader and demoralizer of decent men and called for an end to the accumulation of capital in private hands with its inevitable concomitant of exploitation, and *General Idea of the Revolution in the 19th Century*, in which he was the first to expound revolution as not merely historically inevitable (Marx) but as a part of the natural order, thus foreshadowing the Trotskyist revolution-in-permanence.

Le Peuple had, of course, been suppressed for telling the French people about the President and emperor-to-be. But while its founder, proprietor, editor and principal contributor was still in prison, Alexander Herzen, the prophet of Russian socialism and subsidizer of a score of later famous socialists, provided him with the money to found *La Voix du Peuple*, thus enabling Proudhon to continue propagating his revolutionary ideas. It quickly attained a daily sale of sixty thousand copies, and on the days when Proudhon himself wrote the leader, it was apt to be sold out so fast that copies changed hands at a premium. Like its predecessors it was suppressed, whereupon Proudhon re-founded *Le Peuple*. But he was running out of money, it did not appear regularly, and was soon suppressed for 'incitement to civil war'.

The next important work of the great libertarian socialist was *On Justice in the Revolution and the Church* in which he derived a plan for a just society from a consideration of immanent and transcendental justice. In this, once again, Proudhon took a serious risk, for in his consideration of religion he argued that if there be a god, he must be anti-civilized, anti-liberal and anti-human, the antithesis of immanent justice. The edition he had printed sold like hot cakes; the police seized what remained of the stock after a few days and arrested its author. Proudhon was fined 3000 francs and sentenced to three years; he appealed, was remanded on bail pending the appeal, and again took refuge in Belgium where revolutionary society in Brussels, including Tolstoy and the painter Courbet, lionized him.

He had by now worked out a system of loose federation of his projected Associations as the absolute safe maximum degree of political organization which could be permitted—safe, that is, for the freedom and self-respect of the individual, i.e. for justice. He wrote and published *Of the Federative Principle* (1861) to explain this, and in the same year took the risk of returning to France in order to campaign against participation of the working class in elections. He held it to be essential for the working class to boycott all bourgeois institutions, whether economic or political: the workers' revolution was to be made by ignoring them, and creating, beside them, those federated Associations which would, in due course, absorb the whole economic life of the nation. At this point a group of his own followers broke from him, very reluctantly and respectfully, holding that it would be useful to have Proudhonian anarchists in the National Assembly.

There were other things, too, which now tended to isolate the great man: the French are a notoriously chauvinistic people and they disliked his anti-Patriotism and anti-Nationalism, and some of his admirers had been alienated by his hostility to the Church. Those attitudes he despised, though they cost him dear for he was now very poor and had difficulty in making a living. But there was one kind of opposition he could not ignore: the argument that even if it were desirable for the workers to opt out of bourgeois society entirely, and create a free Proudhonian society of their own, it was impossible because they had not the ability to do it. In response to that sneer Proudhon wrote his last book, *Of the Political Capacity of the Working Classes* (1865). He was a sick man and before the book was finished he faced the fact that he was dying. But, as he told his friends, 'Despite the gods I will have the last word,' and did so, by dictation, on his deathbed.

It seems possible, considering the forms which have been taken by socialism in the New Left a century after Proudhon's death, that despite the little tin gods of orthodox, institutionalized communism, the most brilliant of the anarchists may, indeed, have the last word.

BAKUNIN

Mikhail Bakunin was the son of a rich, cultivated and liberal nobleman; he was born at Tver in Russia and was educated for the army as was customary in his class. As a junior officer in a crack Guards regiment, however, he malingered his way out of it and went to Berlin to read philosophy under the same Hegelian masters as Marx. He became an Hegelian, then a Young Hegelian, and then a revolutionary socialist. But he was temperamentally incapable of Marx's kind of patient study, scholarly thoroughness, intellectual power and coolness. Bakunin was a man of gigantic stature and bulk, his character and nature seemed to reflect his physical attributes—he was gigantic in appetites, in vision, in polemical argument and in conspiracy; superficial in his reading and thinking, restlessly active, wildly optimistic at one moment and utterly dejected in the next. He was a romantic in whom violence was for ever immanent.

He is chiefly important in the history of libertarian socialism not for what he achieved in his lifetime, but for his legacy of anarchism in Italy and Spain. Very briefly, his revolutionary career was as follows: he began by dedicating himself to the overthrow of absolutism in Russia, and only some time thereafter to world revolution which, until near the end of his life, he believed to be round the next corner; it would have been intolerable to believe that it was not. It was partly temperament, partly the fact of being a Russian which turned him away from institutional and towards libertarian socialism. His experience of the Tsarist absolutism which had disgusted and enraged him made it impossible for him to see the State as anything but the arch-enemy of freedom and to take revenge on it, try to destroy it for its crimes, wherever and in whatever form he found it.

The revolution of 1848 seemed to be his chance. He did his best to spread it from Germany, where it had arrived from France and Switzerland, into Russia. When that failed he turned up in Dresden early in 1849, took part in an insurrection when it was already too late—all his active works for the revolution was to have that clownish quality—was arrested by the Saxon police, chained in a cell, handed over to the Russians and sent to solitary confinement in the Peter-Paul fortress where he remained for five years and where, at the request of the Tsar, he wrote his *Confessions*: he has been accused of licking the Tsar's boots in that curious work in the hope of pardon. But his very apology for rebellion indicts Tsarism and if he did hope for release he was disappointed. The Tsar passed the *Confessions* to his son and heir with the comment, 'A curious document', and left Bakunin to rot in jail. It was when he seemed to be actually dying of the scurvy (which was as common in the Tsar's prisons as in the King of England's warships until limejuice put an end to it) that he was removed from prison and, toothless, scrofulous but unbowed, was banished to Siberia. It took him five years to work himself to a place which made escape possible. He made that escape by way of Japan and America and arrived in Europe, martyr and hero of the Left, to take up the revolution exactly where he had left off and as if nothing had happened in the meantime. The revolution must overthrow the State by violence, including terrorism, including the assassination of tyrants, and install the Millennium in the form of a federation of collectives based on industries run by their workers. There would be no political apparatus, no police, armies or lawcourts.

I shall say nothing of Bakunin's ideas for the post-revolutionary era, for none of them was his own. One difference from Proudhon is important: collectivization. It is attributed to Bakunin but derives from more than one of the proto-socialists, notably Godwin and Owen. Bakunin was not a maker, he was a destroyer; not that he would have seen it in those simple terms, for to him the whole past, and not only its political and economic legacies, was a decaying mass of poisonous rubbish and the first task of the builder of socialism was to clear it away by whatever means came to hand. In the very first article he wrote as a revolutionary polemicist, when he was still reading philosophy in Berlin, he said this:

> The people ... because of their origin and position have been deprived of property, condemned to ignorance and in practice therefore to slavery. Now they grow menacing ... the air is sultry with storms ... Let us then put our trust in the eternal spirit which destroys and annihilates only because ... it is the eternally creative source of all life. The urge to destroy is also the creative urge.*

Destruction, root and branch, of established society including its culture became Bakunin's object. In all his writings, whatever relates to construction can be traced to Proudhon or another libertarian philosopher. The works of the institutional socialists he read chiefly in order to attack their *étatisme*: this was especially the case with Karl Marx, although Bakunin was capable of expressing the greatest admiration for Marx's works when he was trying, for example, to infiltrate the International, and even of seeming to repudiate his own libertarianism. On one occasion he even undertook translation into Russian of the first volume of *Das Kapital*. But flattering Marx was an unprofitable exercise, for he never gave anything in exchange.

Bakunin first met with an exposition of communist socialism in the writings of Weitling and commented: 'His is not a free

* This essay was published in the *Deutscher Jahrbucher*, 1848.

society, a live union of free peoples ... but a herd of animals
united by force ...' And after he had met and talked with Marx
and other institutional socialists who sought to install socialism
by leading the proletariat to seize upon and elevate the State
as the sole economic and political power, Bakunin called them
'strangers to the fundamental demands of human dignity and
freedom'.

A Pan-Slav until he tired of that cause, he went to Prague
to help the Czechs in their revolt against the Hapsburg tyranny
and in his *Appeal to the Slavs* he traced the way to libertarian
socialist internationalism through triumphant nationalism—that
notion, at least, he held in common with Marx: first dismantle
the Empires: the socialization of the nationalist fragments could
come later. And in the spirit of that doctrine he made an attempt
to lead an expedition of revolutionaries to liberate Lithuania.
Like so many of his militant enterprises it was a fiasco, and from
it, abandoning the Slavs, he went to Italy (1863) and there started
a number of secret revolutionary societies which were to bring
about the Millennium by means of terrorism. These societies,
at least one of which never even existed excepting on paper or in
his head, were at the origin of his International Alliance of Social
Democracy, planned as an international 'federation' of National
(Anarchist) Bureaux whose task was to destroy their own national
States, abolish social classes, install absolute social, economic
and sexual equality, and compose an international society without
frontiers and free from the incubi of institutions. The Alliance
was also to join the International in a body and, despite Marx
and his followers, make libertarian socialism master of its membership.

Bakunin's attempt to do this is glanced at in the chapters on
Marx and Marxism. A condition of membership made by Marx
was dissolution of the Alliance: Bakunin conceded this. His
powers of oratory and his hold over the Italian and some other
delegations to Congresses did not enable him to take over the
International—Marx out-manœuvred and out-talked him—but,
resulting as it did in the withdrawal of the Italian and some other
delegations, it mortally weakened the International. Foiled, but
with every intention of trying again, Bakunin retired to Switzerland where his doctrine was as popular and enduring as among

the Jura smallholder watch-making artisans (see under Kropotkin) and among the Italian industrial workers and, for that matter, in Spain (where anarchism was so much the strongest of the socialist doctrines that a chapter is devoted to it in Part Two).

It was in Switzerland that Bakunin fell under the influence of the youthful terrorist and revolutionary charlatan, Nechaev, who gained such power over the older man that George Woodcock (in his *Anarchism*) suggests a sort of Oscar Wilde/Alfred Douglas relationship as the explanation. It is a fact that Bakunin gave his imprimatur to Nechaev's *Revolutionary Catechism*, a document in which the revolutionary is required to divest himself of all personal feelings, all emotion but a passion for the revolution, all morality, all shrinking from such crimes as murder, blackmail and extortion,* for he has no right to the luxury of a bourgeois conscience while suffering mankind waits to be saved from governments and capitalists.

A brief quotation from one of the pamphlets which Bakunin wrote at this time will serve to reveal the nature of his revolt against established society:

> The brigand is always the hero, the defender, the avenger of the people, the irreconcilable enemy of the whole State regime both in its civil and in its social aspects ... The brigand ... is ... the revolutionary without phrase-making and without bookish rhetoric ... and the world of brigands alone has been in harmony with the revolution ...

The influence of Nechaev is obvious, but there is no doubt that Bakunin did think in those terms, for he returns to the theme of the brigand revolutionary more than once, though when it came to practice—for example when Nechaev used blackmail to get money for Bakunin to enable him to give up the uncongenial task of translating *Das Kapital*, and when Marx used this disgraceful incident to discredit Bakunin with the International and have him drummed out of it—the Russian declared that he knew nothing of these goings-on and repudiated them. Yet writing for Nechaev's *Narodnaya Rasprava* he tells his readers that everything which stands in the way of freeing the people must be destroyed without sparing lives or shrinking from the com-

* See my *Terrorists and Terrorism*, Dent, London, 1974.

mission of crimes. What is absurd and distasteful in Bakunin is the difference between theory and practice: he frequently engaged in open insurrection, but never in the kind of terrorism which he licensed in his writings. He was a bit of a fraud.

Nevertheless, some of his achievements were positive: his creation, through James Guillaume, of the anarchist Jura Federation gave Europe an anarchist power base for a decade. He was, as I have said, at the origin of the great anarchist movements in Italy and in Spain, and, as will appear, the libertarian movements in those countries did far more to advance the people towards the socialist Millennium than did the Marxists.

Yet it is difficult not to see this gallant, clumsy, floundering and blundering giant as a comic figure, the clown of socialism repeatedly and risibly astounded by his own failure to accomplish the impossible with manifestly and utterly inadequate means; but a sublime clown, tumbling and suffering and grimacing and somersaulting his way towards the golden age of his hazy visions.

MALATESTA

Enrico Malatesta—no connection unless a very remote one with the infamous tyrant of Rimini—was born at Santa Maria Catua Vetere in 1853 into a family of landed gentry. He read Medicine at the University of Naples but was expelled for republicanism before taking his degree.

The anarchism which Bakunin had implanted in Italy had flourished and Malatesta, attracted by nobly libertarian doctrines, became an anarchist. Since the Socialist Congress held at Rimini in 1872, Bakunin's disciple Costa had made the Romagna a hotbed of anarchism and of revolutionary anarchist militancy. Under this influence a majority of Italian socialist workers had repudiated the authoritarianism and *étatisme* of the International's (Marxist) socialism, and opted for a Proudhonian-Bakuninist libertarianism. The anarchist movement has become associated in our minds with terrorism, but it did not, despite Bakunin and Nechaev, begin like that. It began with the idea of open insurrectionary warfare on the bourgeoisie only as the *ultima ratio* should peaceful means fail; it was as pacific and restrained in its revolutionary methods as parliamentary socialism, until terrorism was forced on it.

Shortly after joining the anarchists Malatesta's sincerity was put to the test: his parents dying, he inherited the family estates. The young man was not found wanting. He immediately divested himself of his wealth by presenting the deeds of his farms to their tenants—he had read his Proudhon—and, in order to have a trade by which to earn a living, apprenticed himself to an electrical mechanic. But from that time onwards more of his time was given to socialism than to electrical fitting.

Malatesta began his career as an active revolutionary by leading a number of anarchist insurrections, raised by his own oratory working on the ghastly misery of the poor peasants and farm-workers, in Apulia. Having made Italy too hot to hold him, he moved on to Spain, another land where the Bakuninist seed had fallen on fertile soil, and thus began a long evangelical journey of preaching and agitating which carried him to Greece, Egypt, Syria and Turkey. Probably no single man did more to carry the libertarian socialist message of a Millennium to come, a world without the degrading and demoralizing scourges of capitalism, kings, presidents, policemen, lawcourts and magistrates, Churches or armies or the thousand other ills which institutionalized man is heir to; a world in which men and women with love in their hearts and all the best that had ever been thought in their minds would work freely together for the good of all. From time to time his wanderings brought him back to Italy and he took some part in almost every socialist insurrection, demonstration or riot of the eighteen-seventies.

In 1881 an anarchist Congress brought Malatesta to London and there he fell in with an old comrade of the Italian barricades, Costa's chief colleague Cafiero. Together they founded the magazine *Insurrezione* which circulated among the socialist, communist and anarchist *émigrés* in London which was second only to Switzerland as an asylum for revolutionary socialists 'wanted' by the police of their own countries. But in 1883 he decided that he would have to return to Italy. A number of anarchists in that country had gone over to the parliamentary socialists, more seemed likely to do so, and he felt it essential to do all he could to stop that drift: to that end he founded another journal, *La Questione Sociale*. Its matter and manner were too much for the Italian government and Malatesta was arrested for 'membership of an illegal organization'—the International Alliance—and sentenced to three years' imprisonment. He appealed against the sentence and pending the hearing of his appeal, carried on with his anarchist propaganda until the outbreak of the terrible cholera epidemic in Naples in 1885. Accompanied by his closest friends, he went to Naples and there worked, at the risk of his life, among the sick until the epidemic was over. His courage and humanity did not, of course, make any impression on the government—no bourgeois establishment can, by its very nature, put up with consistent and effective attacks on the institution of property in land and plant and the paramount status of property-protection law—and since Malatesta had no intention of wasting years of his life in prison, he had himself nailed into a large crate and, labelled 'sewing-machines', taken aboard a ship commanded by a sympathizer and bound for Argentina, one of the lands of election for Italian emigrants driven from their own land by the reign of exploitation which Malatesta was fighting to bring to an end.

There was already a *Circolo Communista-Anarcho* in Buenos Aires. Malatesta joined it and set up shop as an electrical mechanic, at the same time starting a local edition of *La Questione Sociale* which he printed in Italian and Spanish. Both the paper and the movement were desperately short of money, and he made a characteristic decision to deal with that crisis: men and mining companies were finding gold in Patagonia to enrich themselves; why should not the anarchists be as lucky and so enrich the cause? He and some other members of the *Circolo* went to Patagonia and, improbable as it may seem, quickly found gold in a river which other prospectors had neglected. They applied to the authorities for a concession to work their 'placer', but came up against a manifestation of capitalism which they had not reckoned with: an established mining company bribed an official to convey the concession to them and Malatesta returned to his workshop no richer than he had left it.

In 1889 he returned to Europe and began to publish another anarchist journal, *Associazione*, first in Nice and then, being persecuted by the French police, in London.

There were more years of wandering evangelism. In England, Switzerland, France and, of course, Italy he fought tirelessly against the bourgeoisie and capitalism with one strong arm, against Marxist State socialism with the other. He was in prison for his inflammatory agitation among the workers of Ancona when, to avenge police massacres of workers and poor peasants who had risen against their miserable condition in Tuscany and Lombardy, the anarchist Bresci assassinated King Umberto. Although his time was up, the authorities were much too afraid of him to let him go, and he was sent to the penal colony on the island of Lampedusa for five years. He did not stay five months. He and three other anarchists stole a boat and put to sea, were picked up by a ship, and landed in Malta. From there Malatesta sailed to the USA.

The silk-weavers of Patterson, New Jersey, whose anarchist cell had organized and financed the assassination of Umberto— Bresci was one of their members—were mostly Italians and for the most part socialists of one kind or another. So it was to Patterson that Malatesta made his way. But there he came up against a measure of libertarianism which went far beyond his own. Among the Patterson anarchists were a few who had been influenced by one of the most extraordinary books in the history of dissent, the German Max Stirner's *The Ego and his Own*. I have no room for Stirner in this book, but he had argued that absolutely the only reality which any man could know, and should therefore serve, was himself and that the only tolerable form of society must therefore be that of an order created by the mutually balancing tensions of conflicting, self-assertive egos. So the Stirnerist extremists rejected not only political and economic organizations, they also rejected co-operation. In a dispute with one of these ultra-libertarian fanatics Malatesta was shot and seriously wounded.

Being Malatesta, he recovered and in 1900 returned to London, again set up shop as an electrical mechanic, and for the next twelve years bombarded Italy with anarchist writings in both pamphlets and periodicals so effectively that he was a sort of one-man *Agitprop* and no other socialist had anything like his influence, his 'legend', in all Italy. He converted literally millions of Italian workers to his brand of libertarian socialism. Yet it was not until 1913 that he returned there, settling in Ancona. He was sixty.

In June 1914 the police in Ancona fired on a crowd of unemployed workers who were demonstrating against the miserable condition to which the exigencies of capitalism had reduced them. A number were killed. The ageing lion was roused. As the head of the anarchist Unione Sindicale Italiana which he had founded in opposition to the timidly socialist General Confederation of Labour (the Italian TUC), Malatesta called for, obtained and led a general strike which, as it included the railway workers, paralysed the central government. The strike spread swiftly through the Romagna to all but the remotest parts of Italy, both town and country. Police terrorism provoked violence from the strikers, and there was serious fighting in a score of cities, the anarchists being everywhere in the forefront of the battle. This continued for a week subsequently know as 'Red Week'. The workers were almost everywhere victorious and the socialist Millennium seemed to be almost in sight so that Malatesta declared that when the fighting ended 'we shall see our ideal shining clearly'.

It was not the Italian government, reduced to impotence by the paralysis of the public services, the 'unreliability' of the army, and the sheer size of the revolt, which beat the anarchists and prevented the revolution. It was—and this sad story was to be repeated a score of times in the next half-century—the leaders of the General Confederation of Labour, who were the sort of trade-union leaders we are all too familiar with in Britain where their price is a knighthood. They ratted on the revolution by ordering their members back to work, and although many persisted in revolt, a majority loyally obeyed orders, and the government was able to crush the insurrection.

Malatesta returned once again to London and there he spent the years of World War One. But in 1919, at the age of 66, with all working-class Europe responding hopefully to the stimulus of the Russian Revolution, Malatesta returned yet again to Italy to found its first anarchist daily newspaper, *Umanità Nuova*. He had the dual task of promoting revolution but preventing the Marxists from getting control of it. His Unione Sindicale

Italiana was still very much alive and under its leadership there were strikes all over the industrial north. What terrified the Italian bourgeoisie was that these strikes were of a new kind: the workers remained in occupation of the factories and, under anarchist leadership, began to run them as industrial co-operatives. Was this the libertarian socialist revolution at last? 'If,' Malatesta wrote in *Umanità Nuova*, 'we let this favourable moment pass, we shall later pay with tears of blood for the fear we have instilled in the bourgeoisie.' He never wrote truer words.

Once again the General Confederation of Labour lost its nerve and ratted, making itself the agent of the management in passing on promises to meet the workers' demands touching wages, hours and conditions if they would restore the factories to their 'owners'. The men began to waver, and the moment of their opportunity passed. Then came hundreds of arrests. Malatesta himself was held for eight months without trial and then released. Why released when the militants of his movement, despairing of peaceful means, turned at last to terrorism and began to throw bombs? For one thing he had always deplored such methods and might be expected to use his great influence to stop terrorism; for another, the authorities did not want to provoke the workers too far and it would have been dangerous to maltreat their hero. When the bourgeoisie found a bully-boy, a Bonaparte, to crush the revolution for them, in the renegade socialist Benito Mussolini, not even that sawdust Cæsar dared to touch the old dreamer of the Millennium, and Enrico Malatesta was left, under discreet observation, to live in peace until his death at the age of 79.

THE JURA FEDERATION

When, to meet the conditions which Marx had made for the admission of Bakunin and his followers to membership of the International, Bakunin 'dissolved' the *Alliance*, he did so in name only. In Spain and in Italy where his kind of socialism was paramount, nothing was changed, nor did that paper dissolution make any difference to his adherents in South-East France and Switzerland.

Among the most faithful of Bakunin's disciples were the men of the Fédération Jurasienne. They were small farmers and watchmakers of the Franco-Swiss mountain villages, led by the dedicated anarchist James Guillaume who first came under Bakunin's influence at a Congress of the League for Peace and Freedom (a short-lived organization which attempted to combine radicals and liberals of all factions in united action for peaceful revolution) held in 1867.

The very nature of their lives as freeholding small farmers and craftsmen made the Jura mountaineers a sort of model of what the Proudhonian man should be like : free, no man's servant and no man's master, able to procure an adequate livelihood for their families without either degrading and hopeless drudgery or demoralizing wealth. In anarchism as preached by Bakunin and Guillaume they saw the means to establish social justice without losing freedom and it was about the nucleus offered by their conference at Sonvilliers in 1871 that the Anarchist International was formed by the adherence of the Spanish, Italian and Belgian Bakuninists. It was James Guillaume who, I believe, first developed the early English socialists' idea of the general strike, subsequently adopted by the syndicalists, as the workers' best means of pulling down the whole capitalist structure.* Moreover the Statutes of the Jura Federation formed the model for those of the later Spanish and Italian Federations.

Not the least of the Jura Federation's works for the Millennium was the conversion to anarchism of the gentlest and noblest of the anarchist prophets, Peter Kropotkin.

KROPOTKIN

Prince Pyotr Alekseyevich Kropotkin was born in 1842 in the Kaluga province of Russia, his father being General Prince Aleksandr Kropotkin, a stern and arrogant martinet of the kind favoured by that stern, stupid and arrogant autocrat, Tsar Nicholas I. The General's pride was the great antiquity of his family, perhaps because the family had nothing else to be proud of but the extent of its estates and the number of its serfs. Pyotr,

* Geneva Congress 1873.

like his brother Aleksandr, was brought up by the house-serfs and given a primary education by tutors. He was picked by the Tsar for the élite Corps of Pages and consequently, as a youth, saw nothing whatever of the world beyond the Court circle. But that was in St Petersburg, and thanks to the writings of the novelist Turgenev, of Bakunin, and above all of one of the greatest of Russian and European socialist pioneers, Aleksandr Herzen, the St Petersburg intellectuals were leaders among the few Russians in touch with Western culture and the revolutionary unrest in the leading European countries. The young Pyotr Kropotkin, under his brother's influence, became a St Petersburg liberal; and a liberal he would have remained had his mind been subservient to Aleksandr's, for the elder brother saw the revolution of the proletariat coming, but, unable to believe in socialism, would not, as he put it, 'raise my banner'.

But Aleksandr's influence was not paramount; Pyotr had the stronger mind, and much stronger feelings. He had himself posted to Siberia, giving up all idea of being a 'fashionable' officer in a crack regiment, and for five years (1862-7), still a soldier, devoted himself to exploring a vast range of the north-east and its coloni-zation, to geophysical science, and above all to geography, in which he became an authority recognized with respect all over the civilized world. He abandoned his military career, returned to St Petersburg and then, during the early seventies, travelled in Western Europe, studying conditions, reading the history of the International, and meeting Russian and French political exiles in Geneva. In his *Memoirs of a Revolutionist* he tells us:

> I was profoundly influenced by the theories of Anarchism which were beginning to be formulated in the Jura Federation, mainly through the work of Bakunin; and also by criticism of State Socialism which threatened to develop into an economic tyranny even more terrible than political despotism; and finally by the revolutionary activities of the Jura workers.

And, a more immediate impression,

> The egalitarian relations which I saw in the Jura mountains, the independence of thought and expression which I saw developing in the workers and their unlimited devotion to the cause appealed even more strongly to my feelings; and when

I came away from the mountains after a week's stay with the watchmakers my views on Socialism were settled: I was an Anarchist.

As such, then, he returned to St Petersburg and (see Chapter Fourteen) joined the *narodniki* of the Chaikovsky Circle, to live among the St Petersburg workers as one of them, propagating socialist ideas. But his ideas were not the moderately constitutional ones of the other *narodniki*: they were in essence those of Proudhon, modified by Godwinian (albeit called Bakuninist) collectivism. At this stage of his life, while he repudiated terrorism, he did not exclude the use of violence along the road to the Millennium and, influenced by Bakuninist ideas on the uses of brigandage, he even suggested the recruitment of bands of armed peasants who, moving from the country to the great cities, collecting more and more recruits as they went, would form the nucleus of a great revolutionary peasant army: it is a curious foreshadowing of the revolutionary method of Mao Tse-tung and Ché Guevara. For two years, calling himself Borodin and dressed as a peasant, Kropotkin stuck to his 'evangelical' work until he was arrested (1874) and sent to the Peter-Paul fortress. There he spent another two years, towards the end of which he managed to convince the authorities that he was so seriously ill that he must be moved to the prison ward of the St Petersburg military hospital. From there he made a spectacular escape and returned via England, to the Jura. He wrote for the Federation's *Bulletin*, then the most important anarchist periodical, accepted office in the Bakuninist *Alliance*, attended International congresses and then settled for some time in London where, working in the British Museum Reading Room, he began to develop the idea of anarchism as a general philosophy, a way of approaching not only politics and economics, but the natural sciences. Out of this early work developed the theme of one of his later books, *Mutual Aid*, in which he argued against Darwin that the most successful species were the co-operative not the competitive ones.

Restless for want of action, in 1877 he went to Paris and there joined Bakunin's disciple and Malatesta's comrade Andrea Costa and the French anarchist Jules Guesde in forming anarchist 'cells' among the Paris workers. When Costa was arrested

Kropotkin again took refuge in Switzerland: but Guillaume was gone, withdrawn into an inactivity which was to last twenty years, and the Jura Federation was withering. Still, there was work in Geneva, helping to write and edit the anarchist *Avant-garde* for clandestine circulation in France.

When the *Avant-garde* was suppressed by the Swiss government and Kropotkin's fellow-editor Brousse arrested, Kropotkin founded his own journal, *La Révolte*, which then became the principal organ of anarchist propaganda in Europe. Its perennial theme was that the first duty of the revolutionary must be the destruction of those embodiments of social injustice, the Nation States. From his articles in *La Révolte* came two books, *La Conquête du pain* and *Paroles d'un révolté*. (Kropotkin wrote equally well in four languages.) In them, and in all that he wrote at this time, there were two dominant themes. First, *the revolution, having been thoroughly prepared by education of the workers*, must be sudden and total, even though that meant the use of violence, for the gradualism favoured by parliamentary socialism would inevitably incorporate in the post-revolutionary epoch all the evils of bourgeois 'democracy'. That, as is vividly clear from the history of France, Britain, Scandinavia and some other countries during the past half-century, turned out to be a true foresight: few men have done more to perpetuate those evils than Léon Blum, Ramsay Macdonald, Clement Attlee, Harold Wilson and Willy Brandt. Secondly, the revolution must at all costs avoid the fundamental blunder of establishing a 'revolutionary government'. What did he mean by this? There is a story of two Cockneys strolling in a graveyard, one of them reads aloud a tombstone inscription—*Here lies a lawyer and an honest man*, on which his friend comments, 'Blimey, two blokes in one grave.' For Kropotkin as for Proudhon, 'revolution' and 'government' were utterly incompatible and the very object of revolution must be to get rid of government once and for all.

It is for this reason that Kropotkin's work is of the first importance today, in the New Left context: the New Left is that very revival of genuine socialism which, as an old and dying man, he foresaw after the Bolsheviks had, in his own words, 'buried the revolution'.

The first step in his plan would be for 'a whole region, great towns and their suburbs, to shake off their rulers', for rulers are parasites, are incubi. That accomplished, the task before us is clear. First, all industrial plant must return to the community: 'The social means held by individuals must be restored to their rightful owners—everybody' so that production shall continue and all have their full and fair share in consumption, and 'Social life, far from being interrupted, may be resumed with the greatest energy.'

It is easy to talk of the means of production being restored to 'everybody', but what, given the dismantling of the State which Marxism has taught us to think of as the only possible trustee for the people and was basic to Kropotkin's revolution, does that mean? He did have a clear notion in mind. He was, in fact, the pioneer (after the old proto-socialists) 'anarcho-communist'. The word community in his context means what other socialists meant by *commune*: it was virtually the Proudhonian free and voluntary association of all workers in a federated network of industrial communes, but with one very important difference which made it 'communist'. Proudhon, using the People's Bank as a clearing house for his Mutualists' labour-value cheques, retained income differentials, for obviously the harder or cleverer worker accumulated more labour-value than his lazy or stupid fellows. Kropotkin rejected this. Every man would receive from the common pool not the equivalent in labour-value of what he had put into it, but what he needed. In other words Thomas More's (*Utopia*) free distribution of goods. To Kropotkin it seemed absolutely essential to get rid of the idea of wages even after capitalism, that verminous parasite on labour, had been mercifully exterminated: for the 'no work, no pay' rule is a form of oppression, of constraint and, as such, demoralizing to those who apply it. Proudhon had shown in *What is Property?* that the accumulated wealth of the past—whether land made cultivable, or plant—was the work of mankind as a whole and must therefore belong to all men equally, for it was not only undesirable but impossible to apportion shares according to contribution. Above all, such apportionment of unequal shares would be unjust: a man is not the maker of his own capacity, he is born with it, good or bad, great or little:

All things are for all men, since all men have need of them, and all men have worked in the measure of their strength to produce them ...

The usual objection to this is 'What about the work-shy?' I think that Kropotkin would have replied that in the first place they are not numerous enough to matter, and in the second, they are a sort of moral cripple: would you withhold his share from the cripple? Moreover, shirking is a by-product of capitalism. In a co-operative anarcho-communist society pains would be taken to make work interesting and pleasant; man is *Homo faber*, it is his nature to enjoy making things; and finally, in such a society every man would enjoy the feeling of being useful to his fellows, of making a good contribution to the common wealth. There is much that bears this out in the experience of modern China. And much hope, in automation, for the future of these ideas.

A question raised by Kropotkin's theories is that of supply: would there, in fact, be enough to go round, enough, that is, to ensure a decent standard of subsistence for all equally? His view was that under capitalism much labour is diverted to luxury production and that if that were stopped production would be equal to the task of supplying all with what they really needed (note that the word is *needed*, not *wanted*). Moreover he believed, and this was a century ago, that a universal five-hour day would be sufficient. Whether he was correct for 1870 I have no idea, but time and technology have made him right. We have a world of gross excess consumption on the one hand (USA, Western Europe, Australia, etc.) and gross poverty on the other, both as between social classes and as between rich and poor nations. If *need* and not *want* was the criterion of distribution, a five-hour day would supply it for all mankind.

What—since we are here concerned with the establishment of an absolutely free society and the Millennium of liberty—what of the dissenter, the maverick, the outsider? Kropotkin said this:

If you are absolutely incapable of producing anything useful, or if you refuse to do it, then live like an isolated man or like an invalid. If we are rich enough to give you the necessities of life ... we shall be delighted to do so ... But since you wish

to live under special conditions and leave the ranks, it is probable that you will suffer for it ... will be looked upon as a
ghost of bourgeois society ...

This has made some libertarians uneasy. George Woodcock
points out in his *Anarchism* that 'There enters the serpent of
public opinion which Orwell detected as one of the inhabitants
of the anarchist paradise ...' Now we do have evidence of this
evil in all societies and particularly in post-revolutionary societies.
It is a fact that in the post-Revolutionary (English) New England
communities this serpent was the most poisonous of vipers, that
it was venomously active during the French Revolution (see, for
example, Anatole France's *Le Lys rouge*), and we see it most
unpleasantly active in the post-revolutionary Russia of Pasternak's
Doctor Zhivago, for example. But since man has to live not only
gregariously but communally or fall back into the condition of a
predatory beast, since all social and herding animals have a sanction equivalent to our 'public opinion', and since in any case the
nature of that opinion is formed by the nature of the society
people are living in, I find this uneasiness at Kropotkin's 'puri-
tanism', and Orwell's reservations, a shade precious. What is it
really but a secret nostalgic harking back to the nearly absolute
freedom of the 18th-century rich as the ideal (if only it had not
been supported by gross exploitation) or to the Athenian gentleman (if only he had not been supported by slavery)? Short of the
fantasies of a Max Stirner* there can be no absolute freedom,
and even in the world imagined by Stirner your freedom would
have been constrained by the threat of the other man's intellectual
or moral or even merely physical superiority. What Kropotkin
envisaged and planned was the nearest attainable approximation
to freedom within the context of social justice.

I do not propose to tell the whole story of Kropotkin's life of
devotion to the cause but there are certain moments of it which
are important in our context. When, with 53 other anarchists, he
was tried in Lyons on a trumped-up charge following some terrorist outrages of which he knew nothing, he made a speech to
the Court which revealed the principles of all the accused and
of anarchists everywhere. First, he indicted both capitalism and

* See *The Ego and his Own*.

formal government as the prime enemies of that equality which
is the precondition for freedom. The anarchists, he told the *Cour
correctionelle* at Lyons where the trial took place, demanded
'the substitution in all human relationships of perpetually revis-
able free contracts, for administration, the tutelage of law, and
imposed discipline'. And he concluded his address: 'Yes, we are
scoundrels, indeed, for we demand bread, liberty and justice for
all.'

Kropotkin, after serving three years of a five-year sentence,
during which he wrote for *The Times*, the *Encyclopaedia Britan-
nica*, the *Nineteenth Century* and other publications, taught
languages, geography and cosmography to his fellow prisoners
and experimented with intensive horticulture in the prison garden
(in later life he became a famous gardener), and was released
after a long battle between the pressure of world public opinion
and the French and Russian governments. He spent the rest of his
life in England and Russia, writing, lecturing, gardening and
entertaining socialist and anarchist friends—Shaw, Morris, Keir
Hardie, Frank Harris and many more. He reversed an opinion
of his earlier years to become a gradualist, but none of his
anarchist views. He returned to Russia at last, after the February
revolution, but his pro-war policy—he wanted the Russians to
continue to fight Germany—and of course his libertarianism
made the Bolsheviks not persecute him, they did not dare, but
ignore him. His last political act was to publish, all over Western
Europe, a 'Letter to the workers of the world' calling on them
to use their power to put a stop to counter-revolutionary wars
of intervention in Russia, and then set out his ideas for a stateless,
co-operative and wholly free and democratic Russian society.
And he summoned the world's workers to create a new International of free trade unions bent on emancipating production
from its enslavement to capital.

Kropotkin died aged seventy-nine in February 1921. A pro-
cession of mourners five miles long followed his body to the
grave. Conspicuous among them were the anarchists, not yet
suppressed, bearing aloft the black flag of their movement, and
carrying black banners on which were written in red letters this
self-evident proposition:

WHERE THERE IS AUTHORITY THERE IS NO FREEDOM.

Part Two

THE PRACTITIONERS

It will be clear from Part One of this history that while all kinds of socialists accepted a body of common doctrine—for example, restoration of the means of production to the community as a whole, and equality in the distribution of consumer goods—there was considerable diversity among them concerning both means and, at least in detail, ends. The Marxist socialists wanted to achieve socialism by seizing the power of the State apparatus for the proletariat and making it paramount in their interest; the out-and-out communists (here used in its pre-Bolshevik meaning: a communist was one who wanted people to live in communes run as collectives on the principle of absolute equality) were for 'to each according to his needs' equality, while the more moderate socialists like the Proudhonian Mutualists were for 'to each according to his work'; the syndicalists saw socialism installed by means of the economic power of democratic trade unions, and rejected political action as futile and pernicious; the anarchists wanted to begin by demolishing the State as the embodiment of social injustice and to run the world as a loose federation of industrial and commercial co-operative associations. I propose in Part Two to deal with the practitioners of each of these theories and to begin with the Social-Democrats.

NINE

The Rise of the
Social-Democrats

Social-Democrats are gradualist, constitutional, or parliamentary Marxists, or near-Marxists. They began their career in Germany.

In the 1860s there were two socialist political parties in Germany: the General German Workers' Union founded by Ferdinand Lassalle, and the Social Democratic Workers Party, founded by August Bebel. Both men were remarkable.

Ferdinand Lassalle was a Jew born in 1825 and like Marx he was educated at Berlin University under Hegelian masters but, unlike him, never rejected Hegel's 'idealism'. He made his revolutionary debut in 1848 as a Left republican democrat and was arrested and imprisoned when the Prussian government recovered its nerve (King Wilhelm had bolted but halted in his flight when he saw that the revolutionaries were making a mess of the revolution) for 'using a call to arms against the King's sovereignty'. A meeting with Marx converted him to socialism yet he never became a Marxist; in fact his programme had a good deal in common with Proudhon's although he was certainly no libertarian. He and Marx exchanged numerous letters, for just so long as Marx hoped to make Lassalle the agent of Marxist socialism in Germany. But it could not work. Lassalle was no man's disciple, and as for Marx, he was increasingly repelled by Lassalle's conceit and by his 'Jewish' flamboyance—Marx was always a bit of an anti-semite *à sa façon*. The sort of thing Marx detested in Lassalle was this, in one of the latter's letters:

I am the servant and master of an idea, the priest of a God, myself. I have made myself both actor and plastic artist, all my being is a manifestation of my will, expressing whatever meaning I wish to give it. The shaking of my voice, the flashing

brilliance of my eye, the least quiver of my face, all must
slavishly convey the dictate of my will.*

One imagines the shrug of those burly shoulders as Marx read
this effusion. But as it happened the very qualities which he
detested in Lassalle were the foundation of that young man's
extraordinary success as a socialist evangelist. The Berlin workers
adored him, followed him, and obeyed him: from 1861 his
success in converting them to socialism and recruiting them into
what was first called the Association General of German Workers
was so spectacular that Bismarck was forced to take account of it.

The two men had a good deal in common: both were highly
emotional; both were shrewd beyond the point of scrupulous-
ness, that is, were exceptionally adroit politicians; and both were
absolute dictators of their respective parties—Lassalle was no
more a democrat than Bismarck, believing as he did that the
German workers needed a firm leader who would give them
clear orders, not a mere mentor. Moreover, Lassalle and Bismarck
had an interest in common; they were both anti-bourgeois. The
bourgeois liberals aimed at taking political power from the
Junkers. It was basic to Marxism that the workers should col-
laborate with the bourgeoisie in overthrowing the aristocratic
power before turning on the burgesses. That was not, as Marx
had discovered to his fury, Lassalle's idea, for his aim was to
establish, under the tutelage of his Association, a complex of
workers' industrial co-operatives (of the kind which had been
pioneered in the industrial north of England), and he needed
State subsidies to finance them. Bismarck had a two-headed reason
for favouring the idea: such Co-operatives, while weakening the
power of bourgeois capitalism, would not weaken and might
strengthen the power of the Prussian State. He and Lassalle
carried on a secret negotiation (revealed by the discovery of a
cache of letters in 1927). It did not conclude in a formal alliance,
but at least the Prussian government did not interfere with
Lassalle's work. Perhaps there might have been an alliance, and
God knows what it might have come to—a socialist economy
under Junker political leadership sounds like a more civilized

* *Works*, Lassalle, F. (ed. Hirsch), 1963. Judging by photographs,
Lassalle was a strikingly handsome man.

version of National Socialism of which Bismarck may have had glimpses—but as it happened Lassalle became involved in a personal quarrel, challenged his adversary to a duel, and was shot dead. However, by that time the General German Workers' Party, as it had become, was a socialist force to be reckoned with.

August Bebel was born to working-class parents in 1840, was apprenticed after a good primary education to a wood-turner, worked at his trade, saved money, set up on his own, and made a fortune as a furniture manufacturer. As a worker in other men's undertakings he had become a Marxist socialist; as a capitalist and master of other men, he remained loyal to his socialist ideals —remember Owen—and in 1869 founded the first German political party which was uncompromisingly Marxist—the Social Democrat Workers' Party.

Bebel's party grew steadily and it made so many converts among the people in the German Workers' Union—Lassalle's old 'Association'—that in 1875 Bebel was able to accomplish a merger, the General German Workers providing the industrial wing, the Social Democratic Workers the political wing in a new foundation, the Socialist Workers' Party, which soon became more commonly known as the Social-Democratic Party.

What perhaps I may call Lassallism prevented Bebel from immediately imposing a Marxist programme on the new Party; in any case, he was not, unlike Lassalle, a man to impose any-thing—in his very gradualism, in his insistence on using per-suasion and never swift, direct action, he sowed the seeds of the ultimate failure of the whole 'parliamentary socialist' idea. It took him sixteen years, until 1891, to get the Party to adopt a completely Marxist programme—at the Party Congress in Erfurt that year.

Bebel, then, was responsible for the idea of installing socialism by taking over, within the constitution and the law, the bourgeois parliament. That was already his intention when, with another member of his Party, he stood for election to the Reichstag in 1871 and, with his comrade, was elected. So, then, in 1871 the Social-Democrats had two members in the Reichstag while there was not a single socialist in any national assembly (unless you count the short-lived Constituent Assembly of the Paris Com-

mune) anywhere in the world. Yet in 1912, following the last
election before the outbreak of World War One, the Social-
Democrats, having polled over four and a quarter million votes,
had one hundred and ten out of the 397 seats in the Reichstag, were the most numerous single Party in that Chamber, and
would, therefore, have formed the government had they not
been excluded from power by a coalition of the Centre and Right
Parties.

It may be taken as a rule that in the following years Social-
Democrat parties were repeatedly kept out of office despite their
majorities by coalitions of the Right and the Centre, the Centre
being the liberals best described (this vulgar adjective will be
appreciated by former Naval ratings and, for all I know, soldiers
and airmen) as half-hard.

The successes of German Social-Democracy had led to the foundation of Social-Democratic parties all over Europe. I do not
propose to trace their progress year by year but simply to give
some idea of their success by looking at their position twenty
years later, just before World War One. It should be remembered
that they went to the electorate with a clear and definite Marxist
policy—class war, nationalization of the means of production,
distribution and exchange, plus welfare legislation far in advance
of anything Marx had envisaged. And the figures can have only
one meaning: that between a quarter and a half of the population
of Europe had been converted to socialism and saw in it the way
to the Millennium.

The Austrian Socialists were quick to follow the German lead
and, with a form of franchise heavily loaded against the working
class, by 1912 had 82 members in a Reichstag of 512. This
relative weakness by comparison with Germany was due to the
influence of the Roman Catholic Trade Unions. There was a
Social-Democratic party in Hungary also, but I have been unable
to find the figures in this case.

A Danish Social-Democratic party was founded in 1889. By
1914 thirty-two of the 114 members of the *Folketing* were
Social-Democrats. The Swedish Party was founded in the same
year: in 1914 it had 87 of the 230 members of the Swedish
parliament. The Norwegian *Storting* with 123 members had 23

socialists. To complete the Scandinavian picture: in 1914 the national assembly of Finland had 200 members, 87 of them were Social-Democrats; Finland had conceded full civil rights to women in 1907 and nine of these socialists were women.

In Belgium the figures were 39 out of 166, but in Holland only seven out of 100. Forty socialist deputies sat in the Italian parliament of 508, but most socialists in Italy were anarchists and they boycotted elections. The same is true in Switzerland where fifteen of the 160 members of the National Council were Social-Democrats.

It should be remembered that in every case the electoral system was loaded against the working class; that is, it took many more votes to elect a socialist than to elect a deputy of the Centre or the Right.

We now have to consider some special cases in Europe and the socialist situation outside Europe. The special cases are those of Britain, France, Russia and Spain.

In Britain socialism was never wholeheartedly Marxist. The British, or rather the English, did not like the idea of class war; or perhaps one should say, rather, that the English working class, very much gentler than the middle class, was prepared to suffer class-war attacks without hitting back, just as, to the contempt of Hippolyte Taine (*Notes sur l'Angleterre*, 1871) they were unique in Europe in being grateful for the cast-off clothing of their 'betters'. Maybe the English workers were more 'Christian' —English socialism was rooted in Nonconformist Christianity and Chartism—than their European fellows; or more cowardly; or just so snobbish that they could not bear to wage class war on a bourgeoisie they aspired to join. It may be significant that Britain had a larger class of domestic servants than any other European country—lackey is a word of abuse among socialists.*

A Social-Democratic Federation was founded in Britain in

* It is only fair to add that after long experience of the British working class and British institutions, Karl Marx and, less surprisingly, Kropotkin came to believe that in Britain—but only in Britain—it was conceivable that socialism would be installed peacefully; the bourgeoisie as well as the proletariat seemed to be less ferocious there than elsewhere. Both men were, it is true, very old when they reached this happy conclusion. But one recalls the opinion of a clever Scot, A. J. Macdonell, that all Englishmen are born two whiskies below par.

1881; the famous Fabian Society of gradualist socialist intellectuals in 1884; and Independent Labour Party in 1893; a number of more revolutionary socialist groups, such as the Socialist League, thereafter; and the Labour Party in 1900. Owing to the anti-revolutionary trade union feeling—British workers were extremely reluctant to take political responsibility and have too much plain horse-sense to think that they could accomplish anything much if, under capitalism, they did—the Labour Party was not immediately able to adopt a Marxist programme and did not do so until 1914. It then did so on paper, but its Marxism has never been convincing. But there is this to be said; in 1914 the Labour Party was at least a great deal more socialist than it is in 1973. It had forty-two members of Parliament, all Social-Democrats.

The difficulty experienced by the French in accepting Social-Democracy was twofold: in the first place it was not French, it was German. In the second place the French are too clever and at the same time too cynical to believe that socialism can be installed without a violent revolution; the French worker knows that if he had as much at stake as a rich burgess, he would fight tooth and claw and with no holds barred to defend it and to hell with the proletariat. In the third place there was a native socialist tradition much older than Marxism. In the fourth place a very large proportion of the French working class was syndicalist, which meant that it did not believe in the socialist efficacy of political action of any kind: the revolution was to be made by industrial action. Even so, there were, in a *Chambre des Députés* of five hundred and ninety-seven, one hundred and two Social-Democrats in 1914.

In Russia, as will appear in its place, the Tsar Nicholas II, for whom it may fairly be claimed that he was the stupidest man short of imbecility ever to rule an empire, was forced by the terrorist activities of the Social-Revolutionary Party rather than by the propagandist activities of the Social-Democrats to concede a Duma (national assembly); he repeatedly dissolved it and held new elections under more and more restrictive rules, in an attempt to procure a Chamber like Louis XVIII's *Introuvable* which was 'more royalist than the king'. In 1914 there were four hundred and thirty-two Duma members of whom only sixteen were Social-

Democrats; but there were also twice as many Social-Revolutionaries.

Then there is the Spanish case: a solitary Social-Democrat sat in the Cortes in 1914 but the progress of socialism in Spain cannot be judged by that. The overwhelming predominance of anarchism over parliamentary socialism has already been referred to, and in 1914 the most powerful and effective socialist movement in Spain was anarcho-syndicalism. The men of that persuasion, following Proudhon, and like the syndicalists in France, boycotted elections as a matter of policy.

So much for Europe. In Australia a Labour party with a Social-Democratic (that is parliamentary Marxist) programme was founded in 1885 by an English immigrant political journalist (who subsequently tried to found a New Australia in a Paraguay depopulated by lunatic dictators trying to play Napoleon), and some immigrant British who had been members of the extreme Left Socialist League in Britain. In 1890 the Party organized the great strike of sheep-shearers, an undertaking in which it was strengthened by the 'Wobblies' (see Chapter Eleven) and in the following year a nation-wide shipping strike; there again 'Wobbly' (anarcho-syndicalist) influence was a factor.

The shearers' strike, involving twenty-six thousand men, developed into a mini-revolution: squatters' stations were attacked by armed bands which fought battles with the police and troops, wool-sheds were burnt, and there was talk of setting up a communist republic in West Queensland. 'Banjo' Paterson's song *Waltzing Matilda*, commemorates a martyr of the strike, Frenchy Hoffmeister. The colonial government had to use all the military force at its command to crush the revolt. That public support was strong is clear, for in the same year thirty-seven Social-Democrats were elected to the State Legislature of New South Wales and in 1904 the Labour Party won the general elections and founded the Commonwealth Government. It formed its second government in 1908, and a third in 1910 with a majority in both Houses, but then came hard up against the snag in the 'gradualist' policy which Kropotkin had foreseen: it inevitably entails persistence of the evils of bourgeois government. The Party made the blunder of submitting the Marxist part of its programme to referendum

and was defeated. There had been almost no education of the
workers for democratic responsibility and what they wanted was
a hand-out, the right to put their hands into capitalist pockets,
not the responsibility of administering their rightful heritage.*
As a result of this referendum, the Australian Labour Party virtually dropped its Social-Democratic policy, and moved Right
into the Radical-Liberal slot.

In the United States Social-Democracy was feeble and short-
lived, starved in infancy by the conservatism of the American
Federation of Labour, a Congress of craft unions quite as determined to keep the proletariat and their democracy in subordin-
ate places as any bourgeoisie could have been. The inflow of
European immigrants under the illusion that a westward migra-
tion in space was a quicker way to the Millennium than a movement in time made slow by the constraints of the human
condition, while it provided America with genuine revolutionaries
like the Patterson Italian anarchists who assassinated both King
Umberto of Italy and President McKinley of the United States,
or Jacob Most, the former Reichstag Social-Democrat author of
a remarkable handbook for anarchist terrorists, did nothing for
Social-Democracy: did not the First International die of neglect
in New York? Thus American socialism was forced to be revolutionary and conspiratorial willy-nilly, and anarchist movements
were, for two decades, quite strong. Industrial unions—as distinct
from craft unions—were briefly socialist and in the Presidential
elections of 1912 the Social-Democratic Party formed by Eugene
Debs put up their founder as a candidate for the third time: he
polled 800,000 of the seventeen million votes cast, a tenfold
advance on his first attempt.

Thus the only Social-Democratic party to win executive power
before 1914 was the Australian Labour Party, and that was
emasculated of its socialism in the manner described. In the half-

---

* In developing and very sparsely populated countries special conditions prevail. Men who really want to be free of exploitation can be
so by going into the bush, clearing land and making a farm, while the
service trades will be taken on by like-minded artisans. The failure of
socialism to develop strongly in the USA may have been due in part to
this same cause.

century of its career to 1914 Social-Democracy had advanced towards power, towards the moment when it would be able to begin to bring in the Millennium, but was to be halted abruptly in its advance by the outbreak of World War One, in which the major capitalist-imperialist powers fought for mastery. With a modicum of revolutionary courage the Social-Democrats might just possibly have prevented that war but revolutionary courage was precisely the quality which had been sacrificed to the policy of gradualism.* That accusation needs justification.

In 1899 all the European and some other Social-Democratic parties, acting at the instance of British socialists in the trades unions, sent delegations to a Congress held in Paris to form a new International, known thereafter as the Second International. As a result of nationalist bickering there were at first two rival Internationals, but their differences were resolved and a Congress of the Second International, the one and only, was held in Brussels in 1891 where the anarchists, too, were accepted as members. But, Marxist exclusiveness coming into play once again, they were expelled in 1893, thus causing the secession of nearly all Italian and Spanish socialists, and about half the French socialists who, as syndicalists, were lumped with the anarchists since their principal crime, in Marxist eyes, was repudiation of the Marxist instrument of proletarian dictatorship, the political State.

In 1910 the exclusively Social-Democratic rump of the Second International—still, of course, a powerful organization representing many millions of workers—met in Congress at Copenhagen: thirty-three national parties were represented, including those of Persia and Japan and some Latin American republics. It began to look as if the gradualist socialist advance towards the Millennium, which was now being cheered on by the GOMs of the Millennial dream, like Kropotkin, who had grown tired of the 'sudden-and-violent' solution, was making headway all over the world. And it was at this Congress that a resolution was voted

* Those German Marxists who, characteristically, interpreted Marx too literally, were in part responsible: they argued that since, according to *Das Kapital*, capitalism was bound to collapse as a result of its inbuilt contradictions, a matter dealt with in a later chapter, there was no point in making a revolution: why shed one's blood trying to kill an enemy certain, given a little more time, to commit suicide? It was this 'Revisionism' which Lenin had the insight to resist: but of that, later.

which did, indeed, seem to mark a grand stride forward. For at least fifty centuries the kings and emperors, the tyrants and aristocrats, the bankers and burgesses had been able to use the workers as assegai-fodder, bow-and-arrow-fodder, cannon-fodder in their wars for mastery of territory and loot. Now, at long last, taking note of Marx's call on the workers of the world to unite (and of his implied call to make war, class war, on their real enemies, their own capitalists and their own governments, instead of on each other), the Second International resolved to call a halt to this slaughter: Social-Democratic parties in all thirty-three countries resolved that they would oppose declarations of war by their national governments and even use, if necessary, the general strike to make this sensible and humane ban effective. The resolution was not taken in the class-war spirit, however: it was, rather, as if a meeting of responsible adults resolved to use their economic power as the providers of pocket-money to stop the juvenile hooliganism of gang-warfare. That spirit was appropriate: for if ever there was a world war between rival gangs of hooligans, albeit genteel ones, it was the war of 1914-18.

It was on this resolution that the Second International was wrecked: when the Austrian Empire delivered its deliberately provocative ultimatum to Serbia and the German Empire declared its support for Austria, in other words when Europe's Continental empires, joined shortly by France and Britain, finally got themselves into the fight they'd been spoiling for, the leading and strongest (German) Social-Democratic party ratted on its undertaking and, with the brave and honourable exception of one member, Karl Liebnecht, voted war credits, just like any bourgeois 'patriot'. The French socialist leader, Jean Jaurès, did his best to stop the rot and was murdered by a French 'patriot' for his pains—patriotism, said Sam Johnson, is the last refuge of a scoundrel. The other Social-Democratic parties, again with one brave and honourable exception, the British Independent Labour Party, tamely followed the German example. And, once again, the workers of the world, instead of using their strength to impose civilized behaviour on their governments, were cutting each other's throats for the benefit of their masters.

The Russian workers, led by the Bolshevik ('Majoritist') branch of the old Russian Social-Democratic Party, by the Socialist-

Revolutionaries and the anarchists, were the first to come to their senses; but the October Revolution is the subject of a later chapter.

In November 1918, as the result of a revolution, the Social-Democrats took office in Germany for the first time. Since the days of August Bebel they had been preaching Marxism to the workers who now, therefore, expected their socialist mentors to nationalize the means of production, distribution and exchange immediately, and loudly summoned their leaders to get on with it. But once again Kropotkin was vindicated: the policy of gradualism rather than revolution had cost the Social-Democratic leaders the courage of their convictions and, frightened of falling into the morass of difficulties in which the Bolsheviks were floundering in Russia, they set up a commission to advise on ways and means of socialization. The commission advised against it for the time being: let capitalism do the work of restoring production and trade, and only then undertake a cautious, step-by-step approach to socialism. A ridiculous sort of 'joint-control' system of industrial management by State, workers, bosses and even consumers was tried. It resulted, as perhaps it was meant to, in the capitalists retaining all their old power.

Very much the same kind of thing happened in Austria where the Social-Democratic administration of Otto Bauer, long the leader of the Austrian socialists, did make a half-hearted attempt to socialize a part of Austrian production by setting up managements composed of State, co-operative societies, and trades unions. When they showed signs of being successful, they were discontinued and the industries reverted to the capitalists. Only the Social-Democratic municipality of Vienna had some positively socialist measures to its credit: their workers' housing became a model for the whole world: it was the first thing to be destroyed (by artillery) when the bourgeoisie hit back in the class war, using a mini-bullyboy, the dwarfish but ferocious Chancellor Dollfuss, as their leader.

It was not that men like Bauer were insincere or treacherous: gradualism, it must be repeated, had debilitated their will. They probably knew, in their hearts, that unless the socialist is prepared to change the economic and social structure of society in one fell swoop, at whatever cost in chaos and suffering at the start, then he had better abandon all but the welfare part of his programme. The Social-Democrats did not have, and never have had, the courage to take responsibility for the initial strife and misery which lay between them and the Millennium: when the bourgeois Appolyon bestrode their path and declared 'Here will I spill thy soul', they made deprecating gestures and suggested getting round a table for talks. When a socialist consents to get round a table with the burgesses, he should leave his wallet at home; unless, of course, his object is to fill it.

The Social-Democrats in Sweden took office in 1920, having already shared it as members of a coalition government. They followed the German example, set up a permanent commission to examine ways and means to socialization, and did nothing to introduce socialism for six years, when they were defeated in elections. Later Swedish Social-Democratic governments made Sweden the first model Welfare State, but within the context of capitalism: the Swedish workers have the highest standard of living of any working class in the world, taking both personal incomes and public-service benefits into account; it is notorious that they are forced to work at such pressure that Sweden has become infamous for the unhappiness of its population and its high suicide rate. In short, exploitation continues with, apparently, the mesmerized help of the exploited.

In Denmark, where the Social-Democrats took office in 1924 with a clear majority in the *Folketing*, the story was much as in Sweden: welfare, certainly; socialism, not bloody likely.

The British Labour Party held office with a minority supported by the Liberals in 1924, and a small majority in 1929. It did nothing whatever to realize its Marxist programme although the 1929 capitalist collapse offered a magnificent opportunity to bold and determined socialists who believed in what they were doing. But if you were a mere cautious reformer, and not a revolutionary, the slump was a paralysing disaster: it enabled you to claim that this was not the right moment to try anything new and that we must wait for better times. Socialism was abandoned by all but a rump of the Party, the majority of Labour members joining with the Conservatives in policies which enormously increased working-class misery. That majority slowly faded out under the guise of a 'National' Labour Party which was firmly anti-socialist.

The rump, under Clement Attlee, remained Social-Democrat on paper until its Right-wing, led by Gaitskell, forced it to abandon the socialist part of its programme after six years of office following World War Two.

So what went wrong? Throughout most of Europe Social-Democratic Marxists were given the legal power to transform their societies into socialist ones and so, if they believed in their doctrine, to take a giant stride towards the Millennium which socialists had dreamed of since the 18th century. They made no use of their opportunities. Why? There are probably three answers:

(*i*) The Social-Democratic leaders and the trades unions allowed themselves to be deeply discouraged by the Russian economic disaster although it was, clearly, quite irrelevant to their own case.

(*ii*) They were frightened of provoking the ferocious bourgeois and capitalist backlash of the kind which elevated Mussolini to the dictatorship of Italy. They would not face the necessity of violent class war, although it does seem that in most cases a majority of the workers were ready for it.

(*iii*) The corrupting and debilitating effects of gradualism which have already been sufficiently discussed.

TEN

The Anarchists in Action

At the end of the last chapter I suggested certain reasons why the Social-Democrats failed to have the courage of their old conviction that the installation of socialism would be the first and most important step towards the Millennium of freedom and social justice, and I have tried to show that anarchist socialists who approached the problem of ensuring social justice by way of the demolition of the State detected just those weaknesses in the Social-Democratic case and foresaw just those failures which must arise from them.

These libertarian socialists were of several kinds and therefore their attempts to demolish the politico-social-economic apparatus so that a free socialist society could take its place must be looked at in different places and contexts. There was the work of Malatesta, Costa, Cafiero and others, following Bakunin, in Italy; there was the Spanish case—by far the most important, for the Spaniards came nearer to succeeding than any other anarchists; there were the Russian anarchists; and finally those countries in which anarchism was marginal, effective only in promoting libertarian ideas among other socialists.

The brief account of Malatesta's career only touched on Italian anarchism because Malatesta was one of the great internationalist revolutionaries whose work in the 19th century transcended all nationalism and all nationality. When Italy was united under the monarchy of Savoy, with the concurrence of Garibaldi and despite the opposition of Mazzini who remained a 'classical' Republican, the workers and poor peasants had, in their innocence, expected some benefit from this, as it were, modernization and bourgeoisization of Italy. They were not to know that the poor do not benefit from a bourgeois 'revolution' unless and until they assert themselves by industrial or political action backed by the threat of violence. Nor did the romantic Republican Nationalism of Mazzini, harking back to the imaginary virtues of pre-Imperial

Rome, offer them anything. The 'Liberty' proclaimed by Mazzini and his kind would not even feed, let alone liberate, the poor worker or peasant. So that by the 1860s when Bakunin arrived in Italy spoiling for a fight there were not only strong surface eddies and whirlpools of superficial revolt, but below that a deep and rising swell of working-class and peasant resentment. There would, therefore, seem to have been much good material to Bakunin's hand; yet his International Brotherhood, though it attracted a respectable number of men dedicated to the demolition of the State and the repudiation of capitalism as an economic system and to the use of violence in achieving those ends, did not, in practice, accomplish anything more than the sowing of the seeds of libertarian socialism in Italy.

A more substantial anarchist than Bakunin, Proudhon, influenced Italian socialist thought through the translations published by a hero and martyr of the *Risorgimento*, the Duke of San Giovanni, better known as Carlo Pasacane, who, following his great master, preached that all property but that acquired by the work of a man's own hands was theft; that the land should be cultivated in common, all industrial plant become common property, and society be administered by free communes. Pasacane was in one sense a follower of Nechaev, for he believed in what he called 'propaganda by deed', so that Italy would move into the Millennium by way of terrorism.

Anarchism grew more slowly in Italy throughout the 1860s but there was no effective militancy until the seventies and the leadership of the movement by such men as Malatesta, Costa and Carmelo Palladino. Most of the militants were, like the 'Weathermen' in the USA and the Latin-American Tupamaros a century later, the well-educated sons of burgesses, often rich burgesses. These were the people who refounded the Bakuninist International Brotherhood in Naples, and were only slowly winning recruits for anarchism when Mazzini, never a social-revolutionary and now, in old age, a conservative Republican, attacked them and their movement in print. That gave them just the publicity they needed. Bakunin riposted in newspaper articles and a pamphlet and thereafter the movement grew so much more rapidly that the Italian delegation to the First International was wholly anarchist, voted consistently against participation of the workers in elections and, in general, opposed the Marxist way to the Millennium as more likely to lead to hell than to heaven. It was useless to talk of reforming the State and taking it into proletarian hands: the State, any State whatsoever, was necessarily a tyrant; it must be destroyed by armed force and the army to do that job was waiting in the industrial towns and in the countryside—'fourteen million peasants ... waiting in the agony of fever and hunger for the hour of their emancipation'. Socialist principles must be affirmed by insurrectionary deeds, not words and votes. A Committee for Social Revolution was formed by the Brotherhood, in 1883, to plan a course of violent action.

The first such action (1884) was abortive. The Bologna anarchists were to have risen and seized the city and that was to have been the signal for armed risings in Rome, Florence and the Sicilian towns, and in certain regions of the countryside but a police spy gave the game away and Andrea Costa and Enrico Malatesta, leaders of the conspiracy, were arrested along with many other militants. Unfortunately for the authorities the monarchy was so unpopular with the bourgeoisie as well as the working class that juries consistently found accused anarchists 'not guilty' without the slightest regard to the evidence, and they all had to be released.

But the police continued so active against even the most peaceful anarchist operations that the Congress of 1886 had to be held in an Appennine forest and Costa was arrested while on his way to it. Fifty delegates from all over Italy reached the rendezvous and Malatesta and Cafiero persuaded them to vote a policy of open insurrection and also to adopt, for the post-revolutionary phase, a Kropotkin-style anarcho-communist society in which every man would have the right to 'all his needs in the measure conceded by the state of production and social capacity'. The insurrectionary action which followed consisted in recruiting armed bands of peasants led by anarchists who moved from village to village trying to raise the countryside. They were greeted rapturously as liberators by the villagers, nearly always led by their priests who were as poor as themselves. In some of the larger villages or small towns the municipal offices were raided and the tax-records were burned. Arms were captured from the police and distributed to the peasants. What this amounted to was guerrilla warfare of the kind we are familiar with today in the Latin-American countries, of the kind, in fact, which accomplished the Cuban revolution. We are too inclined to believe that Mao Tse-tung and Ché Guevara invented the idea of the peasants bringing the revolution to the urban workers (in defiance of the Marxist rule that the proletariat is necessarily the militant class). In fact, both in Italy and Spain, this method was normal anarchist practice. The great difference, of course, is that the Chinese and Cuban communists succeeded, the Italian anarchists did not, and for the obvious reason that they were in too much of a hurry and had not prepared their revolution. The nation-wide revolution which was planned during this guerrilla phase never even started; the masses were miserable, even desperate. But for want of education in the social and economic realities their attitude was negative. Instead of rising, they despaired: theirs was the despair of the same Calabrians and Sicilians whom Carlo Levi described in *Christ Stopped at Eboli*. It still hangs like a storm which will not break over those same countrysides; the patience of the poor with their maltreatment at the hands of the rich and mighty is very long.

The anarchists, then, took to terrorism. A first attempt to assassinate King Umberto was made and there were bombings and shootings in Florence and Pisa of the indiscriminate kind employed by the IRA Provisionals in Ulster in 1972-3—propaganda by deed. These acts, those of the extremists, alienated some of the leaders who repudiated individual terrorism not only as immoral but as useless. Costa defected and became a gradualist and co-founder of the Italian Parliamentary Socialist Party. Cafiero also defected but then went mad and spent the rest of his life in a lunatic asylum. There was a similar falling-off among the rank and file.

Yet the *idea* of anarchism as the only way to the Millennium persisted: propagated by anarchist journals, spread abroad by such anarchist evangelists as Malatesta, kept alive by such acts of propaganda by deed as the assassination of Sadi Carnot, the French President (1894), of the Spanish Prime Minister Canovas (1897), of the Empress Elizabeth of Austria, poor scapegoat (1898), of King Umberto of Italy (1900) and others. What had those victims of fanatics, who were so dangerously pure in heart, in common? Each was the personification of a tyrant State; each, therefore, was the devil, the great enemy of mankind.

The country in which anarchism came nearest to success in its purpose—destruction of the State and its replacement by a free society of co-operatives and communes, was Spain. Half a century after it had ceased to be in a position to compete with Marxism, whether communist or Social-Democratic, everywhere else in the world, it was the principal socialist movement in that country. It was not, perhaps, killed outright by the combined efforts of the Stalinist Marxists and Franco Fascists in the Civil War (1936-9). It still remains to be seen whether those enemies of freedom only succeeded in stunning it; if violent uprisings against the trium-virate of capital, the Falange, and the Army gathers momentum, it may still do so in anarchist terms. At all events, there was a moment in time when it looked as if the theories of Proudhon, Bakunin, Kropotkin and Malatesta might be given a trial in Spain.

The story begins in 1845 when Proudhon's disciple Ramon de la Sagra founded an anarchist newspaper, *El Provenir*, in Corunna. Those who read it became familiar with the idea of 'Mutualism' as a possible way of life. Next came the translator of Proudhon's most important works into Spanish, Pi y Margal who, however, also had his own ideas of how to arrive at a libertarian society: the way to rid mankind of the scourge of the State was by 'dividing and subdividing power, by making it changeable and progressively destroying it'. In short, by planned, progressive decentralization, the transfer of power from the nation to the province, from the province to the city municipality, from the municipality to the parish, to the village and finally to the workers' and peasants' commune. To the best of my knowledge this was an original suggestion, a new means of 'revolution' without blood-shed.* Pi y Margal's followers were recruited among Aragonese, Castilian, Galician and, above all, Catalan separatists, just as, in Britain today, he would have found his first supporters among the Welsh and Scottish 'nationalists'. They were called *Federal-istas* (the name implied federation of communes, not autonomous provinces). From about 1854 these *Federalistas* set about de-molishing established society by organizing general strikes in

* And, I suggest, one well worth re-examination today.

industrial cities, peasant insurrections in the countryside; and a number of urban riots. All this culminated in a great *jacquerie* in 1867. Meanwhile co-operative, trade unionist, and political socialist movements were springing up and spreading all over Spain, some of them affiliated to the First International in which Bakunin's influence had not yet been destroyed by Karl Marx.

In 1868 came the army *coup* under General Prim which rid Spain of the impossible Queen Isabella, set up a provisional government, and invited Prince Amadeus of Savoy, Duke of Aosta to accept the Spanish throne. Bakunin seized the opportunity to send evangelists into Spain; the most successful of these was an Italian, Giuseppe Fanelli who is regarded by most historians as the founder of anarchism in Spain. Out of his work (accomplished, God knows how, without a word of Spanish), and out of Bakunin's meeting with the Spanish delegates to the First International's Basle Congress of 1869, emerged the Spanish Federation of the International and the Spanish Alliance of Social-Democracy, both wholeheartedly anarchist. At a Congress held in Barcelona in 1870 the Spanish Federation adopted the Statutes of the model Jura Federation. Bakunin was losing to Marx in most of Europe: in Spain he was completely victorious, and the Spanish revolutionary working class remained largely anarchist until it was bashed into a kind of resignation by the saviour of the bourgeoisie and of capitalism, Francisco Franco.

Amadeus of Savoy, having first refused the Spanish crown and then on second thoughts accepted it, was forced to give it up in despair in 1873 when a Republic was proclaimed and the Federalist Pi y Margal became its President. His government was pledged to the Federalist policy of progressive decentralization with an ultimate aim of Proudhonian 'Mutualism'. But the very attempt to form a government for the purpose of abolishing government was absurd: men, even of the highest principles, always find admirably highminded reasons for not divesting themselves of power, which is why all the great anarchist thinkers have insisted on the need to make the destructive part of the revolution at one stroke, despite the dangers of the phase of chaos which must follow. Pi y Margal's administration was unable to control its own revolution and was, at the same time, attacked from the Right by a Carlist armed rising in the North. In the South the anarchists and Federalists set up communes run by Committees of Public Safety, closed the churches, imposed penal taxes on the rich and, in short, took the revolution seriously. Meanwhile the Carlists were scoring successes in the North. It is a wonderful instance of the corrupting influence of power which the anarchists' theorists were so very right to be afraid of, that the administration, faced with a choice of crushing the Carlists or crushing their own revolutionaries, since they had not the military force to do both, chose to crush the revolution. Pi y Margal himself would have preferred to use the army against the Rightists, but he was simply overruled by a majority of his ministers, whereupon, again demonstrating the futility of 'gradualism' in revolution, he could think of nothing to do but resign. The southern *Federalistas* might have survived had they had wholehearted anarchist support, but in fact the 'Alliance' held aloof there, although where they were in strength they raised insurrections and, for example, seized the town of Alcoy, burnt its factories and the houses of the rich, killed the government's officers and carried their heads on pikes in triumph through the town, a somewhat *outré* manifestation of revolutionary exuberance which shocked more anarchists than it amused.

An army *coup* restored order in the familiar style of such *coups* by the faithful mastiffs of the burgesses (the carefully nurtured dogs of Comrade Napoleon have but one style and these Spanish ones relied on it), by imprisoning or shooting all the socialists and liberals the troops could get their hands on, suppressing working-class movements of all kinds and banning all socialist and anarchist organizations whatsoever. Yet anarchism survived the most ferociously vengeful reprisals which the army-sponsored Bourbon restoration could devise, notably in Andalusia, nursery of fierce malcontents: there were underground Congresses, an underground press, and an effective network of underground anarchist schools which taught thousands of people to read and write—skills rightly abominated by all good Spanish conservatives as dangerous. This activity produced a kind of revolutionary euphoria:

Every new movement or strike was thought to herald the immediate coming of a new age of plenty when all—even the

Civil Guard and the landowners—would be free and happy.*

Nothing in the history of socialism is more moving, and more
productive of despairing laughter or tears according to temperament, than the faith of simple, decent men in the existence of a
fund of goodwill (O! that wicked myth of immanent justice ...)
even among autocrats, even among the rich burgesses. Yet it is
not surprising: how are the have-nots to understand the corruption of the human heart which is an inevitable consequence of
the kind of property which implies the exploitation of other
men? It is good anarchist doctrine that the exploiters are as much
the victims of capitalism as the exploited.

The Bourbon restoration put Alfonso XII on the Spanish
throne: in 1878 the anarchists tried to kill him, the authorities
riposted with counter-terrorism, whereupon the anarchists
organized strikes in the cities and burned manors in the countryside—and so on, until the workers' organizations were again
legalized (1881). By far the most important of these was the
anarchist Federation of Workers of the Spanish Region, whose
militant wing, *Los Desheridados*, became active in 1882. It is
curious to note the duplication of the Russian pattern: Populist
moderates and *People's Will* extremists (see below). This terrorist
wing was repudiated by the body of the movement. To deal
with the 'Disinherited' the police seized the occasion of the
murder of one of their political informers who had been found
out by the comrades and disposed of, to invent a secret revolutionary society, *La Mano Negra* (this Black Hand has, of course,
nothing whatever to do with the Serbian terrorist organization
of the same name): and then to imagine assassination plots
planned by it, and to arrest anarchists in order to prevent them.
If this seems improbable, the sceptical reader is referred to the
well-documented history of Evgenio Azef in Russia, who was
at once the ablest and most trusted Socialist-Revolutionary
organizer of assassinations and other acts of terrorism, and the
principal and highly-paid Okhrana informer against himself and
his activities. His dual role was sustained for twenty years. The
Black Hand device, conceived by an exceptionally clever Civil
Guard officer, was remarkably successful: in 1882 the Federa-

* Brenan, Gerald, *The Spanish Labyrinth*, London, 1936.

tion had thirty thousand members; four years later three thousand.

But this was not owing only to police successes: with the spread in Spain of Kropotkin's anarcho-communist ideas large organizations like the Federation tended to break down into small groups of conspirators. There were bombings, assassinations, general strikes, riots and, in Jerez, a sort of *jacquerie* in which five thousand peasants led by anarchists took part. This was put down by troops but as the poor wretches captured were clearly not anarchists, and what the Civil Guard had promised the government was anarchists, a number of genuine ones who had been in prison at the time of the rising were taken out and shot for provoking it; shot, or, in some cases, garrotted. In Catalonia at the same time, the police overdid the ordinary practice of torturing prisoners to such an extent that a lot of them died before they could be brought to trial (the reputation of the Civil Guard for sadistic cruelty still endures). The news of this atrocity reached the outside world, the Spanish government was condemned by the world's press as barbarous; its fellow governments doubtless deplored the gross carelessness of letting such news get beyond the walls of the Montjuich prison and probably explained apologetically to the Spanish ambassadors that they would have to make protesting noises. The Spanish Prime Minister held responsible for his policemen's excesses of zeal (the politicians' International had not quite the solidarity it has today) was assassinated by an anarchist to almost universal applause.

On the intellectual front, the anarchist *Revista Blanca* was being written by the best brains in Spain. Spain's young painter of genius, Pablo Picasso, was an anarchist supporter, and the anarchist Francisco Ferrer's *Escuela Moderna* schools, co-educational, banning any kind of punishment, offering a free choice of work to pupils and a measure of pupil-power control, anticipated all the educational advances of the next century. Ferrer, an anticlerical, of course, and clearly an immoralist since he neither beat children nor despised women, was subsequently judicially murdered by means of a rigged trial at the instance of the Spanish hierarchy.

The success of the next anarchist organization, *Solidaridad Obrera,* belongs, in my view, to the chapter on syndicalism. Out of its one-week revolution in Catalonia, its deliberate attempt to put a stop to the Government's imperialist war on the Rif, and its fearful aftermath of mass arrests, torture and judicial murder, arose the *Confederacion Nacional del Trabajo*, a sort of 'TUC-with-guts' composed mostly of anarchist, or anarchist-dominated trades unions. Its organization was strictly anarchist in that it had no bureaucracy (there was a single paid official), and was run by direct democracy with all the executive work being done by members designated for special tasks. The means which it adopted to attain worker-power were industrial and economic; it would have nothing to do with politics. Its plan was to call general strikes, lead the strikers in taking over a town, set up communes of workers to run the administrative region—parish, village, town or province—and co-operatives to run industry and agriculture; and then to repudiate the Spanish State by declaring itself independent. This was Kropotkin's idea of revolution-by-opting-out, an idea which, in another form, is to be found also in Proudhon. There were also echoes of Pi y Margal's *Federalismo*, but the danger of gradualism was to be avoided by direct action. By 1912 the CNT was so numerous and so powerful and growing so fast that, in a panic, the Prime Minister, Canalejas, banned it.

The CNT demonstrated the failure of the ban by calling a general strike. Since the railway workers, always to be relied on for militancy, were among the strikers, the country was paralysed. Canalejas mobilized them for military service so as to put them under military discipline, a trick which can always be used in countries which tolerate conscription. The anarchists dealt with him in the only possible way: they shot him dead, whereafter the strength of the CNT continued to increase until, in 1919, it had about three-quarters of a million members.

But the whole anarchist movement, within and outside the CNT, was being penetrated—one is tempted to add 'and corrupted' —by the Marxists, both Social-Democratic and Bolshevik communist, urging the need for political action, the seizure of the State for the proletariat, not its demolition. The success of the Russian October Revolution—its failure had not yet become apparent—gave them heroic haloes and all the glamour of victory over the arch-autocrat, over the bourgeoisie, over capitalism.

For a time the Spanish workers were shaken in their hostility to the Statist Marxists and in their repudiation of political means. But soon the haloes began to wane, to become invisible in the glare of the Bolshevik terror. The news reached Spain that the anarchists were being persecuted; anti-Marxism revived, and in 1922 the Spaniards withdrew from the Third International (Comintern) and affiliated the CNT to the German International Workers Association, a syndicalist organization.

Bolshevik success, then, failed to attract Spanish workers into the Communist Party. It became clearer and clearer that the great anarchist theorists had been right: communism triumphant had created, in the revolutionary government, a State as tyrannous as the Tsar's—the poor Russian frogs had exchanged King Nicholas Log for King Central Committee Stork. Or, to use another of the great proverbs which tell in a few words the eternal tale of the relationship between man-thesis and State-synthesis, the Bolshevik boys like the Tsarist boys threw stones at the proletarian frogs in fun, and although the stones were hand-picked by the dedicated mentors of the proletariat, still, most disconcertingly, the frogs died in earnest.

For another fifteen years the anarchists and the CNT fought the good fight of the common people of Spain for a libertarian Millennium against the experienced torturers of the Civil Guard, against the capitalists' hired pistoleros who, in Spain as in the United States, shot down strikers to send up dividends; and against whatever government contrived to get control of the State apparatus. The story of their failure belongs to another chapter, to that second crisis of socialism, the Spanish Civil War.

Although three of the great anarchist theorists, Bakunin, Tolstoy and Kropotkin, were Russians, anarchism remained always a marginal and eccentric doctrine among the various brands of Russian socialists. In the nihilists Russia produced her own kind of anarchists who, like the anarchists elsewhere in the world, believed in a Millennium which would be golden because it was at long last free of that reservoir and fount of social injustice, the State.

It has been pointed out by George Woodcock, quoting Isaiah

Berlin's introduction to Franco Venturi's great work,* that the
whole Populist movement which, for half a century prepared the
Russian Revolution, was permeated by libertarianism. Isaiah
Berlin wrote of the Russian revolutionaries of the 19th century
that 'anarchism, equality, a full life for all, these were universally
accepted'. Moreover the *obschina*, the ancient peasant commune
which had certainly endured since the very beginning of agriculture among the North Slavs, whatever its 19-century reality,
was, to refer to Woodcock again, idealized as 'the magic link
between a sort of age of gold and a future of idyllic promise'.
Furthermore, it was Alexander Herzen, the 'father' of modern
socialism in Russia who, it will be recalled, financed Proudhon's
La Voix du peuple. True, Herzen was equally generous to revolutionaries of other persuasions, but he certainly did distrust any
kind of authoritarian government, calling the communist State
as, according to Marx and his followers, it was going to be,
'Russian autocracy turned upside down'—exactly, in short, what
it turned out to be.

Bakunin, working chiefly with Russian political exiles in Switzerland made a number of attempts to implant his ideas among
his own people. His propaganda had an, as it were, anarchizing
effect on some groups of revolutionaries inside Russia, but it
created nothing like even the merest beginnings of a mass movement. There were isolated anarchist-led insurrections: at Chigrin,
near Kiev, Bakuninists exploited the peasants' innocent faith in
the good will of the Tsar to involve them in a rising against the
landowners in which, they were convinced, the Tsar was on their
side against their oppressors. Bakunin's propaganda had some
influence on the militant wing of the Populist movement,
Narodnaya Volya (the People's Will). But the position in Russia
was never, until 1917, as clear-cut as it was in Spain: all kinds
of socialists, from the gentle Chaikovskists and the Social-Democrats, to the *Narodnaya Volya* terrorist who assassinated Tsar
Alexander II on the very day he signed a preliminary draft of
the Constitution drawn up for him by the relatively liberal General Loris Melikov, were working for a libertarian Millennium
and the differences between their aims would not become important until Tsarism had been overthrown.

* *Roots of Revolution*, London, 1960.

To our ancestors of the 1870s, and for a long time thereafter, the word nihilist evoked the vision of a ferocious-looking revolutionary ruffian with a bomb in his hand; and doubtless some anarchist terrorist who had read the nihilists believed that they were practising nihilist principles by destroying lives and property which were elements of the established society. The nihilists properly so-called were the philosophers who wrote and edited the review *Russkoe Slovo* in the 1860s and their followers in the intelligentsia.* Their leader was a brilliant young thinker called Pisarev who argued that the day of the arts and of the feelings associated with them was over and done with; the honest revolutionary realist must repudiate art and give himself up to the only form of useful human activity, scientific utilitarianism. Now in his novel *Fathers and Sons*, Turgenev attacked the people who thought like that as 'nihilists', borrowing the word from the critics of the Neo- or Young Hegelians with whom he had mixed in Berlin. (It was not a new coinage even there; it can be traced back to the 18th century.) Pisarev accepted the word to describe his following, although far from believing in nothing, which is what the word implies, they had a passionate faith in the revolutionary value of materialism and positivism. These nihilists, then, held that the task of the revolutionary intellectual was to demolish the ideology on which established society rested by the coldest and most calculating scientific criticism. Such a man must emancipate himself from the whole culture of the past, must become a free mind thinking critically. What the revolution needed was an elite class of such free thinkers applying economic calculation and scientific utilitarianism to the problem of society's organization; all the rest was romantic nonsense. How could such ideas lead to violence? Very simply: the Darwinian 'struggle for existence' was good, modern science.

Although the Russian anarchists, like all other Russian socialists, had some hand in the Revolution of 1905, there was no specifically anarchist contribution, no rising under the black flag as such. In fact it was not until the Revolutions of February and October 1917 had released all Russian revolutionary movements from constraint that the difference between the anarchists, includ-

* A Russian word almost synonymous at the time with 'nihilists'.

ing those in the Socialist-Revolutionary Party (see Chapter Thirteen) on the one hand, and the Social-Democrats, whether Bolshevik or Menshevik on the other, tacitly ignored in the long struggle against Tsarism, were allowed to emerge clearly: it was the old difference, the one which had separated Marx and Bakunin. For the Social-Democrats, the State as an instrument of the proletarian dictatorship was all; for the anarchists, even as that instrument, it was the enemy and what they wanted from the Revolution was decentralization down to commune level and loose federation of workers' communes. But were not the Soviets, which included anarchist and Socialist-Revolutionary workers as well as Bolshevik workers, the nuclei of such communes? At first the anarchists thought that they might be and for that reason they allied themselves with the Bolsheviks, reassured by such acts of Bolshevik amity as the almost royal public reception given to the aged Kropotkin when he returned to Russia to salute the Revolution.

In 1917 the movement was strongest in Moscow and in the Ukraine. In Moscow its strength was in the anarcho-syndicalist trades unions; in the Ukraine, in the Federation of anarchist groups. In the Ukrainian town of Gulyai-Polye—thirty thousand inhabitants—anarchists had been at the head of the peasant revolution since February, and the town Soviet was chaired by the anarchist Nestor Makhno. And when the *Nabat* (Tocsin) movement, the Confederation of Anarchist Organizations emerged in 1918, it was centred in Kharkov. There is not much doubt that the Bolsheviks identified Ukrainian anarchism as Ukrainian separatism. In theory the 'nationalities' within the Russian Empire were to be free and autonomous: time has made Lenin seem to have perpetrated a cynical joke when he made Joseph Stalin People's Commissar for the Nationalities. There was never, from the beginning, the least chance for the provincial Soviets of any real freedom from the central government.

That this was so is clear from the subsequent history of Nestor Makhno. Following the Treaty of Brest-Litovsk which handed over the Ukraine to the Central Powers (Germany and Austria), Makhno recruited a band of anarchist peasants and began one of the most effective guerrilla warfare campaigns in modern history. He raided large estates and killed the counter-revolutionary landowners, captured his old home town of Gulyai-Polye, and engaged whole divisions of the German Army. One is reminded of Tito's guerrilla campaign in Yugoslavia in World War Two. In November 1918 the German and Austrian armies were withdrawn; for the next seven months Makhno controlled the whole region east of the Dnieper and set about creating a federation of free communes composed of ten families of peasants and workers —an average of 200 people, according to Makhno's own account.* Each commune was allotted land, tools and cattle from the great expropriated estates. The attempt to install something analogous in the industrial towns which Makhno captured was a failure: it was too rustic, too unsophisticated.

By 1919 Makhno's original guerrilla band had grown into the Revolutionary Insurrectionary Army numbering fifty thousand, and was helping the Red Army in its war with the counter-revolutionary 'Whites' under General Denikin. In June of that year the anarchists decided to hold a Congress in Gulyai-Polye. It was then that the Bolsheviks showed their hand: Trotsky forbade the Congress and ordered Makhno to resign his command. He appeared to obey, crossed to the west bank of the Dnieper, summoned some of his units to join him, and continued to wage guerrilla war on the Whites, but also to remove the communist administrations from the places he controlled, replacing them with anarchist communes.

Meanwhile the Red Army had failed to defeat Denikin. Makhno summoned the remainder of his units to leave the Red Army and rejoin him and began an independent war on Denikin's armies. He retreated in the face of a White attack, gathered his strength, counter-attacked and in a matter of weeks had scored a whole series of fast victories, cutting clean through Denikin's lines of communication and supply and forcing him to retreat, leaving the Revolutionary Insurrectionary Army in control of an enormous region in which communist authoritarianism was immediately abolished and the peasants and workers left to form their own free communes.

When, in December 1919, the Red Army again appeared on the southern scene, Trotsky tried to get rid of Makhno by ordering him and his army to the Polish front. Makhno refused to

* *La révolution russe en Ukraine*, Paris, 1927.

go and there began a nine-month civil war between the anarchists and the communists. This madness was stopped, by treaty, when General Wrangel at the head of a new White army emerged from the Crimea as a dangerous threat to the Revolution. The communists kept the treaty until Makhno had enabled them to defeat Wrangel, then arrested all the anarchist leaders in the territory they controlled and, having summoned the anarchist senior officers who had been detached by Makhno to a military conference in the Crimea, seized and shot them all out of hand. At the same time the Red Army began an attack on Makhno and the main body of the Revolutionary Insurrectionary Army. For nine months, until his supplies were exhausted and most of his men killed, he carried on the war which had been forced on him and then, only when he could do no more for the libertarian cause, slipped over the frontier into Romania and, after many vicissitudes, to exile in Paris where he lived on the charity of Spanish anarchists, wrote his book, and at last, a drink-sodden and tubercular wreck, died in 1938.

Kropotkin, while supporting the Revolution and calling on the workers of the world to stop their governments from counter-revolutionary military intervention in Russia, was publicly condemning Bolshevik terrorism and the tyranny of the new proletarian State. It became clear to all Russian anarchists that the Soviets (Workers' Councils) far from being the tenants of power, were being used by the Bolsheviks as tools. *Nabat* ostentatiously withdrew all its members from the Soviets on the grounds that they had become organs of the all-powerful State. Persecution of the anarchists began very discreetly and tentatively; their journal, *Anarchy*, was suppressed, but for some time longer they were left free to say what they liked, even in public, although they were kept under observation by the Cheka. The two events which frightened the Bolshevik government into full-scale persecution of anarchists were the anarchist demonstration at Kropotkin's funeral—those terrible black flags bearing, in red, the legend *Where there is authority there is no freedom*—and the insurrection of the anarchist sailors at the Kronstadt naval base, against oppressive 'revolutionary discipline'.

The Bolsheviks cracked down on all anarchists and Socialist-Revolutionaries, one of whose militants, Dora Kaplan, so nearly succeeded in assassinating Lenin that his wound contributed to his premature death. Within one year the libertarian opposition had been wiped out. The anarchists had been murdered in the cellars of the Cheka, driven abroad, or terrified into silence, all with a thoroughness which the Tsars, looking up from hell, must have admired and envied.

In short, the tyrant communist State was behaving precisely as the anarchists had predicted that it would and must. For the State is not merely permissive of social injustice; it cannot but embody social injustice.

Tom Paine, one of the theorists of anarchism, was an Englishman but he spent a great part of his life in the United States and there planted his creed. Native American intellectuals adopted it: one does not think of Emerson as an anarchist, yet it is a fact that he held the State, and for that matter any formal apparatus of law, to be the great enemy of liberty. The State—any conceivable State—was necessarily corrupt. The good man, he wrote, should be careful not to obey the laws too well. Emerson's grounds for these views were moralistic: only complete liberty could develop the individual conscience, source of the only true virtue. Where there is law man has only to obey, the operations of conscience are dulled for want of use; thus law is the enemy of virtue.

Yet Emerson is very much in the margin of our subject for, if he was a sort of moral anarchist, he was no socialist. The same is true of other American moral anarchists such as Thoreau, for example, who held 'that government is best which governs not at all'.* For both men socialism would have been beside the point or perhaps, since it involves the tyrant law, pernicious.

But there was also a native American anarchism which was not arch-individualist. Robert Owen had his disciples. His own socialist colony of New Harmony had been a failure, coming to grief in disharmony. From that failure American theorists, notably Josiah Warren, drew lessons which led them to conceive an economic system based on labour-value exchanges, making possible co-operation without derogation of personal freedom while tending to the elimination of capitalism. In other words,

* *On the duty of civil disobedience* (1849).

Warren and his friends arrived at much the same sort of conclusion that Proudhon was to reach; and their solution had the same flaw—it entailed economic inequality.

But we are here concerned with anarchism as the libertarian manifestation of socialism, and of that there is no native tradition in the USA. It was introduced by German and Italian immigrants and in its extremist, terrorist form by that remarkable exponent of revolution by terrorism, Jacob Most, and the Italian anarchist silk-weavers of Patterson, New Jersey, who were responsible for the assassination of King Umberto of Italy and had some influence on the assassin of President McKinley.

In 1881 the socialists and anarchists among the Germans, Austrian and other middle-European immigrant workers who were being cruelly exploited by American capital, formed an International Working Men's Association better known as the Black International. It was not, at first, downright anarchist, many of its adherents favouring Marxism. But a year later Jacob Most arrived in New York and, under his unfortunately sinister influence, the Black International became anarchist, which might have been all to the good, and terrorist, which turned out to be disastrous.

Jacob Most was an extraordinary man. The pleasure he took in urging the most outrageous, and even base, forms of violence on all revolutionary workers recalls the abominable Nechaev; but at least Nechaev had a noble, if self-destructive and very dangerous, ideal of dedication. I suppose that Most was feeding a huge appetite for vicarious power of the most unpleasant kind: the power of the hangman.

He had been a Social-Democratic member of the Reichstag but the anarchistic violence of his speeches and writings led to his expulsion from the Party and flight from the police into refuge in England (1879). In London he founded and edited *Die Freiheit* which preached terrorist revolution for two years, at the end of which time a rapturous leader which Most published on the assassination of Alexander II resulted in his arrest, trial and imprisonment for 'seditious libel'. While Most was in prison his deputy editor, enthusiastically determined to out-Herod Herod, published a fulsome congratulatory leader on the Irish Invincibles' assassination of Mr Burke and Lord Frederick Cavendish in Phoenix Park. That was going too far: *Die Freiheit* was suppressed, and when Most came out of gaol he had to go to New York in order to refound it and continue his campaign, which found much more response in America than it had done among German immigrant anarchists in England. Most reinforced it by touring the country to address meetings of workers whom he urged to take up the bomb and gun against their capitalist oppressors. And, with German thoroughness, he took a job under a false name in an explosives factory and from what he learned there wrote one of the remarkable manuals of revolutionary technique in the history of revolution, *Revolutionäre Kriegswissenschaft*, which includes instructions on the manufacture of nitro-glycerine, the construction of bombs, on burglary, arson and the use of poisons against the class enemy.

Most seems to have been responsible for the almost hysterical tone of the German and English anarchist-communist press in its preaching of immediate class war. But still there is every excuse for workers' leaders driven into a frenzy of rage and hatred by the great American capitalists, the most heartless ruffians ever to disgrace a system never remarkable either for justice or compassion.*
By 1885 the Central Labour Union dominated by anarchist leaders, and pricked by the same spur as the anarchist and socialist press, was passing such resolutions as:

> We urgently call upon the wage class to arm itself in order to put forth against their exploiters such an argument as alone can be effective—*Violence!*

That would have been fair enough if what the workers were being called to was a mass armed rising; but again the response was terrorist, as will appear, albeit provoked by the police-plus-gangster terrorism used by the great employers against their workers.

Most was not, of course, the only articulate anarchist in the United States; far from it, there were both native and immigrant propagandists preaching the coming of the libertarian Socialist Millennium. I do not propose to spend time, however, over a movement which had remarkably little effect in the long term:

* The reader who doubts this should read Gustavus Myers' copiously and carefully documented *History of the Great American Fortunes*, New York, 1936.

the fact is that anarchism was virtually killed in the USA by the events which have still to be recounted. But three of the immigrants should be mentioned: Alexander Berkman, Leon Czolgosz and Emma Goldman.

Berkman and Emma Goldman were Russian immigrants and anarchists of the highest ideals. Their lives are reminiscent of those led by the non-violent Russian Populists of the 'going-to-the-people' movement. Both people of education and middle-class origin, both shed their class, became factory workers and lived on what they earned in order to bring their message of hope to the poor. Emma, indefatigable teacher, writer and orator in the cause, if she did not repudiate terrorism in so many words, certainly did not encourage it, although the assassin Czolgosz claimed to have been influenced in his deeds by her fiery speeches. Berkman, at heart a pacifist, was driven by anger and despair to a single and futile act of violence.

As for Czolgosz, he was of a very different kind: a brooding loner, a close student of every act of anarchist violence of the past decades, a man who waged single-handed war on established society out of hatred for the perpetrators of the social injustice which that society embodied and protected.

The rising shrillness of the call to arms which Most had initiated had, as I have said, disastrous consequences for anarchism in the United States. On May Day 1886 police in Chicago, city of criminal as well as revolutionary violence, opened fire on a peaceful and indeed rather depressed crowd of workers demonstrating against the employment, by the McCormick Harvester Company, of three hundred gunmen recruited for them among the criminal element by the Pinkerton agency, to terrorize them into accepting starvation wages following a lockout, against the employment of blacklegs to enforce a cut in their already miserable wages, and against the vicious practice of 'trucking'.* A number of workers were killed and many more wounded. At a protest meeting held the following day someone, assumed to be

---

* Trucking: the employer runs a shop at which the workers, on pain of dismissal, are forced to buy their groceries and hardware at inflated prices. Another system was to pay wages in vouchers which could only be used at the firm's shop. It was made illegal in Britain by the Truck Act of 1887.

an anarchist but possibly an *agent provocateur* employed by McCormick, threw a bomb into a detachment of police marching into the Haymarket where the meeting was being held. Police and Pinkertons, and some armed workers who had followed Most's advice, began shooting. In all seven policemen and about thirty workers were killed, and many more wounded. The police, unable to find the bomb-thrower, arrested known anarchists at random and, after a mockery of a trial, four completely innocent men were judicially murdered by the State. This official counter-terrorism was effective: anarchist terrorism subsided.

But in 1892 the poor wretches of workers in Henry Clay Frick's Homestead Steel Plant went on strike for a living wage. Frick, like McCormick and other great American capitalists, employed Pinkerton gunmen to 'protect' the plant, that is to shoot down strikers, which they very effectively did. Berkman decided to avenge the dead, tried to assassinate Frick, and failed. And, but for one more act of violence, that was the end of anarchist terrorism as a way to the Millennium in the United States: Czolgosz, determined to strike at the very incarnation of the State which protected the great moneymen against the people, took advantage of a handshaking session laid on by President McKinley's PR staff to shoot the President dead at the certain sacrifice of his own life (1901).

Anarchist activity continued however. Anarchists organized and led strikes, published newspapers and addressed meetings. They renounced the bomb and the gun, but too late. The ordinary American worker, the native better paid than and indifferent to the lot of the immigrant, was frightened and disgusted by terrorism and henceforth whatever he, too, might suffer at capitalist hands until the power of his unions won him the means to ape the burgesses, he would not listen to argument from a source tainted by association with terrorism.

In other countries of the world anarchism was, at least in our context, marginal. There was a considerable anarchist terrorist movement in France, but its history is so impure that it belongs to criminal rather than to political and economic history: it is impossible to separate anarchists from criminals calling themselves anarchists. In Britain, land of anarchism's origin and greatest poet, it became a doctrine for intellectuals who were never likely to have to suffer for the cause; it had some influence in promoting the libertarian idea among socialists, even in Fabian tracts. In Germany, land of the Social-Democratic triumph and disaster, it remained marginal. In Switzerland, it waned and died and it never even got a footing in Scandinavia. Perhaps the writings of the anarchist theorists had some influence on Chinese and Indian socialism.

Are we then to conclude that the anarchists lived and thought and wrote and bombed in vain? I do not think so. It has taken more than half a century of failure by the Social-Democrats to resist the corrupting effects of gradualism which have hamstrung them in their dealings with capitalism in its Imperialist (in the Leninist sense) and Fascist phase, and by communists to resist the corrupting effects of State power, to make vividly clear the urgent need to return and take another look at the path pointed out by the anarchists. For we are confronted by a choice : either the capitalist–communist hive, anthill, territory; or a society which is free, if relatively poor, because it denies authority to any power but the individual conscience implanted in men by the beautiful fiction of immanent justice.

ELEVEN

Syndicalism

'*That I may remain free,*' wrote Proudhon, '*that I may be subject to no law but my own, and that I may govern myself, the edifice of society must be rebuilt on the idea of contract.*'

What kind of contract? For an anarchist the individual is sovereign: but sovereign individuals could, at the voluntary sacrifice of a minimum of liberty, associate together in communes of mutual aid in industry and commerce. Those communes would be linked together in a world-wide federation, which network should be the uttermost measure of organization either desirable or necessary.

Syndicat is the word which the French use to mean trade union; the same word is used in Italian and in Spanish. A syndicalist is a socialist for whom the power-base for the making of the revolution and for managing mankind's affairs after the revolution has succeeded, is the trade union. The principal weapon of syndicalism is, therefore, the general strike. The syndicalist is also an anarchist-socialist in that he repudiates the State as well as repudiating capitalism. So by use of the general strike he aims to ruin the capitalist and thereafter to install his system of contracts between free unions of free men and thus deprive the State of its *raison d'être*. For imposed law backed by force, he substitutes free contract freely entered into.

Modern syndicalism—for there were some primitive forms of it *avant la lettre*—originated in the setting-up, by French socialist trade unions, of *Bourses du Travail*, sorts of labour-exchanges which, by taking the business of placing labour away from the capitalist-controlled or government agencies, would in due course control the 'labour market' and so take economic power into their hands, the hands of the workers. These *Bourses* were set up between 1888 and 1892. Two kinds of socialism were then strong in France: Social-Democratic and anarchist. The anarchists very soon won control of the *Bourses* and they linked them together in a *Fédération Nationale des Syndicats*. The idea of controlling all labour as a means of denying hands to the capitalist and so destroying him was not new; it is implicit in the very earliest English universal trade-union idea. But it had certainly never been tried in practice on such a scale.

The Secretary-General of the Federation was an anarchist, Raymond Pelloutier. He had made thorough trial of Social-Democracy and been a socialist *député* and, thoroughly experienced in the corrupting and debilitating effect of conventional political means, rejected them in favour of industrial action, with the national general strike as the *ultima ratio*.

Pelloutier became the most important theorist of syndicalism, but he was not the only one. Georges Yvetot, his successor as Secretary-General of the Federation, was another, laying stress in his propaganda on the need not only to deny labour to capital, but to deny soldiers to the generals and their political masters. So great was the appeal of the arguments put forward by these two men and others of like mind, and by Pierre Monatte of the socialist-controlled but anarchist-infiltrated *Fédération Nationale des Syndicats*, that they were soon able to unite the whole French trade-union movement in a *Confédération Général du Travail* (CGT) and to dominate its policy through anarcho-syndicalist officers.

Syndicalism has its mystic philosopher, another Frenchman, Georges Sorel. He made a study of Marxism from the point of view of a professional engineer and inventor with business experience and, in philosophy, a Bergsonian, with results which are faintly absurd in his *Reflections on Violence*: he approves of the syndicalist general strike, and of the Marxist class war on the grounds that only in acts of violent strife does a man encounter those moments of truth which form the character of the individual and therefore, since society is composed of individuals, advance society. The class war would be eternal: the idea that the general strike could accomplish the purpose for which the syndicalists advocated it was an illusion; but the general strike was a valuable 'social myth' because the prospect of it inspired the workers to keep up the struggle which is the stuff of life. Sorel's principal contribution to syndicalism, if contribution it can be called, is that he made it into suitable material for the kind of refined scholasticism which has debilitated Marxism. He was never a socialist in our sense of the word, turned monarchist and Rightist in later life, and his writings gave Benito Mussolini an ideology for Fascism and other Fascist leaders an ideology for the Corporate State.

In 1906 syndicalist policy was formalized in the resolutions adopted at a Congress held in Amiens and a rigorously anti-political programme was adopted. The working class, in so far as the CGT spoke for it, repudiated political parties of whatever colour and boycotted elections; it would make its own way into revolution by gaining control of industry, and thus of economic power, the only reality.

But there were forces other than anarcho-syndicalist at work in the unions, officers, or officers-to-be who believed that the official policy was wrong-headed and that the French unions should follow the example of the older and more experienced British unions, and should take part in politics through a specifically socialist party. Now these were the men who took over the leadership when, as a result of a campaign of strikes—the opening of a cold war of industrial action against capital—which failed dismally, all the anarcho-syndicalist leaders were arrested and imprisoned.

Yet anarcho-syndicalism continued to be on the cards as the choice of the revolutionary French workers until the outbreak of World War One. But at that crisis the syndicalists failed in precisely the same way as the Social-Democrats in Germany. Instead of repudiating the war as a bourgeois and capitalist madness in which the workers would have no part and which they would do all in their power to prevent, they turned out as good patriots ready to lead their flock to the slaughter.

And that, really, was the end of the syndicalist movement. There was still a syndicalist group, the *Centre Syndicaliste Révolutionnaire*, within the CGT after the war. It later withdrew from the CGT to form a rival CGT *Unitaire*. But it was unimportant: the fact is, the day was now to the communists, glorified by the grandeur of the Russian Revolution and not yet discredited by its miseries.

Syndicalism, originating in France, proved exportable. Early in the first decade of our century *Camerali di Lavoro* were set up in Italy, on the French model, by one group of trades unions. The unions concerned proposed to destroy capitalism by deliberate use of the general strike. But there was another group of unions with a British-style policy—political rather than industrial action, by means of parliamentary socialism. It was this group which proved the stronger when a General Confederation of Labour was formed to unite all the unions (1905). Unable to win control of the CGT, the anarcho-syndicalists established a Committee of Resistance Societies, based on the *Camerali di Lavoro*, to save the Italian workers from the disaster of *étatisme*. Recruits poured in, notably the whole railwaymen's union, and by 1908 the syndicalists were strong enough to call a strike of all farm workers throughout Tuscany, and a general strike in Milan. The strikers were attacked by armed police, there was serious fighting, heavy casualties, and the workers were beaten. Enfeebled by this defeat, the syndicalists rejoined the CGT for another attempt to dominate and take it over. When that failed the railwaymen, still loyal to their anarchist and syndicalist principles, led the way out of the CGT (1911), were followed by others, and a year later founded a union federation of their own at Modena. It was called the *Unione Sindicale Italiana* and had a hundred thousand members. Its policy was general strike and armed insurrection as 'the only way to accomplish the expropriation of the bourgeoisie'.

Such was the attraction of this call to arms that by the end of the war the *Unione Sindicale* had half a million members, despite the serious defeat which it had suffered during 'Red Week' in 1914 described in my account of Malatesta. But what, from 1918, happened in France also happened in Italy: Bolshevik success in Russia tempted anarcho-syndicalist workers away from their principles and towards Marxist communism. It was taking leave of their libertarian ideals but the extent to which that was the case was not yet apparent.

In Spain anarcho-syndicalism in act preceded the theory, born during the general strike in Barcelona in 1902 and the urban and rural strikes which spread down to Andalusia during the next couple of years; all failed, crushed by ruthless and prompt Civil Guard action. George Woodcock has pointed out (*Anarchism*) that, on starvation wages even when they were at work, the strikers did not have the stamina for a sustained struggle. Yet the anarcho-syndicalist movement grew and in 1907 was formally embodied as *Solidaridad obrera* which first made deliberate use of the general strike in Catalonia (1909) to fight against conscription for the imperialist war against the Rif in Morocco where the Rif forces were inflicting defeat after humiliating defeat on the Spanish army.

That strike developed, under the provocation of police violence, into a miniature revolution. There were five days of serious warfare, two hundred workers were killed and thousands wounded. The army, late in arriving because the workers had torn up miles of railway line, 'restored order'. In the course of its revenge on the Catalan workers the government perpetrated such atrocities of torture in the Montjuich prison (and also made the blunder of judicially murdering the educationalist Francisco Ferrer), that a European-wide outcry forced the Maura ministry to resign.

Out of this defeat of *Solidaridad obrera* there arose, in 1910, the anarcho-syndicalist *Confederacion Nacional del Trabajo* already discussed in Chapter Ten. Unlike the trades unions we are familiar with, those composing this confederation were *sindicatos unicos*, that is they united in one union all the workers, of whatever trade, in a particular plant or a particular region. Thereafter the development of syndicalism in Spain was so indistinguishable from that of anarchism that there is no need to go over the ground covered in Chapter Ten.

Meanwhile the syndicalist idea had spread into Russia where, about 1905, it emerged as an underground revolutionary movement spreading rapidly. There was in that country and in the conditions then obtaining very little question of effective use of the general strike; the syndicalists engaged, like the other revolutionary parties and movements, in terrorism, while maintaining the principle that the proper weapon for the workers was the general strike. The influence of syndicalism in the trades unions grew steadily during the next twelve years and was fairly strong at the moment when the October Revolution put power into Bolshevik hands. That syndicalist strength, dangerous to their dictatorship, was certainly one of the considerations which led the Bolsheviks to initiate the brutal repression of anarchism —and with it syndicalism—which resulted in its extinction in Russia.

In Germany syndicalism of a kind appeared as early as 1890 among a group of Social-Democratic 'dissenters' who opposed the centralism and *étatisme* of the official party policy. They formed the *Freie Vereinigung Deutscher Gewerkschaften* (FVDG), with a programme of anti-parliamentarianism and industrial revolutionary action; but it does not seem to have become a force there until after World War One. Just before that war the German anarchist theorist Rudolf Rocker was living in England —had been for some years and had, indeed, become a greatly loved champion of the poor Jewish workers in London's East End (he was not himself a Jew, though he learned Yiddish for the sake of his work). He was interned during the war but immediately after it went to Berlin set on saving the German revolution from going the way of the Russian one and making the disastrous blunder of setting up yet another tyrant State.*

By that time the FVDG, renamed *Freie Arbeiter Union*, had a growing membership which reached 120,000 in 1922 when an International Syndicalist Congress was held in Berlin; by 1933 when Hitler came to power there were 200,000 anarcho-syndicalists in the German working class. The movement, like all the other socialist movements, was stamped out by the Nazis, bullyboys of German capitalism and the German bourgeoisie.

A native American syndicalist movement can be identified in the Industrial Workers of the World—'Wobblies' for short—who found their revolutionary work waiting for them in the atrocious working conditions in the mines and lumber-camps of the newly opened West late in the 19th century. The IWW emerged as a revolutionary syndicalist force in 1905 with a programme of founding industrial unions dedicated to the destruction of capitalism, the demolition of the political State, and the management of the society's business by trades unions running their own industries as trustees for the community at large, linked in a network of contracts with other trades unions to form a loose federation. There was a measure of originality in the IWW's method of attacking capitalism—sabotage of plant—but like the European syndicalists their ultimate weapon was to be the national general strike which would ruin capitalism by depriving it of labour, and the State by depriving it of law-abiding citizens.

* See his *Nationalism and Culture*, Los Angeles, 1937.

The strength of the IWW unions was in the mining, harvester and timber industries—it had a particularly strong case in the lumber-camps because the forests had quite simply been stolen and looted from the national domain by the lumber companies. That strength continued to grow until 1917 when the United States entered World War One. IWW anti-war propaganda— the Wobblies held that the workers of the world had nothing to gain and their lives to lose in the ferocious brawling of the world's capitalist empires over sources of loot, thus showing themselves to be better Marxists than the Social-Democrats—enabled the authorities to crack down on them, and after the war the socialist movement in the United States, in so far as it existed at all, was —again as a consequence of the successful October Revolution in Russia—communist orientated.

The only other country to which the IWW form of syndicalism spread was Australia, and there it had some influence not in forwarding the cause of anarcho-syndicalism but in making Australia the first country in the world to have a socialist government.

It was from Australia that syndicalism reached England where it made almost no impression. Britain has a distinguished record in the field of theoretical anarchism, from Thomas More's *Utopia* to William Morris's *News from Nowhere*. And there is a syndicalist element in the Guild Socialism of William Morris and G. D. H. Cole.* But the Guild Socialists were guilty of 'archaizing'—golden-agers if ever there were any, they seemed always to hark back to an imaginary world of noble-hearted craftsmen-anarchists, rather than think forward to a world in which machine industry would not just go away. The truth is that, as socialists, such men thought and wrote in vain, for they were not dealing in realities. There was never, in England, any attempt at anarcho-syndicalist practice, and the 'Wobbly' brand of syndicalism, introduced from America via Australia by Tom Mann in 1910, albeit one of the most practical and interesting forms of socialism ever put forward, gained no mass following.

From 1911 Mann's ideas were aired in a journal, *The Industrial Syndicalist*. He advocated the formation of industrial trades unions of the kind which the IWW had created in America and

* Morris, however, was a Marxist which Cole was not.

Australia which would manage their own industries, a solution to the problem of liquidating capitalism which Mann thought much less dangerous to individual liberty than nationalization, which merely strengthens the tyrant State. The transfer of power from the capitalists to the unions was to be accomplished by repeated strikes followed by a national general strike. Much the same ideas were being advanced in another journal, Guy Bowman's *The Syndicalist*; but Bowman's followers were favouring not Wobbly-style industrial unions but something like the Spanish *sindicatos unicos* so that local and regional interests could be given more importance than national industrial interests.

Two other European countries gave syndicalism an inadequate trial. When in 1891 the Swedish anarchists were, with the anarchists of other countries, expelled from the Second International for their wicked and pigheaded opposition to the Social-Democratic glorification of the Marxist-Hegelian State, they turned their energies onto the trades unions: in other words, they became anarcho-syndicalists. Attributing the failure of the General Strike of 1909 to the fact that they did not direct it, they broke with the body of the trade union movement and formed one of their own, the *Sveriges Arbetares Central* with five hundred members and a militant policy of strike plus insurrection. The policy was attractive, and by 1924 the SAC had nearly forty thousand members, was affiliated to the German Syndicalist International, and was publishing a daily newspaper, *Arbetaran*.

But, like every other anarcho-syndicalist movement the Swedish one was, as it were, washed away by the rising tide of Marxism—parliamentary or Russian communist. The SAC still exists, still pays lip-service to anarcho-syndicalist principles. In practice, however, since its component unions behave in exactly the same fashion as Social-Democrat unions, syndicalism is as moribund in Sweden as it is elsewhere.

In Holland syndicalism derived from the work of a Lutheran minister turned anarchist, Ferdinand Domela Nieuwenhuis who, in 1879, abandoned a successful career as the most fashionable preacher in The Hague to devote his life to the working poor. He began by founding a Christian-Socialist journal, *Recht voor Allen* and in due course became leader of the Dutch Socialist League. It was because the League's work was chiefly in the trade union movement, with the parliamentary method of forwarding social-ism, that after three years as a socialist MP (1888-91) he turned to syndicalism. In 1893 the Socialist League split, the minority forming the Social-Democratic Party (the least successful in Europe), the majority following Nieuwenhuis into syndicalism. Work in the trades unions had continued steadily and was success-ful enough for the syndicalist *National Arbeids Sekretariat* to be founded in 1893. That organization produced in one of its officers, Christian Cornelissen, one of syndicalism's best theorists who made an international reputation by his contributions to the Sorelian *Le Mouvement socialiste*. Unfortunately Dutch syndical-ism threw away much of its popularity by taking sides in World War One—the Allied side.

By then, however, it had already seriously damaged itself by a premature and disastrous attempt at militancy: in 1903, with twenty thousand members, the NAS challenged Dutch capital and the Dutch government by calling a general strike, completely underestimating the strength of the reaction which this would provoke. The government used soldiers and blacklegs to operate the railways and arrested all the syndicalist leaders. The strike accomplished nothing, with the result that workers began to turn away from Nieuwenhuis and put all their hopes in the parliamen-tary socialists.

Finally, there is the Latin-American case. During the great emigration movement of the 19th century the South American republics were as much the lands of election for Spanish and Portuguese emigrants as were North America and Australia for the British and Irish. Emigrants carried European revolutionary ideas to the New World—it will be remembered that when Mala-testa arrived in the Argentine he found an Italian anarchist move-ment already in being and there were similar groups in Mexico, Cuba, Brazil and Uruguay. Thus when the time came to organize trades unions in those countries the organizers were not men committed to parliamentary socialism or revolutionary Marxism but anarchists, with the result that the unions were, from the beginning, anarcho-syndicalist. It was in Argentina that the anarcho-syndicalist movement was most successful, and in 1901 its unions were united in the *Federación Obrera Regional Argen-tina* which rapidly outstripped such Marxist labour organizations as there were, and within a few years had a membership of quarter of a million.

For seven years the *Federación*, using the usual syndicalist means—the general strike—fought a determined war with Argentine capital, that is with the Argentine government which fought back with armed police attacks on strikers, the use of troops as strike-breakers, and a series of anti-union laws. This class war culminated in 1909 in a major battle in the streets of Buenos Aires in which there were heavy casualties on both sides with the workers getting much the worst of it. To avenge the deaths of so many of his comrades a Polish member of the *Federación* assassinated the chief of police, a soldier infamous for his brutalities in handling labour demonstrations, and the government reacted by making all anarchist and syndicalist organizations illegal.

But the FORA proved to be too strong to kill with a single blow and it endured until 1929 when it lost its identity, and its libertarian principles, by merging with the socialist unions to form the General Confederation of Workers.

If and when we are finally driven to face the fact that while Social-Democracy in both its parliamentary and communist forms has accomplished much in the field of welfare legislation, it has entirely failed to achieve the fundamental aims and purposes of millennial socialism, it may be that anarcho-syndicalism, as a possible way to egalitarian social justice combined with the optimum measure of personal liberty, should be one of the roads to re-explore.

TWELVE

Russia: to October 1917

The socialist idea, and with it the vision of the Millennium, reached Russia from Europe in the writings of intellectuals who saw in it the means of overthrowing the Tsarist autocracy and giving their fellow countrymen a decent life in a just society. The most important of these writers was Alexander Herzen (1812-70) who after being educated at Moscow University became a civil servant (1835) but did not allow this to prevent him from expressing 'westernizing' ideas. Labelled a liberal, he was denied the normal advancement in the service, but in 1847 he inherited a considerable private fortune whereupon he left Russia to live for the rest of his life in London and Geneva. In both places he gave asylum and money to revolutionary exiles, and meanwhile he was writing essays in various journals which were printed in England and then smuggled over the frontier into Russia to do their work of propaganda. As he wrote extremely well, with great clarity and decision, his writings were effective and made thousands of converts to socialism, each one of whom carried on the good work, so that Herzen's influence was enormous and enduring. One of his most remarkable foresights was in his judgement that Russia, despite what Marx might say about it, was, with her traditional primitive communes, clearly more fitted to be the first socialist country than any of the advanced industrial countries which, if they had ever had such collectivist traditions, had long since forgotten them.

The revolutionary struggle in Russia, then, the struggle to free, educate and raise the peasants out of misery and ignorance, to raise the new and growing industrial proletariat out of the slough of vile conditions, semi-starvation and humiliating subservience was carried on by intellectuals, young men and women of 'good' family and education driven to sacrifice their own comfortable privileges by a sense of guilt towards the majority of their countrymen. The several and different movements which they formed between about 1865 and the first decade of the 20th century are collectively called Populism. It will be necessary here to take a very quick look at some of the Populist movements which prepared Russia for that socialist revolution which was to usher in the Millennium.

Nozdenie v narod in Russian means 'Going to the people'. Between 1872 and 1876 a large number of the young social missionaries of the Populist movement 'went to the people' with teaching and preaching; accordingly they were called *Narodniki*. These narodniks were people who felt that the burden of obligation to the poor peasants who produced the wealth of Russia, received almost none of it and yet paid 90 per cent of the empire's taxes, was so heavy that they must spend a part of their lives trying to discharge it by bringing to them the new message of hope—socialism: and by teaching to enable them to understand that message and, in due course, to act upon its social imperatives. The narodniks lived among the peasants and workers, dressed like them, ate what they ate, and worked at the trades which they practised.

But the narodniks had little success. The peasants failed to understand what they were talking about and usually mistrusted them, and the narodniks made very little impression. After 1876 those narodniks really dedicated to gentle means continued in their course under the name of Lavrovists, after a theorist of the movement. Others turned to Bakuninist anarchism, that is to preaching and practising violent revolution including the use of assassination. In 1877 revolutionaries of the latter persuasion succeeded in provoking an armed rising of some thousands of peasants in the Chigirin region near Kiev. It was put down by the military, there were widespread arrests of narodniks and anarchists, and the narodnik movement ended with the 'trial of the 193' (St Petersburg 1877) which, however, the accused managed to convert into a forum for their ideas. One of their number, Ippolit Myshkin, won fame by his denunciation of the court:

This is no trial but a farce or something worse: more revolting and shameful than a brothel where a woman sells her body because she is poor. Whereas here judges, out of base slavish-

ness, for the sake of promotion and high pay, trade away other
people's lives, truth and justice ...

The narodniks had not been quite the first of the Populists in
the field. In 1861 a movement called Land-and-Liberty, inspired
by the writings of the nihilist Chernishevsky, had set out to free
the peasants from the crushing burden of redemption payments
for their land following the emancipation of the serfs in that year.
This same name, Land-and-Liberty, was taken by a much more
effective movement started in 1878, and originally called the
Revolutionary Populist Group of the North. (It was also known
as the Troglodytes because it worked 'underground'.) From quite
early in its career Land-and-Liberty was split into two factions.
The first remained faithful to the original idea of the movement,
the peaceful propagation of socialism by teaching and propaganda; the other faction, growing impatient at the slowness of
progress and repeated setbacks due to ruthless police persecution,
turned to the use of terrorism. At a meeting in Voronezh in
August 1879 this division was made formal: the moderates, led
by the Social-Democrat Plekhanov, called themselves Black
Partition; and the terrorists, led by the anarchist Andrei Zhel-
yabev, called themselves the People's Will. At its inaugural
meeting the People's Will solemnly and formally condemned
Tsar Alexander II to death as an enemy of the people and, after
a long campaign of attempts, carried out the sentence with a
bomb. All the revolutionaries involved in this were executed.
  But by far the most important of the many pre-Marxist
(Bolshevik and Menshevik) revolutionary parties in Russia was
the Social- (sometimes Socialist-) Revolutionary Party. It had its
origin in the bitterness of a rich young nobleman of Rostov-on-
Don, Valerian Andreyevich Osinsky, who was devoting his life
and fortune to the education of the poor peasants and workers,
and to familiarizing them, once they had learnt to read, with
liberal, socialist and democratic ideas from the West. The police
were uneasy about his activities, and when one of their spies, an
informer planted in Osinsky's staff, revealed the extent and
seriousness of the work, they pounced, raiding his offices, destroying his books and papers and arresting his helpers. The first signs
that this had driven Osinsky to the terrorist solution were the

finding of the body of the informer who had betrayed the organization and the plastering of Rostov with posters announcing that all traitors would be treated in the same way. The posters were signed 'Executive Committee of the Socialist-Revolutionary Party'.

For the next forty years the Party itself propagated socialism, of a much more libertarian brand than Marxism, often more or less anarchist, in print and by the spoken word among the people. Meanwhile its Executive Committee, that is its activist and terrorist wing, not only engaged in fomenting and leading strikes, riots and local insurrections, but carried out a long list of assassinations of high-ranking police officers, of generals, of cabinet ministers, culminating in the killing (1905) of the Grand Duke Sergei, the Tsar's brother and Governor of Moscow. For twenty of those forty years the Executive Committee, known simply as Organization, was dominated, and for ten of them led and managed, by the most remarkable double-agent in revolutionary history, a ghetto-born Jew named Evgenio Azev who, while organizing assassinations on the one hand, was the most valued of the Okhrana's counter-revolutionary informers on the other with immediate access to the Minister of the Interior whom, in due course, he had assassinated. As for the success of the Party's non-violent wing, it is sufficient to say that in the 1900 election for the Duma which Organization had terrorized the Tsar into calling, it won 37 of 288 seats and that in the Moscow and Petrograd Soviets following the October Revolution it had almost twice as many worker-delegates as the Bolsheviks.

The first real chance that the Russian socialists had to break the power of the autocracy came in 1905. Tsar Nicholas II had aggravated revolutionary feeling and activity by his stupidly obstinate refusal to concede even the mildest of liberal constitutions until the Russian people, prepared by the Populists, the Social-Revolutionaries and by the Social-Democrats, were in a mood to force his hand by violence. This situation was made even more tense by the gross misconduct of the war with Japan, both on land and at sea, with its humiliating defeats of the Russian forces. Finally, the last straw, came the 'Bloody Sunday' massacre of half-starved workers who were marching peacefully, led by the priest Gapon, to the Winter Palace, to petition their Little White Father to do something to relieve their miseries. Of that mass-murder Lenin later wrote that it advanced the political education of the proletariat further in a single day than years of propaganda would have done.

The fact is that Nicholas and his ministers were more afraid of revolution at home than of defeat abroad: to be defeated by another imperial power was one thing—it would not damage the idea of imperial autocracy; to be defeated by the common people would be much worse. The autocrats and the bourgeoisie have always understood, much more clearly than have the proletariat, that class war is a more serious matter for them than international war. If any reader doubts this, in the case of 1905 Russia at all events, he should note the following striking fact: following receipt of the news that Admiral Togo had completely wiped out the whole Russian Imperial Fleet in the Pacific at the battle of Tshushima, stocks on the Moscow stock exchange rose two points. Togo, by winning the war for Japan, had freed the Russian Army to deal with the Russian workers and peasants.

Its services were urgently needed. By September 1905 strikes and riots had paralysed all the railways, most of the industries and, incidentally, all the universities. The workers and students were stating their demands in loud, clear voices: a Constitution based on universal suffrage, including votes for women; workers' Soviets in permanent session as a sort of second chamber; immediate abdication, or alternatively forced deposition of the Tsar and the declaration of a Russian Republic. Nicholas, his soldiers and policemen unable to stem the rising tide of liberalism and socialism, announced a Constitution in an October Manifesto. The deputy-chairman, soon to be chairman, of the St Petersburg Soviet of workers, a fiery young Jewish intellectual named Bronstein but known as Leon Trotsky, immediately denounced this document as 'a Cossack's whip wrapped in a piece of parchment'. His Soviet, and the Moscow one, demanded immediate withdrawal of all troops from both capitals, a political amnesty, withdrawal of the decree placing all Russia under martial law, immediate legislation for an eight-hour day for the workers, and the calling of a Constitutent Assembly.

But the Soviets were whistling in the dark: the industrial

capitalists were starving the workers into weakness by means of the lockout, while in the countryside Nicholas was having some success in distracting the rebellious peasants by unleashing his Cossacks on the Jews in a series of pogroms—a device subsequently used by the Nazis on a much more impressive scale. Then a mutiny of revolutionary sailors at the Kronstadt naval base was crushed by the Army. Trotsky tried to hamstring the capitalists and bring down the government by organizing a run on the banks, but failed to get enough liberal bourgeois support. The Tsar was recovering his nerve. On 3 December troops of reliable Guards regiments surrounded the St Petersburg building where the Soviet was in permanent session. The members were armed and ready to fight for their lives and their golden vision of freedom and plenty. It was Trotsky, seeing clearly that they would merely be massacred, who persuaded them to throw down their arms. The entire Soviet was arrested.

Meanwhile, in Moscow, the anarcho-syndicalists had called a general strike. Troops began a massacre of the strikers, heavy artillery was used to shell the workers' quarters of the city and the government used mass-execution of worker-prisoners to terrorize the revolutionaries into surrender. Thus the revolution was crushed in both capital cities.

But not yet in the country at large: strikes, riots and insurrections broke out all over the empire, and troops had to be sent into nearly every province to help the local forces crush the rebellion. In two months of 1905, November and December, there were 1,372 peasant risings in which manors were looted and burnt, their proprietors hanged or shot and their land distributed to the peasants. But in the rural areas, too, the recipe of shootings and hangings of rebels was effective. By early 1906 Tsarism and capitalism in alliance had blocked the way to the Millennium which, for a few weeks, the socialists had seen open before them.

For the next decade the social and economic situation in the Russian Empire remained continuously potentially revolutionary. There were innumerable strikes, some of them on a huge scale, urban riots, peasant revolts and, in retaliation, Cossack and Guards massacres of the rebels and strikers. On the non-violent level there was the struggle between the progressive wing of the Duma and Nicholas II for a genuine parliamentary and more or less democratic constitution, the former supported by the liberal bourgeoisie (Kadet and Octobrist parties) the latter by the Tsarina who urged her husband to be another Ivan the Terrible, by her *ame damnée*, Rasputin and by the reactionary wing of the nobility. The political, social and economic fever came to a head after two years of World War One, chiefly because the people's miseries were aggravated by ever-worsening conditions: the appalling hardships suffered by millions of soldiers ill-supplied and worse led; severe shortages due to mismanagement of the economy, leading to starvation at home; more strikes in all the industrial centres; defeat on the German and Austrian fronts; industrial breakdown and grotesque bureaucratic muddle and inertia and general defeatism leading to loss of all interest in the war. These factors combined to create an explosive revolutionary situation, especially in St Petersburg. The Duma progressives warned repeatedly of impending revolution and denounced the Tsarist absolutism which was exasperating the people. Even the British Ambassador warned the Tsar, in a private audience, of what would happen if he did not grant an immediate constitution and hand over the executive power to a responsible administration. Nicholas remained obstinately blind to the truth, even when plots to depose him in favour of his son or his brother were exposed and when Rasputin was assassinated. Social-Revolutionaries, Mensheviks, and the few Bolsheviks on hand, organized street demonstrations threatening revolution.

Bolshevik, Menshevik?

Like socialists in all the European countries, the Russian socialists had been impressed by the successes of the German Social-Democratic Party and had (1899) formed one of their own, in exile of course, under the influence of Marxist philosophers like Plekhanov and Lenin. In 1903 the Party held a Congress, its second, in London and the principal question discussed was whether to install socialism gradually by making peaceful and legal use of bourgeois parliamentary institutions, or by promoting violent revolution to be followed by a dictatorship of the proletariat. The latter plan, passionately advocated by Lenin with all the prestige of his revolutionary Marxist writings behind him, prevailed with a majority of the delegates (the Russian word for 'majoritists' is *bolsheviki* and for 'minoritists', *mensheviki*). It should be made clear at once that these terms applied only to the delegates at the Congress and were, at the time and for some years, misleading as to the Party at large inside Russia, for there the Mensheviks had a majority and it was the Bolsheviks who were in a minority.

The most successful socialist revolutionary of all time, Vladimir Ilyich Ulyanov, known as Lenin, was born at Simbirsk in 1870, son of an Inspector of Schools and after a middle-class upbringing and secondary education, read law at Kazan University. He became a dedicated Socialist after the execution of his elder brother in 1887 at the age of twenty-one, for implication in a plot to assassinate the Tsar. Sent down for 3 years for revolutionary activity in the University, Lenin spent the time studying Marx, became a Marxist and after finishing his education as a law-student at Samara went to St Petersburg and was soon a Marxist leader among the revolutionary intellectuals. His first Marxist book, *Who are the People's Friends?*, was published in 1894 and put the Marxist case against the Populists and the libertarians. For two years he worked among the St Petersburg factory hands, teaching them Marxism, forming a 'Union of Struggle for the liberation of the working class', and preparing them for revolution. He was then picked up by the police and deported to Siberia— almost as intensive a forcing-ground of Socialist revolutionaries as the British Museum Reading Room—there wrote *The Development of Capitalism in Russia* (1899), was released in 1900 and joined Plekhanov and other Social-Democrat and anarchist Russian exiles in Switzerland. He also spent much time in London —the BM Reading Room again—in France and in Germany. Founder and editor of *Iskra* (The Spark) in which he and other Russian Social-Democrats preached revolutionary Marxism and which was regularly smuggled into Russia, he emerged as a leader and, as described above, as the majority, i.e. *bolshevik*, leader at the 1903 Congress of the Social-Democratic Party.

Lenin was in Russia for the 1905 revolution, though he played a less important part in it than Trotsky. On the other hand he learnt more from it, and getting out of the country following its defeat wrote a classic manual on the proletarian takeover of

bourgeois revolutions, *Two Social-Democratic Tactics in Democratic Revolution*, and at the same time one of his philosophical
Marxist works, *Materialism and Empiriocriticism* (1909). At the
Prague Conference in 1912 he took the Bolsheviks out of the
Social-Democratic Party to found a separate Bolshevik Party,
later renamed the Communist Party. Meanwhile he had been
adding more didactic and polemical writings to his very substantial *œuvre*. He spent World War One in Switzerland, campaign-
ing against worker participation in the war which he hoped to
stop by persuading the world's workers to sabotage it by refusing
to fight or to make munitions, and against the 'opportunist' policies of the Second (Social-Democratic) International, policies
which he had been denouncing since 1903. He made a
thorough re-examination of Hegel and he wrote what, in the
revolutionary context of 1973, is his most important book,
Imperialism, The Highest Stage of Capitalism, in which *Das
Kapital* is, as it were, brought up to date. That was published in
1916; others of his works also date from that period.

  In 1917, when the February Revolution broke out in Russia
—the liberal preliminary to the Socialist Revolution—Lenin was
in Switzerland. A distinguished German Social-Democratic member of the Reichstag, Parvus by name, suggested to the German
High Command that Lenin and other Russian socialist exiles in
Switzerland (there were thirty-two on his list) be enabled to
return to Russia: Lenin's anti-war policy was notorious, his
influence great, he might be expected to take such a hand in the
revolution that Russia would back out of the war and liberate all
Germany's Eastern front forces for the Western front. The pro-
posal was accepted and Lenin and his friends, put into a sealed
train as if they were dangerous bacteria, were conveyed across
Germany to the Russian frontier. There he found the sort of
revolutionary situation he could exploit.

  By 22 February 1917 tens of thousands of starving striking
workers were on the streets of both capitals. Troops and police
were attacked but soon began going over to the revolution. Even
the Cossacks proved 'unreliable'. On 27 February the crack
Volynsky regiment mutinied and a few days later the whole
Petrograd garrison of 170,000 were refusing orders and shooting
officers. Michael Rodzyanko, president of the Duma, telegraphed

the Tsar that the city was in anarchy, the people starving, the troops in full mutiny, and asked for the government to be dismissed and a new, responsible, administration appointed to meet the demands of the revolution. Nicholas, who could always be relied on to play into revolutionary hands, prorogued the Duma. It refused to disperse and asked the Grand Duke Michael to declare a military dictatorship. Michael wasted time trying to persuade Nicholas to agree and so lost his chance. On 27 February the Duma party leaders formed themselves into a provisional government, mostly Kadets and Octobrists (Liberals) and the socialist revolutionaries formed their own 'government', the Temporary Executive Committee of the Soviet of Workers' Deputies, mostly Social-Revolutionaries, Mensheviks (Social-Democrats) and Bolsheviks. The principal men of the provisional government were Milyukov, Guchov and Kerensky and they immediately promised the people an amnesty, freedom of speech, press and assembly, a people's militia to replace the police and no victimization. This provisional government forced the Tsar to abdicate with the intention, later frustrated by the Soviets, of crowning the Tsarevich under the regency of Michael.

The Soviet Executive Committee held an election of Workers' and Soldiers' Deputies—one worker for every thousand per factory, one from every factory with fewer than 1,000 workers, and one soldier from every company. The 1,500-strong Soviet which resulted consisted mostly of Menshevik or Social-Revolutionary soldiers, fewer workers of the same persuasion and only 40 Bolsheviks. Its Executive Committee immediately organized companies of soldiers to protect the revolution, who were to obey the provisional government only for so long as the Soviet endorsed its orders. The Soviet was inclined to support the provisional government provided it carried out its promise and added to its programme equality of rights, abolition of minority nationality disabilities, democratic elections for a Constituent Assembly and no Romanov restoration. It was not yet demanding socialist measures, the Menshevik majority holding that it was their duty at this 'bourgeois' stage of the revolution to support the bourgeois liberals. The real differences between the two bodies did not emerge until late April: the Soviet, representing the war-weary workers, peasants and soldiers, wanted immediate peace with

Germany; the provisional government, under severe Allied dip-
lomatic and financial pressure, wanted more efficient prosecution
of the war. Meanwhile outside the capital the revolution was
welcomed, though in some places with reservations. Peasants and
industrial workers set up their own Soviets. By the end of April
it was clear that, having completed its basic programme of legislation, the provisional government had accomplished nothing in
the fields of economics and war politics, were jibbing at fixing
a date for the Constituent Assembly, were hostile to the en-
franchisement of the soldiers and were still playing with the idea
of a Romanov restoration. This meant stalemate, for as Prince
Lvov, the president of the provisional government, put it, 'The
Soviet has power without authority; the Government has authority without power.' This was the uneasy situation which Lenin
and Trotsky were able to exploit from May until their triumph
in October.

Which brings us to the second great man of the Bolshevik, that
is communist Revolution : we have already met him as chairman
of the St Petersburg Soviet in 1905.

Lev Davidovich Bronstein, *nom de révolution* Leon Trotsky, was
born in 1879, son of a prosperous Jewish farmer in the Kherson
province. In his autobiography he has evoked his youth and
education with a talent which might have made him one of the
epoch's great writers. At the village school he learnt arithmetic
and to read and write Russian and Hebrew—the household's
language was Yiddish. He was sent to the Lutheran *Realschule*
in Odessa and there spent most of his time writing poetry, and
some of it leading a schoolboy revolt against the injustice of a
master to one of his schoolmates. When his health broke down (it
did so at critical moments during his whole life except when he
was commanding the Red Army in its sixteen separate wars
against White Russian and foreign interventionist counter-
revolutionaries), his father provided him with a tutor at home—
a tutor whom he easily 'subverted' so that he was free to read
what he liked or to loaf if he wanted to. He was the antithesis of
Lenin, a brooding, fiery, free-thinking romantic who, if he very
early realized that if the revolution was to remain pure in heart,
it must be permanent—his own ultimate solution to the problem

which the anarchists solved by repudiating the State entirely—
was perfectly willing to concentrate on the present phase of it
and overlook the fact that his colleagues' aims were not his own.

It was during a final year of education at the Nikolaev Gym-
nasium that he read political economy and became a socialist
à sa façon. As soon as he left school he began to work as a
political agitator among the workers while living what we should
now call a 'hippy' life with a few friends, disowned by his father
whom he did not see again until the old man called on him when
he was one of the two masters of the Russian empire. But he was
full of the purpose of overthrowing Tsarism and the installation
of socialism and, to that end, founded the South Russian Workers'
Union. Imprisoned in Odessa in 1898, he married a fellow-
prisoner and revolutionary, Alexandra Lvova. And there he first
read some of Lenin's writings.* In 1900 Trotsky and Lvova were
exiled to Siberia where she bore two daughters and he wrote
socialist tracts, some of which reached Lenin in London and
were printed in *Iskra*. Lenin got a letter through to the young
man urging him to escape and join him. With Lvova's agreement
Trotsky did so in 1902. He descended on the Social-Democrat
offices in Vienna demanding a loan of money, got it and went to
London, there to work with Lenin, Martov and other Social-
Democrat exiles, writing for *Iskra*, lecturing to Russian and German immigrants in the East End, and also in Brussels and Paris.
What impressed his new colleagues was his great power of
oratory, the ease with which he could seize and hold an
audience.

At the 1903 Party Congress in London he represented the
libertarian branch of the Social-Democrats. He took the middle
position between Lenin (Bolshevik) and Martov (Menshevik)

* The reader, living in an age shaped by Stalin and Hitler, can, unless
he has read history, have very little idea of the scandalous laxity with
which, with exceptions, political prisoners were treated in the 18th and
19th centuries. One recalls John Wilkes, editing the *North Briton* anti-
government journal from prison, and the revolutionary work done by
Russian deportees to Siberia. There is, of course, the case of Hitler
writing *Mein Kampf*, that paranoid work of Gothic fiction, in prison.
But then, the Weimar Republic was the last of the political foundations
which had libertarian and humanitarian ideals; besides, Hitler was at
least anti-communist and anti-semitic, a fact his captors no doubt took
into account.

trying, not very successfully and to Lenin's annoyance, to reconcile the two parties.

He was in Geneva in January 1905 when the 'Bloody Sunday' massacre of workers occurred in St Petersburg. He returned to Russia on a false passport, wrote pamphlets for the underground Bolshevik press in Kiev, worked with both Bolshevik and Menshevik factions in St Petersburg, went into hiding in Finland when hunted by the police, returned to St Petersburg to organize and edit a revolutionary press and became president of the Workers' Soviet. Arrested in December 1905, he continued his revolutionary studying and writing in prison, relaxing occasionally with French novels. He acquired fame by his conduct at the trial of the workers' delegates, which was described as 'heroic'. Exiled again to Siberia, *en route* at Berezov he evaded the guards and made a spectacular escape by reindeer-sledge and horseback, riding 700 kilometres to a railhead in the Urals. He met Sedova, his second wife (he appears to have forgotten the first one), in St Petersburg and with her and their children went into exile lasting ten years. He continued his revolutionary work, with Rosa Luxembourg, Karl Liebknecht, Kautsky, Bebel, Lenin, Zinoviev and others in Germany, France, England, Belgium, Romania and other countries. It was in this period that he developed those ideas of 'permanent revolution' which separated him from Stalinist Russian communism. He also wrote for the legal, liberal press in Russia. On the outbreak of World War One Trotsky moved his family to Switzerland but was able, as war correspondent of the *Kievskaya Mysl*, to work in France until expelled, at the instance of the Tsarist government, for editing the revolutionary *Nashe Slovo* for Russian political exiles. He and his family were put over the Spanish frontier, arrested by the Spanish police and put on a ship for New York. There he wrote and spoke for the socialist cause and joined the editorial board of *Novy Mir*, a Russian-language socialist paper. On the outbreak of the Russian Revolution in February 1917 the family set out to return to Russia but were arrested by the Canadian (he himself says British Naval) authorities and put into a concentration camp at Halifax, Nova Scotia. At the instance of the Russian provisional government under pressure from the Petrograd Workers' Soviet, they were released and went to Petrograd* where Trotsky became president of the Soviet in which the Bolsheviks were in a minority. In the following months he took the leading Bolshevik role, and in the October Revolution the role second only to Lenin's.

The Bolsheviks had set up their HQ in a villa near the Peter–Paul fortress. From there Lenin promulgated his 'April Theses': no support for the war effort since the provisional government was still capitalist; concentration on the immediate overthrow of capitalism in Russia; all power to the proletariat and the poorest peasants, and therefore overthrow of the provisional government; expropriation and nationalization of the land and its control and management by peasant Soviets; formation of a revolutionary International to spread the revolution abroad. These theses, at first rejected as too extreme, were accepted by the end of April. The task then became to win control of the Petrograd Workers' Soviet from the Menshevik and Social-Revolutionary majority. The first open breach between the Petrograd Soviet and the provisional government occurred when the government published its war aims, including 'adherence to all obligations assumed towards our Allies'. The war-weary people and soldiers rioted and there was much street fighting (18 April). The Bolshevik Central Committee seized the chance to point out that the provisional government was 'bound hand and foot to Anglo-French and Russian capital'. The government knew that it was losing control of the armed forces even at the fronts where troops were becoming mutinous. It was decided to save itself by taking three Social-Revolutionary and Menshevik Ministers from the Soviet into the administration. The small Bolshevik minority in the Soviet rejected the idea of any such co-operation with the bourgeoisie; in Lenin's view the socialist parties which consented to this arrangement were putting themselves 'outside the revolutionary pale'. On 5 May, while the Executive Committee were commending the proposed coalition to the chamber, Trotsky, arriving from his concentration camp in Halifax, was given a standing ovation and at once spoke against the coalition. It was, he said, 'a capture of the Soviet by the bourgeoisie'.

* From its foundation in 1703 by Peter the Great the city was known as St Petersburg. In 1914 the name was changed to Petrograd, and in 1924 changed again to its present-day name of Leningrad.

The coalition continued its predecessor's war policy. Even the All-Russian Congress of Soviets held in June rejected the proposals for an immediate, separate peace with Germany made by the Bolsheviks, and Lenin was denounced as a German agent. Nevertheless, Bolshevik committees were steadily gaining strength in the armies and factories and their press under Trotsky's guidance was growing in influence. When the Congress elected a new Executive Committee it included 35 Bolsheviks, 104 Mensheviks and 99 Social-Revolutionaries. But the principal Congress resolution—for complete workers' control of industry and confiscation of capitalist profits and which was carried by an enormous majority—was drafted by Lenin and Zinoviev. Now the Bolshevik cry of 'All power to the Soviets!' was raised. As these cries grew louder Lenin, suffering from overwork, went for a short holiday to Finland. Soldiers were everywhere deserting the fronts, peasants seizing the land, workers the factories. When in mid-June Kerensky, as War Minister, ordered a general Russian offensive against the German fronts, the soldiers showed extreme reluctance to obey orders and the moment the Germans counter-attacked, ran away and kept on going until they reached home. By July the Petrograd streets were crowded with revolutionary soldiers and sailors ready to attack the government. But neither Lenin, back from Finland, nor any other Bolshevik, despite the cry 'All power to the Soviets', thought the moment had come. Whereas a new socialist-dominated but bourgeois-orientated government now decided on firmness, suppressed all publications calling for disobedience to military orders or violent overthrow of government, banned street meetings and processions, condemned land-seizure by the peasants, took powers for arrest and deportation of violent revolutionary leaders, published partly authentic and partly forged documents connecting Lenin with the Germans, and again raised the cry that Lenin was a German agent. The Soviet Executive Committee and the Executive Committee of the Peasant Soviets joined heartily in this denunciation. Lenin was forced to go 'underground' and Trotsky and other Bolsheviks arrested and imprisoned, though soon released again. As a result, Lenin now proclaimed a new Bolshevik policy: no longer 'All power to the Soviets', the Petrograd Soviet's leaders had turned it into 'a fig-leaf of counter-revolution'

and it was unfit to hold power. Instead, 'Victory for the workers':
armed uprising must transfer power into the hands of the proletariat and the poor peasants, 'to put into execution the programme of our party' (Trotsky, *History*). In short, a revolutionary
dictatorship of the proletariat.

Stalin put this policy to the 6th Bolshevik Party Congress held
illegally in June, but the majority was still too unsure to take
the leadership of an insurrection. But the people were soon
pushing them into that coveted but uncomfortable position. As
shortages became worse, prices rose three times as fast as wages.
Tension between labour and employers became intolerable, and
workers seized control of the factories while employers retaliated
by lock-outs. Factory workers' committees became increasingly
Bolshevik while in the country the peasant Soviets were seizing
not only land but control of local business and overruling or
ignoring government agencies. When Chernov, the Social-Revolutionary leader in the cabinet, tried to legalize their seizures
there was a cabinet split and Prince Lvov resigned. The right-
wing Kadets, dominating the next administration, tried to veto
'all basic social reforms' until the calling of a Constitutent
Assembly which they had no intention of calling. Kornilov, the
only Russian general still effectively fighting the Germans, called
for a 'restore order' programme. Kerensky appointed him Commander-in-Chief, whereupon he announced from Moscow that
the time had come to hang Lenin, the German agent, disperse
the Soviets and restore the death penalty for soldiers disobeying
orders. When it looked as if he was trying to impose a military
dictatorship, Kerensky dismissed him (26 August). Kornilov
refused to go and made a cavalry advance on Petrograd. This
caused a strong pro-Bolshevik swing in public opinion. The
Soviet, that 'fig-leaf of the counter-revolution', organized workers'
defence squads and sabotage of the railway communications
Kornilov would need. The would-be dictator was arrested without bloodshed.

The Soviet called a conference of all democratic organizations
to decide what form of effective government was now possible;
all that emerged was another coalition under Kerensky and
an advisory Council of the Republic. Trotsky immediately
denounced it and again proclaimed the Bolshevik programme:

workers' control of industry, transfer of land to peasant committees, denunciation of secret treaties, an immediate armistice,
arming of the workers, establishment of a Red Guard and self-
determination for the nationalities. All over Russia there were
lootings and arson, banditry, rioting, mutinies and pogroms. Such
authority as existed was in the hands of local Soviets. With two
million army deserters at large, predatory bands of soldiers roamed
the country. Among the seven million men still under arms,
defeatism and then Bolshevism rose like a tidal wave and swept
aside all military discipline. In these conditions Lenin revived
the slogan 'All power to the Soviets', and declared that the
Bolsheviks would take no office in a Menshevik–Social-Revolutionary administration since they stood for the dictatorship of
the proletariat. Those two parties, bound in coalition with the
bourgeois parties, failed, as he knew they must, to respond. At
the September local elections in Moscow the Bolsheviks were
the largest party with a small overall majority. In Petrograd
and elsewhere the story was much the same, although they were
still in a minority in the country as a whole. Trotsky became
president of the Petrograd Soviet and a vote of no confidence
in the provisional government was passed by a large majority.

On 13 September Lenin summoned the Bolshevik Central
Committee to prepare at once for an armed insurrection. It
took him a month to persuade them. It was Trotsky who found
the instrument for the *coup d'état*: when, on 9 October, the
Mensheviks proposed forming a committee for revolutionary
defence, he backed them and then seized on the committee and
turned it, despite Menshevik protests, into a Military Revolutionary Committee. Many of the Petrograd garrison troops and the
Kronstadt sailors were already Bolsheviks; many more came over
when the Bolsheviks first attributed to Kerensky the intention
of sending them to the front, then intervened to prevent this.
On 24 October Colonel Polkovnikov, commanding the Petrograd
garrison, ordered all army units to rid themselves of the political
commissars appointed by the Soviet while Kerensky, declaring
Petrograd in a state of insurrection, summoned loyal troops to
garrison the Winter Palace, government HQ, and take control
of all key points in the city. On 25 October the Council of the
Republic resolved by a small majority to call on the government

to invite the Allies to stop fighting and negotiate a peace with Germany, to legalize all land-seizure by the peasants and to advance the date of the oft-postponed Constituent Assembly— in short, to steal Lenin's thunder. But it was too late: the Military Committee's soldiers and the Red Guard factory-hands were seizing every strategic point in the city, including the State Bank. The government troops handed over to them without a struggle. On the afternoon of 25 October Trotsky was able to proclaim to the Soviet: 'In the name of the Military Revolutionary Committee, I announce that the provisional government no longer exists.'

On the night of 25/6 October the second Congress of Soviets met. The Bolsheviks were the largest single party but in a slight minority to the Social-Revolutionaries, who were split into Left and Right, and the Mensheviks, split into Menshevik-Internationalists (Left) led by Martov and Mensheviks (Right). Martov proposed a commission to form a joint Socialist government; Lenin, playing for time, agreed. The Right Social-Revolutionaries and the Mensheviks walked out, combined with some peasant leaders, members of the Council of the Republic, and trade-union leaders, to form a Committee of Public Safety and denounce the Bolshevik *coup d'état* as undemocratic. This enabled Trotsky to tar Martov with the same brush as the dissident Social-Revolutionary Rightists and repudiate the coalition agreement. During the morning of 26 October a newly elected Central Executive Committee dominated by Bolsheviks appointed an all-Bolshevik government, the first Council of People's Commissars, headed by Lenin and with Trotsky as Commissar for Foreign Affairs. It was a minority government: at the long-delayed election to the thereafter aborted Constituent Assembly the Bolsheviks won 168 seats, the Social-Revolutionaries 299 and all other parties 153. But that was no longer the point—the Bolsheviks had the soldiers, and they ruled as the executive of the proletarian dictatorship. Their first decrees were immediate armistice and abolition of private property in the means of production and in land. Moreover, as all their opponents, Left and Right alike, showed their willingness to call in foreign allies, even Germans, against the Bolsheviks, both the new glamour of the revolution and the older charisma of nationalism came to reside in the Bolsheviks. Furthermore, Lenin and Trotsky, having published the secret treaties with the Allies and exposed their iniquitous horse-dealing, were appealing over the heads of governments to the people all over the world for open diplomacy and 'a just and democratic peace without annexations or indemnities ...' (it is Trotsky speaking not Woodrow Wilson), which was what a majority of the world wanted. The revolution still had to fight the civil war but by November 1917 it had triumphed.

The just society, the Millennium, was in sight.

THIRTEEN

The Vision Fades

The Millennium was in sight: but not yet within reach. The forces of the aristocracy and bourgeoisie inside Russia—the various 'White Guard' counter-revolutionary armies—were gathering their strength to scotch the revolution and prevent the socialist vision from being realized, and outside Russia capitalism was preparing to reinforce the counter-revolution with British, French, American, Japanese and even German armies.

In the longer term the Bolshevik success in Russia did, of itself, more to render the socialist Millennium unattainable than anything else for, the socialist revolution having been made, socialists all over the world for the next two decades felt obliged to defend it, to look to the USSR for leadership. Although the truth concerning the Stalinist tyranny (which we shall come to shortly) was known much earlier, it was not until after World War Two that a majority of socialists were able to bring themselves to admit it. In short, the existence of a nominally socialist great power inhibited revolutionary effort elsewhere by submitting socialism at large to the decrees of a sort of socialist Pope who was just about as truly socialist in practice as the Roman Popes have been truly Christian in practice. As Francis Hope wrote (1972) in the *New Statesman*, itself long guilty under Kingsley Martin's editorship of shutting eyes and ears to the betrayal of socialism in Russia:

> Western Marxists appear to have adopted what I take to be George Lichtheim's position—many of them without his learning—that it is a monstrous irony that so subtle a consummation of Western political thought should have been seized on by a crudely Asiatic state—rather as if the Eskimos had invented nuclear energy. The Socialist sixth of the world has become something like a senile relative, embarrassing to all but attributable to none.

The Bolshevik Council of People's Commissars took Russia

out of the war at the cost of a German and Austrian occupation of the Ukraine by signing the Treaty of Brest-Litovsk, negotiated by Trotsky who turned the negotiations into a propaganda platform from which to appeal to the world's workers to stop fighting each other and make their own communist revolutions. The council redistributed all the land in Russia to the peasants and nationalized the banks and all the means of production and distribution. In short it made the new Union of Soviet Republics economically socialist on Marxist lines, at a stroke.

But this attempt to install a completely socialist economy while fighting a civil war on a dozen or more fronts, facing British and Japanese seizures of Russian territory in support of the counter-revolution, and trying to create both a civil and military State apparatus out of the wreckage of the old, led to the total collapse of the Russian economy in 1920. Lenin then showed his flexibility by introducing the New Economic Policy, in which a measure of private enterprise was legalized. Meanwhile he found time to write *The Immediate Tasks of Soviet Power* (1918) and the polemical *Proletarian Revolution and the Renegade Kautsky** (1919), and to move the whole apparatus of the revolutionary government to the Kremlin in Moscow. That was a significant move: the revolution, instead of being centred on Westward-looking, 'Europeanizing', sophisticated Petrograd, was now embattled in a fortress in the heart of old Russia, anti-European Russia, the Russia not of the great progressives but of the great reactionaries, 'Holy' Russia. It was as if Lenin, Trotsky, Zinoviev, Bukharin—'the darling of the Communist Party' (Lenin)—and the other cosmopolitan internationalists in the Bolshevik leadership were playing straight into the hands of the one 'provincial', the only Russian chauvinist among them: Stalin.

It is time to introduce this man who, having helped to make the revolution, to make the USSR, was to inherit it, wipe out in Russian blood the vision of a libertarian socialist Millennium and, as an arch-tyrant, restore autocratic rule to the empire which was now called a union of workers' Soviets.

Joseph Vissarionovich Djugashvili, better known as Stalin, was a Georgian, son of a cobbler, born at Gori near Tiflis in 1879.

---

* Lenin's reason for calling Kautsky a renegade are set out in Chapter Sixteen.

Intended for the Church by his mother, the effective head of the family, he was sent first to a seminary at Gori, and then to the Tiflis Theological College, which expelled him for revolutionary socialist activities. He read Marx, turned Marxist, and at the age of 19 joined the Social-Democratic Party—it was clandestine, of course—to become a professional agitator and socialist organizer in the Batum oil-field. Until 1912 he laboured to bring the oil workers to socialism. He was arrested five times, escaped from the police or from prison five times. Utterly dedicated to the revolution, when Party funds fell short he organized and led bank-robberies to replenish them, an example which has been much followed by the New Left. Of low stature but powerful build and handsome face, he was passionate, greedy, ruthless in action, yet patient and very cunning, with a cold insight into the weaknesses of his colleagues in revolution, and of his opponents. Finally, unlike all the other leaders of his Party, he was the complete provincial; they were Europeans, socialists who for most of their lives had thought in internationalist terms, like Karl Marx himself; he, though an oriental, citizen of the Eastern empire conquered by the Tsars in the 18th and 19th centuries, was as ultra-Russian, as anti-European as Dostoevsky.

He first met Lenin during the revolution of 1905. Was it, I wonder, with secret inner reservations that he accepted his leadership? By 1912 he was editing *Pravda*, by then the official organ of the Party and was among the secondary Bolshevik leaders, but in the revolution itself he emerged as one of the top twenty and when Lenin formed his first government he made Stalin—who had made himself an expert on the empire's ethnic minorities and Far Eastern provinces—Commissar for Nationalities. From 1918 to 1920, however, he was helping to fight the civil war, and became a member of Trotsky's War Council in 1920, a post in which he did a good deal to hamper the war policy of the cosmopolitan Jewish intellectual whom he detested.

Trotsky had relinquished the Commissary of Foreign Affairs to take on the Commissary for War when the Whites and their European and American allies launched the counter-revolutionary war. This physically delicate, highly strung romantic member of a supposedly unwarlike race turned out to be one of the most brilliant military leaders of all time: if there be such a thing as a military 'genius', which I doubt, Trotsky was one. Out of the ragged and half-starved remnants of the Tsarist armies, out of wandering peasants and workless factory hands, he forged the Red Army. In his Ministry, the *Predrevoyensoviet*, a special train composed of offices, sleepers, kitchen and dining car, radio-car, emergency supply wagons, engineering workshops, and garage-car, he rushed from one to another of sixteen war fronts during more than two years of desperately hard fighting. In the worst crises of the war he took personal command, leading actions at the head of his comrades, turning defeats into victories. It was he who forced General Yudenich to raise the siege of Petrograd, not yet called Leningrad. He had the star-quality, possessed by very few, which can inspire men to fight to the death without yielding chiefly because, even in the young socialist republic's darkest hour, his vision of the just and brotherly society of equals remained bright and shining and his personal ambition for power was wholly invested in that vision. From among his common soldiers he picked the men who would be good generals—the flamboyant Budyenny, a peasant and yet last of the cavalry commanders in the dashing tradition of Prince Rupert; and Tukhashevsky who not only drove the Polish Army out of Russia with a *sans culotte* army starved of rations and weapons and ammunition, but would have taken Warsaw had not Marshal Weygand been rushed from Paris to command the defence of the Polish capital and push the Red Army out of Poland.*

Thus Trotsky, absent from the Kremlin power base during the critical years 1920-22, was at an enormous disadvantage in the power-struggle with Stalin. From time to time he made flying visits to Moscow to consult with Lenin; but he could not, short of abandoning the war for socialism into the hands of lesser men, remain on the spot to counter, with his passionate belief in a socialist world, the intrigues of the man who had made up his mind to succeed Lenin and be master of Russia and never mind the international proletariat and world revolution. Trotsky could and did appeal to Lenin to check Stalin's interference with his war strategy and, on occasion, tactics. But Stalin's strength was in the Central Committee of the Party, and Lenin had a

* Stalin, in due course, was to murder Tukhashevsky by judicial means, and his leader by means of a secret police assassin.

doctrinaire respect for the Party democracy as deep as his distrust of the Party bureaucracy.

By 1920 Stalin was busy creating the very bureaucracy of competent, faceless men which Lenin, in his last writings, was to see as the mortal danger to socialism. Those Party hacks looked to Stalin for advancement, for their share of power. Coarse, clever, brutal, a natural enemy of refinement of thought, of scruple, of sensibility, in short a 'boss' of the kind that made millions for themselves and misery for millions in late 19th-century America, Stalin was just such a leader as the bureaucrat looks to. Trotsky required of his comrades that they respond to his fire, that they put their hearts into the intellectual effort of understanding that he was right and sharing his conviction. Stalin asked nothing but that they obey his orders and ask no questions; he was Comrade Napoleon in Orwell's *Animal Farm* who had the foresight to raise and train a pack of mastiffs to tear his old comrades to pieces at a word of command.

In 1918 the Social-Revolutionaries, appalled at the *étatimse* of the Bolsheviks and as desperately determined as ever that the vision of a libertarian paradise must not be betrayed, reverted to their pre-revolutionary tactics and opened a campaign of assassinating Bolshevik leaders, and in August of that year one of them, Dora Kaplan, shot at Lenin. The serious wound she inflicted undermined his health, which was already damaged by overwork and strain. But he continued to work, founding the Third International (Comintern) in 1919 to spread the communist revolution beyond Russia's frontiers, adding half a dozen important socialists tracts to his already enormous *oeuvre*,* and presiding over a government coping with war on sixteen fronts, with famine, plague and sabotage. Stalin was not the least of his burdens; and before he died Lenin warned, in his writing on cultural revolution, against the kind of apparatus Stalin was creating and even, in his Testament (by some thought to be apocryphal), against the man himself.

---

* Thirty-eight volumes. The most important works added in this period were *'Left Wing' Communism, the Infantile Disease* (1920); *The Importance of Militant Materialism* (1922); *On Co-operation* (1923); and *Better Less but Better* (1923).

It was, then, in the decline of Lenin's health, in Trotsky's preoccupation first with the war, then with rebuilding Russia's transport system, and in the subservience of the Party hacks, that Stalin found his chance—in 1922 he was elected Secretary of the Central Committee of the Communist Party of the USSR. He held the post until his death and by its means made himself far more powerful than any member of the executive, the nominal government and, ultimately, absolute autocrat, Dictator.

All the evils of that self-contradictory monster, a revolutionary government, which Proudhon, Bakunin, Kropotkin, Malatesta, and for that matter Godwin and Owen, had foreseen, and which Lenin himself feared, were coming to pass.

Stalin's policy was 'Socialism in one country': he abandoned socialist internationalism to exploit Russian nationalism. Trotsky's policy was not only world revolution, but revolution in permanence—his solution to the danger of the bureaucratic fossilization foreseen by Lenin in his later writings. It is quite possible to see Stalin as the Bonaparte of the Russian Revolution, though what he did was not to save the old bourgeoisie from the people, but to create a new one in the bureaucracy which has—*vide* every Russian writer worth reading from Zoschenko to Solzhenitsyn— become the real heir (ousting the proletariat) to the revolutionary gains. For the rest of his life Stalin used the jargon of socialism to justify his acts and the Marxist economic techniques to control the industry and trade of the USSR. But he had long ceased to be a socialist in the sense in which the word is used in this book. He abandoned the vision of the just society to become a 'realist', that is a cynic who accepts as the only possible level of action that which is set by the basest, and not by the noblest, in human nature. He abused the socialist idea to obtain supreme power for himself and industrial and military strength for the USSR. Now it could be argued that this was a necessary and valuable work, that world socialism needed a power base equal in strength to the capitalist power bases in America and Western Europe, that until such a base existed international libertarian socialism would be dangerously weak in its struggle with capitalism, that the world-wide proletariat needed a fatherland of its own. But means determine ends; after Stalin's work was done, it was impossible for the USSR to revert to socialism: it had fossilized as a State Monopoly Capitalist Imperialism.

Stalin's work is very closely comparable with that of the great American capitalist tycoons in the late decades of the last century and the first of this one; the men who industrialized America and, in so doing, forced their countrymen to abandon the founding father's vision of a just and egalitarian society, asserting instead the colossal wealth and ruling power of the *haute bourgeoisie*. No men were ever more forward than the Astors, the Morgans, the Clays and Fricks, Goulds and McCormicks in appealing, in support of their own power, to the great American vision of equality and justice. In the same spirit, Stalin repeatedly won the support of the Communist Party's Central Committee by appealing to the Marxist-Leninist canon which, in almost every act of his tyranny, he was betraying.

The fact that Stalin, like the devil or Jay Gould, could always quote chapter and verse of scripture to justify his crimes has led to a belief that Lenin, had he lived, would have been no less terrible a tyrant than Stalin; and it will be recalled that all the anarchist philosophers had forecast that because of the Social-Democratic insistence on the need for a political government and the weight they gave to the paramountcy of the Hegelian state, a communist revolutionary government would *necessarily and inevitably* be a tyranny. It will, therefore, be appropriate at this point to take a look at Leninism, or what is now called Marxism-Leninism, as a version of socialism, especially as it is the ideology of the New Left, that is to say the only effective form of revolutionary socialism still active.

In the field of economics Lenin, of course, advocated (and tried to apply) social ownership of the means of production, distribution and exchange. It is important to remember that, equally of course, *he did not believe socialism would have been achieved when that had been secured*. Following the nationalization of the banks and of industry after the October Revolution, he wrote:

Such is the dialectic of history that war, which has strikingly accelerated the transformation of monopoly capitalism into *State* monopoly capitalism, has by the same token brought humanity much nearer to Socialism ... State monopoly capitalism is the most thorough material preparation for Socialism ... Socialism is State monopoly capitalism placed at the disposal of the entire people ...*

So far we have a sort of vindication of Stalinism *excepting for that last and vital phrase.* Stalin chose to mistake state monopoly capitalism for socialism despite the manifest fact that it destroyed freedom and failed signally to ensure social justice. How do we move on from state monopoly capitalism in which the USSR has been bogged down for half a century into socialism? Lenin said this:

> It is not enough that the economic apparatus be managed for the people; it must be managed by the people† ... That man only is a Socialist who relies on the experience and instincts of the labouring masses ... The intelligence of tens of millions of creators provides us with something infinitely more valuable than the most extensive and brilliant theoretical forecasts.‡

Has any modern communist leader attended seriously to this dictum? At least one, Kim Il Sung of North Korea; but of that, later. Lenin, then, was an advocate of worker-control of industry.

When it comes to politics, the spirit of his writings is the same. Once the revolution is accomplished the workers—among whom, by the way, he specifically includes housewives §—must at once begin on their apprenticeship in state management.

> For us, the State is strong only by virtue of the masses' political awareness. It is strong when the masses are informed of everything so that they can form their own judgements and go into action fully aware of what they are doing.||

Marx, despite his inability to reject the Hegelian State was aware of the danger that its bureaucracy would become a tyrant.¶

---

* Works, vol. XXVI, p. 107.
† A curious echo of Lincoln's Gettysburg speech.
‡ *Works*, vol. XXV, pp. 389 et seq, and p. 495.
§ *Works*, vol. XXV, p. 109.
|| *Works*, vol. XXVI, p. 263.
¶ See his *Critique of the Philosophy of the Hegelian State* in which, however, he does not make the point in so many words.

Lenin held that danger to be 'enormous'. The proletarian democracy must, he says, be ever alert to destroy the bureaucracy
root and branch and it is the business of the trades unions to
correct the State's innate tendency to 'bureaucratize'. The implication is, of course, that far from being subservient to the
State the trades unions are free and independent and in a position
to reprove and reform the conduct of the State. But by what did
one replace the bureaucracy in the matter of its essential func-
tions? By the popular democracy,* one must never forget that:

> If the power of the Soviets, the will of the Soviets, is
> victorious, it is because they have from the beginning applied
> the principles long laid down by Socialism ... have striven
> to arouse the most oppressed and burdened classes of society
> to life, and led them into taking the Socialist initiative ...†

In short, socialism either involves the whole people in decision-
making and denies power to the bureaucracy, *or it is not socialism*;
under genuine socialism the bureaucracy is a clerk under orders
from his boss—the people, the direct democracy.

Finally, there is Lenin's treatment of the cultural revolution:
he held that the whole of bourgeois culture should be absorbed
into the new socialist culture as one of the means to build socialism
—socialism could not afford to dispense with it. The worst
danger to socialist culture was communist complacency, the idea
that communism being in power, anything which was communist
was good and everything else bad, and the notion that the leaders
of the proletariat were entitled to dictate the forms of art, literature, music or science, and the styles used by artists, writers and
savants. Lenin says that there is no greater mistake than to
suppose that revolutionary socialism can be built without the
help of non-revolutionaries, non-socialists; the cultural revolution entails an alliance with non-communist creative workers of
all kinds; critical assimilation of pre-communist materialism;
integration of non-communist artists, savants and scientists into
the socialist culture. The catalyst to be used to accomplish this

* *The State and the Revolution*, p. 520.
† *ibid.* p. 483.

synthesis is a systematic study of Hegel's dialectic from the materialistic point of view.

Whether Lenin, had he lived the normal span, would have tried to put his own precepts into practice, nobody now can say; he was not given the chance, communism was still suffering what he called its 'infantile malady' when he died.

Trotsky might have carried out the programme implied in Lenin's writings, but he too was denied the chance. Following Lenin's death in January 1924, he was seriously ill and unable to be at the centre of events in Moscow or to take charge of the Leninist cause in the Central Committee, which enabled Stalin progressively to deprive him of offices, power and followers; he lost the Commissary for War in January 1925 and was given the task of rebuilding the transport network. But, almost continuously ill, with a permanently high temperature, in 1926 he went to Berlin for special treatment. He returned late in the year to try to organize the angry opposition to Stalin's pro-Kuomintang China policy which had led to a massacre of communists by Chiang Kai-shek, and in 1927 became leader of such opposition as there was, in the Central Committee and the CP at large, to Stalin's majority faction which controlled the GPU. This involved him in 'illegal' political agitation which Stalin characterized as 'counter-revolutionary'. At the 15th Congress of the CP in December 1927 he and his party were expelled from the Central Committee, later from the CP and Trotsky and his family were exiled to Alma-Ata in Central Asia. He was still a focus of the anti-Stalinist 'pure' Leninists and acted as such, with the result that in January 1929 he was charged with counter-revolution and forcibly deported to Turkey. During his Turkish exile he wrote *The Permanent Revolution* (1929); the first part of *The Spanish Revolution* (completed 1939); *The Struggle against Fascism in Germany* (not published in book form until 1970); volume I of his great *History of the Russian Revolution* (1931), completed during later exiles elsewhere; and *The Stalin School of Falsification* (1932) which led to his being stripped of Soviet citizenship (1932) in which year he visited Copenhagen to deliver a lecture, and published *Problems of the Chinese Revolution*. In 1933 he founded the International Communist (Bolshevik-Leninist) League from which later derived the Trotskyist Fourth International. In 1933 he was granted a visa for France, there continued his work as an anti-Stalinist pamphleteer, but was so harassed by Stalin's agents, the French government and the bourgeois press, that he took refuge in Norway when its Social-Democratic government invited him to do so, there completing the *Life* of Lenin started in France. He organized the first conference of the Fourth International, although it was not officially founded until later, and wrote *The Revolution Betrayed* (1936).

The first of Stalin's great show trials by which he rid himself of the old Bolsheviks took place that year, and Trotsky was convicted *in absentia* of conspiring to overthrow the Soviet government. As a result of threatening pressure from the USSR and from Norwegian Nazis led by Quisling, the Norwegian government deported Trotsky, on an oil tanker, to Mexico where President Cardeñas had offered him asylum. In 1937 Stalin charged him, *in absentia*, with being a Fascist agent: Trotsky not only exposed the purge trials in the world press as faked, he defended himself against the charges by arranging for a commission of enquiry to re-try the case in the USA under John Dewey: the commission acquitted him and declared the Moscow trial a frame-up. One of his sons, still in Russia, was put into a labour camp where he died; in 1938 another, Leon Sedov, was poisoned by a GPU agent in Paris. In the same year Trotsky published *The Death Agony of Capitalism and the Tasks of the Fourth International*; other works of this period were *In Defence of Marxism* (1939) and *Marxism in our Time* (1939), and several other books were left unfinished at his death. In May 1940 a first attempt by Stalin's agents to murder him failed, but on 20 August a more competent agent succeeded in driving a pick-axe through his brain.

Inferior to Lenin as a philosopher and Marxist theorist, and to Stalin in the baser arts of politics, Leon Trotsky was the greatest revolutionary socialist man of action of the 20th century. He believed that without Lenin the October Revolution would have failed and that with Stalin, it was betrayed. What is likely is that without Trotsky, the supreme organizer of victory in the civil war and supreme advocate of its cause with the workers and socialist intellectuals all over the world, it would have perished in its infancy. Without Trotsky, too, its original purpose and ideal would have been even more completely abandoned and obscured than they were by Stalin—that purpose being socialist revolution continued until the extinction of capitalism everywhere; the ideal, an international, world-wide, communist community, humanist, egalitarian, free from the evils of class and state, and therefore of war. That ideal is very remote and perhaps unattainable, but it remains the hope that springs eternal in the socialist breast and Trotsky did more than any other Bolshevik to keep bright the vision of the Millennium.

In 1925 Stalin, already virtually master of the USSR started a colossal programme of industrialization in a series of Five Year Plans, concentrating on heavy industry. To the accomplishment of his purpose he bound the whole Russian people hand and foot. One of his first acts was to put an end to Lenin's New Economic Policy under which a certain amount of private enterprise was permitted. (Private traders under this policy were called Nepmen and despised as licensed outlaws.) The peasants, unable now to make a profit, simply ceased to produce enough food, whereupon Stalin 'collectivized' the farms and tried to have them run on industrial lines. The result was famine, mass shootings of recalcitrants and mass deportation of others to labour camps. And, using the secret police as a means of terrorizing the whole nation into obeying orders from the Central Committee, in the following ten years Stalin made the USSR into one of the great industrial and military powers. The costs were liberty in all its forms, deprivation of consumer goods, a chronic housing shortage and the reign of fear of delation and the secret police. In 1936 he promulgated the liberal Stalin Constitution; it remained a piece of paper, for in the same year he became what he remained for the rest of his life, dictator in all but name.

The Russian empire which Stalin thus recalled into existence called itself socialist. It was, of course, nothing of the kind, it was what Lenin had called State Monopoly Capitalist. The vision of the libertarian socialist Millennium had by now faded and vanished to be seen no more in Russia. Nor could it shine again outside Russia until socialists all over the world had rid themselves of the illusion that the USSR was a socialist country.

FOURTEEN

Depression, Stalinism, and the Spanish Civil War

Karl Marx had laid it down as axiomatic that capitalism would perish of its own internal contradictions, a dictum which enabled one school of German Social-Democrats to argue that revolution was unnecessary since there was no point in trying to kill a system which was dying anyway. In 1929 it looked as if Marx had been right: those contradictions produced the worst crisis of collapse in capitalism's history. Why, then, in the ruinous condition of capitalism during the following years, did the intellectuals and the proletariat of the Western world not seize the opportunity to install in the place of the system which had failed so disastrously, and of whose failure they were the principal victims, that socialism in which they had invested their hopes of a prosperous, socially just, and egalitarian society? This chapter is an attempt to suggest answers to that question.

First, as to the nature and manner of the capitalist failure: in the decade before 1929 agriculture all over the world was producing more food and fibres than ever before in history yet, as had always been the case, more than half the human race was living miserably, half-starved, under-clad, and under-housed. So unequal to its task was the capitalist system, bound as it was to a 'market' economy and to the gold standard which severely limited liquidity and therefore the volume of trade, and to repudiation of the notion that social need, not profit, should dictate the nature and place of investment, that it could not even distribute the abundance produced by the world's workers, to those workers. While vast stocks of foodstuffs were dumped or burnt in a desperate attempt to force prices up to that 'economic' level which capitalism required to make it work, millions went hungry, roofless and in rags. Because the workers—peasants, farmers, farm-hands—of the world's basic industry, and therefore those of the dependent industries including shipping and haulage,

could not, on the return they received for their labour, afford
to buy the manufactured goods they needed, the deepening
depression in agriculture spread to industry; and since industrial
workers suffering cuts in wages or simply thrown out of work,
could not afford to buy food and clothing, the industrial depression further deepened the agricultural depression. In short,
capitalism had accomplished a miracle of ludicrous ineptitude—
world-wide want in the midst of unprecedented plenty.

Meanwhile, another internal contradiction was at work destroying the system from within. In the United States, already the
greatest and richest capitalist power, there began in about 1927
an extraordinary and very unedifying orgy of gambling by means
of speculation in stocks and shares. The only hope of millions
of people in any capitalist society of enjoying the good things
which are the privilege of the minority at the top, lies in
gambling; hence, of course, the colossal football pools industry
in Britain and the popularity of gambling all over the Western
world. The stock-buying mania affected tens of millions of
people in the United States and to a lesser extent in Western
Europe. It drove up the price of all industrial and commercial
stocks to such a fantastically high level that the whole industrial
plant and commercial apparatus of the Western world was, on
paper, grossly over-valued. That is to say, their entire maximum
product would have been a very insufficient return on the amount
of money which, on paper, appeared to be invested in them.

In October 1929 rumours started a stock-selling panic. The
warnings were hinted at rather than clearly uttered by certain
bankers who, being good business men, saw in the chance to
precipitate a 'crisis' a marvellous opportunity to get control of a
vastly increased share of the economy very cheaply. Then came
rumours, perhaps from the same source, that some of the industrial firms whose stocks had reached such unjustifiable heights
were, on the basis of their paper value, clearly unsound. On 24
October thirteen million shares changed hands and by 29 October
the daily dealings involved sixteen million shares. This unloading
panic was as absurdly excessive as the buying mania had been
and within one week the grotesquely over-blown balloon of the
finance side of American industry and trade had not merely
been deflated—it had burst. The biggest banks, and those indus-

trial concerns whose wealth was substantial, benefited by getting control, at the new falsely low prices, of the financially weaker firms; small banks all over the country broke and there was a flood of bankruptcies. As usual, the price in suffering was paid by the workers and the little people of the bourgeoisie. In the money famine, demand failed, industry was crippled, millions of workers (probably about fifteen million representing approximately fifty million people if we take the worker's household into account) were thrown out of work and left destitute. In the cities of the world's richest capitalist country men who had contributed honourably to the wealth of the community by their labour, and who had nothing, begged for dimes from men who still had a little left.

Let us take a look at this state of affairs from the point of view of an outsider, a Martian if you like, or a real genuine socialist who is, in the state of confusion produced in socialist thought by the combined influences of the Stalinist charade and Marxist scholasticism, almost as rare a bird. The United States had, after the balloon had burst (i) as copiously abundant sources of raw material, including a super-abundance of fertile soil and energy sources, as ever; (ii) an enormous pool of labour, skilled and unskilled, more than sufficient to make use of the above resources; (iii) an equally rich supply of technical skill, i.e. the means to direct labour in the production of wealth in the form of both capital and consumer goods. In other words, it had *all* the elements required for the production of wealth in the form of of both capital and consumer goods. Why, then, our Martian or our socialist enquires, was there semi-paralysis of industry, agriculture, unemployment of workers on a scale until then without precedent?

I refer him to Marx, to those 'internal contradictions': so inadequate was the capitalist system that, as will appear, the breakdown had to be repaired by having recourse to socialist-type measures. I offer a small parable. One day the people who were accustomed to use a certain bus for getting from their homes to their work, got onto the bus as usual, and sat or stood waiting for it to go, but it didn't move. They enquired the cause: was the bus broken down? No, it was in good working order. Was its tank empty of fuel? No, the fuel tank was full. Had the driver failed to report for work? No, he was sitting at the wheel as all could see for themselves. Then why wasn't the bus starting? Because the bus-company had neglected to provide the bus-conductor with tickets.

As I have said above, broken-down capitalism had to be repaired by using socialist-type measures. This influence of socialism on capitalism is an example of a consequence of socialist thought, socialist economics, which will be discussed in a later chapter. The President who had the courage to apply these measures, which outraged the sanctity of 'market' economics, was Franklin Delano Roosevelt, elected in 1933. His policy was called the New Deal. Measures included creation of the Tennessee Valley Authority as a Public Corporation, building dams and hydro-electric power plants to enrich the productive potential of a vast area from which seven States benefited—a typical example of socialist planning; the setting up of a Federal Emergency Relief Organization; the recruiting of two million workers into a Civilian Conservation Corps and of four million into a new Civil Works Administration to carry out public works —another typically socialist measure; passing of a National Industrial Recovery Act to regulate industrial competition; implementation of Social Security measures for the workers and price guarantee machinery for what in America are not called the 'peasants', small farmers. These and other measures were supervised by the state through the Works Progress Administration.

In short, while, despite its catastrophic breakdown, there was no question of scrapping capitalism in favour of socialism, socialist means were used to prop up capitalism. So true was this that Roosevelt had an arduous struggle with the Supreme Court which, acting for the great capitalists who saw the New Deal as a serious threat to their power, and giving expression to the sacrosanctity of the free-enterprise market economy in the United States, did all in its power to block the President's 'social' legislation.

In Europe, meanwhile, the French government, subservient to bankers whose religious respect for bus-tickets was as notorious as that of the United States Supreme Court, had withdrawn short-term credits from an institution with enormous interests in

East European industry, the Austrian Credit Anstalt Bank. As a result, the bank broke, setting up a wave of bankruptcies in trading concerns, quickly reflected in industry, agriculture and all the service industries and trades ...

Thus began the Great Depression which was to last for five years, to reduce tens of millions of workers to near-starvation in demoralizing idleness, and the German bourgeoisie to the desperate measure of giving abolute economic and political power to a vicious demagogue named Adolf Hitler who promised to save them from the only visible alternative to national ruin, communism. Like Roosevelt, Hitler and his ablest economist, the banker Hjalmar Schacht, had recourse to measures of socialist planning. But his backers had been the great capitalist industrialists and, under capitalism, now again triumphant over its enemies, there was only one way left to recover from a major depression and put the people to work: rearmament, leading, of course, to war. Another of Marx's predictions had come true.

Why, in this tragic, this ridiculous and predictable failure of capitalism and of the old bourgeois establishment to control it, did not the majorities, that is the proletariats, of the great industrial nations, organized by powerful trades unions, force a total recourse to socialism instead of being satisfied with the half-hearted socialist measures which were used to save capitalism from the scrapheap? I shall try to give some of the elements of the complex, compound answer to this question.

The socialist intellectual leadership was paralysed by the existence of the nominally socialist USSR; the vaguely socialist inclined rank-and-file, the ordinary industrial or agricultural worker who almost automatically voted 'Labour' (Socialist or Communist in France) was paralysed by the existence of the Labour Party in Britain, the Social-Democrat and Communist Parties in Continental Europe, and the want of a Socialist Party in the USA.

The paralysis of the intellectuals can best be demonstrated by the case of Kingsley Martin and the *New Statesman*. Let us take the matter of the 'Moscow purges', the show-trials by which Stalin rid himself of the men who took their committal to socialism seriously. In April 1937 Martin, the editor of the *New Statesman*, by far the most influential socialist weekly of the

English-speaking world, was in Mexico where he met and talked
to Leon Trotsky who for some years had been busy revealing
Stalin's betrayal of socialism to the world at the risk of his life—
which he lost, three years later, to one of Stalin's assassins.

Kingsley Martin formed the impression of a man who was
vain and very able, of fierce will and unruly temperament.
A man, moreover, who always saw events in relation to his
own career and was incapable of objectivity. He was charming
and friendly and had a high opinion of the *New Statesman*'s
honesty and radicalism. It occurred to Kingsley Martin that
Trotsky had read the *New Statesman* article in which the
evidence at the Moscow trials had been treated with scepticism. He got Trotsky to talk about the 'proofs' he had promised
that this evidence was all faked. Trotsky did talk, volubly, but
not really to much purpose. When Kingsley Martin put it
to him that it was strange that none of the accused men had
behaved like Dimitrov and, since they were going to die
anyway, 'have gone down fighting and appealed to the public
opinion of the world', Trotsky became excited and even abu-
sive, rather than lucid in explanation. He wanted to know how
much 'Mr Pritt, KC had been paid to report the trial as a
fair one'. The Editor defended Pritt as an honest man, and he
and Trotsky had a 'regular wrangle' about this. 'To see him
get up and shout abuse at Mr Pritt was revealing.' Trotsky
clearly thought that anyone who had a word to say for Stalin
or who did not denounce the whole trial as a frame-up, was
in the pay of Moscow.

The conclusion which Kingsley Martin came to after this
interview is important because it must have been one of the
influences which shaped the *New Statesman*'s attitude to the
USSR during the next two years:

When I wrote that I did not know whether or not to believe
in the confessions, I meant exactly what I said. It seemed
to me the only honest thing to say. Trotsky, like other people,
interpreted my scepticism as a vote against Stalin and tried to
remove any lingering doubts. But I came away from our talk

rather less inclined to scout the possibility of Trotsky's complicity than I had been before, because his judgement appeared to me so unstable and therefore the possibility of his embarking on a crazy plot more credible ...

Neither then nor later did the *New Statesman* accept Stalin's case; but nor would it simply reject it. There may well have been a conspiracy against Stalin and the Soviet Government; the court confessions of men like Radek may, after all, have been genuine. Nobody knew, and there was a serious danger that capitalist exploitation of this uncertainty would be used to break with the USSR which, whatever its faults, was a strong ally against the warlike Fascists and Nazis. If the Western democracies and the USSR quarrelled openly, there would be nothing left to restrain the Fascists from plunging the world into war.

'Every effort is of course being made to exploit this proof of difficulty and violence in Soviet Russia. It is grist to the mill of the Conservatives ... there is a great deal amiss and political liberty has a long battle to fight before it becomes a reality in Soviet Russia. But that makes no difference to the fact that Russia is a Socialist country with an overwhelming desire for peace.'

This *New Statesman* attitude, critical but patient, was to infuriate the extremists on both sides. To those who, as the paper put it,

'finding few investments for their spiritual capital, have staked their all on Soviet Russia and may feel spiritually bankrupt when the dividend is beneath expectation ...'

Anything but a fanatical insistence that there was nothing wrong with Russia was plain treachery. To those who knew what was going on in Russia, or what the Stalinist Communists were doing in Spain, anything but open denunciation of these evils was, as George Orwell was to say, 'to have the mentality of a whore'.

The *New Statesman*'s handling of both pacifism and this question of the shot-gun wedding between Soviet Communism and the Western Popular Front, was consistent. In a single issue of the paper 'Critic', applying the method he had devised to deal with his own conflict, might point out that war over Manchuria, Ethiopia, the Rhineland, albeit apparently justified, would probably turn into just another, conventional 'Capitalist' war, while a leading article would suggest that the point had been reached at which resistance to Fascist aggression must stiffen even to the point of war. Similarly, in dealing with Communism, the *New Statesman* favoured the allience between Socialism and Communism because it was expedient, but did not hide from its readers that the Communist ally was no gentleman.*

The state of mind revealed here, and common to socialists all over Europe and in the USA, has been sufficiently discussed in the last chapter. The Communist parties of the Atlantic countries were uncritically and unquestionably subservient to the Comintern. The Comintern had been made, by Stalin, into an instrument of Russian power-politics and had nothing whatever to do with socialism yet the USSR, as the only country which had undergone a socialist revolution, retained a right to the loyalty of socialists who could not bring themselves to face the fact that they must, if they were to act socialistically, begin by writing-off all the apparent gains of the October Revolution and start again from scratch. They took Stalin's State Monopoly Capitalism for socialism because they could not face the consequences of doing otherwise.

To sum up in plain language: that historical accident which made Russia the land of the first completely socialist revolution was the worst disaster in the history of socialism.

Then there was the existence of Social-Democratic parties all over Europe, not unlike the Labour Party in Britain. That is to say of 'Menshevik' parties, committed to using the bourgeois parliamentary apparatus and repudiating violence and which, moreover, had had their confidence in the socialist theory under-

* *The New Statesman: The History of the First Fifty Years, 1913-1963,* Edward Hyams, Longmans, 1963. (This and the subsequent quotation are reproduced by kind permission of the *New Statesman.*)

mined by the quite colossal Russian failure which, had they been able and willing to recognize the fact, was completely without significance for their cause since it was due to forces which had nothing whatever to do with that theory. For example had the British and French working class tried, by electing socialist militants to trade-union office, to use the political instruments to hand to install socialism, that is the Labour and Communist parties, then the Labour parties, helpless prisoners of the bourgeoisie whose parliamentarian system they had accepted, would have broken in their hands, and the Communist parties would have betrayed them to the cause of Russian State Monopoly Capitalist power-politics. I believe it was an 'intuitive' recognition of this which was responsible for their apathy, their failure to respond with righteous anger and a socialist solution to the breakdown of capitalism which was inflicting such suffering on them.

Then there was the success—in Italy, Portugal and a number of other countries, and finally in Germany—of the capitalist-bourgeois recourse to counter-revolutionary violence: the pre-emptive strike of Fascism. In Italy Mussolini was successful in suppressing socialist movements and trade-union socialism by means of illicit gang violence including beating, deportations, torture and murder.* This success was hailed by the middle class in Britain and France as a triumph for 'law and order', that is to say for the reassertion of middle-class privilege. The way had, as a matter of fact, been shown by an economist, Doctor Salazar, in Portugal. Another intellectual, the dwarfish and sinister Doctor Dollfuss, followed suit in Austria with such convincing arguments as the destruction of Vienna's socialist municipality's model housing quarters for industrial workers by a heavy artillery bombardment; then a kind of upper-class gangster, one Codreanu, flaunting Christian morality (a cry which the proletariat should always beware of, although lately the clergy, with the marvellously self-preservatory intuition of the raven in *Animal Farm*, have been tending to swing to the Left) used his Iron Guard bullies to reassert Christian morality and the privilege of the middle class to dominion in Romania by means of club, daggers and guns. In Greece the St George who slew the dragon Socialism, was an

---

* For example the brutal murder of Matteotti in 1924, the Socialist champion in the Italian parliament.

army officer, one Metaxas: it is not beside the point here that, of the original St George (of Cappadocia), a purveyor of bacon to the Roman army, Gibbon wrote: 'His occupation was mean, he rendered it infamous. He accumulated wealth by the basest arts of fraud and corruption ...' Europe had many such St Georges slaying socialist dragons for love of the stout but fainting Maiden Bourgeoisie, in the 1930s; for it is very much to the point of our argument that, in this period when the war between the socialists with their vision of the Millennium, and the capitalists with their 'natural' and historically inevitable determination to hang on to their privileges as long as they could, the most repulsive scoundrels, even psychopathic criminals like Codreanu and, of course, Hitler and his colleagues, became Heroes.*

In some other countries, Poland and Yugoslavia for example, the reassertion of middle-class privilege was managed with more discretion (in the former country by the military intervention of an aristocratic soldier; in the latter by that of a monarch, neither of whom had any need to employ political gangsters of the kind so brilliantly satirized by Brecht in *The Predictable Rise of Arturo Ui*). In short, over a great part of Europe the bourgeoisie had hamstrung the socialist revolution by a pre-emptive recourse to violence, the use of police and para-military terrorism to keep the worker majority in its place—noses to the grindstone when at work, and at leisure sunk in the apathy induced by semi-starvation, worn-out shoes, mean streets, dirt, slums, hovels and the death of Hope.

In Britain, the Labour Party and trade-union committal to 'law-and-order', i.e. to the existing Establishment's right to make the rules, to those parliamentary and peaceful means of installing a socialism which was never convincingly Social-Democratic Marxist, and which are warranted proof against socialism, entailed a handicap of the most crippling kind. The ultimate holders of effective power in any capitalist State are the great money-lenders, the purveyors of bus-tickets at prices fixed by themselves, bankers, and the various controllers of credit. Despite the often-

---

* It is important to realize that this does not make villains of the great burgesses, the truth is much more frightening—when one of them said that what was good for General Motors was good for the United States, *he really believed it.*

repeated demonstration of Labour Party readiness to conform
to the Conservative establishment's rules, and the equally
frequently demonstrated eagerness of the trades unions to compromise over disputes rather than provoke a really grave
confrontation between labour and capital* (since capital meant
the state and they were law-abiding men), the money mandarins
could, when Labour was nominally in power, make sure that
that Party would not govern for long. In 1929, for example, the
British Labour Government was crippled and paralysed by the
malfunctioning of that very capitalism they were, in theory,
dedicated to getting rid of. But there was more to the paralysis
of the British Left than that: we have already noted that in post-
World-War-One Germany, Austria and Sweden, Social-Democratic parties in power lost their nerve and failed to have the
courage of their supposed convictions when offered the chance to
implement a Marxist programme of legislation. It was the same
thing with the British Labour Party: want of real conviction,
loss of nerve among the politicians; decline into Marxist
scholasticism among the intellectuals; apathy among the rank-
and-file, the workers who had never received any kind of political
or economic education, who voted Labour because they vaguely
recognized their enemy in the Conservative Party but who had
no real hope of getting more by it than a somewhat less illiberal
welfare programme. The communists in the working class must
be excepted, of course; but the Stalin-dominated Comintern
which dictated the policies of foreign Communist parties was
increasingly suspected of being what, indeed, Stalin had made
it by the judicial murder of any foreign Comintern officer who
showed signs of thinking independently: an instrument of Stalinist imperialism.

There was still another reason why, during the 1929-34 collapse
of the capitalist system, no real attempt was made to turn to a
socialist programme, an initiative which would have involved the
working class in class war, probably 'cold' but possibly 'hot',
with its own middle class. As I have said above, the hostility of
the older British and French imperialisms to the brash new
imperialisms of Fascist Italy and Nazi Germany cut across those
class lines which, in any case, the British working class had

* Especially since the failure of the General Strike in 1926.

always been reluctant to recognize.* Socialists of all degrees saw in the opposition offered by the British and French governments to Fascism and Nazism, despite the envious admiration with which many Conservatives in both countries regarded Mussolini and Hitler, a possible alliance with the old bourgeoisie against the German and Italian bourgeoisie-in-arms.

But the hope, the vision, the dream of a Millennium of social justice was still there. In Britain it found expression in a merely literary manifestation in Left Bookclubism, *New Statesman*-ship and Fabianism revived; while in France a Popular Front of Left-wing parties, with a negative anti-Fascism rather than a positive socialist programme in common, was in power, under the Social-Democrat Léon Blum from mid-1936 to mid-1937, then led by the Radical (Left Liberal) Chautemps, and Blum again for a couple of months until early 1938 and then under Daladier until October 1938. Some measures of social and economic reform were introduced by these governments, but nothing like a full socialist programme. They were debilitated by a want of the courage of their paper convictions and, as the pioneer socialists had forecast, they had had to trim their ends to match their means. Then, they were afraid that the 'cold' class war would become 'hot': they were not generals able to face the prospect of being responsible for mass slaughter with professional equanimity. Furthermore, like the whole parliamentary system in France, they were corrupt, their institutions penetrated and their individuals subverted by businessmen with the money to buy politicians. When the British national government under Chamberlain realistically recognized the common interest of the whole European middle class and of capitalism at large by surrendering to the Nazis and signing the Munich Pact which handed over Czechoslovakia and ultimately Poland to Hitler's Germany, Daladier followed suit for the French Popular Front government. It is probable that both leaders had the majority of their fellow citizens on their side. The parliamentary Social-Democratic repudiation of Marxist class war and Stalin's revival

* Hippolyte Taine pointed out a century ago that whereas the French working class wore, in its *bleus-de-travail*, distinctively working-class clothes, the English working class wore the cast-off clothes of its betters.

of the autocratic Russian Empire had together seemed to deprive the European working class and European Socialism of anything worth fighting for.

A Popular Front government excluding the communists was formed in Spain after an overwhelming victory for the parties of the Left in the general elections of 1936. Its leaders were Manuel Azaña, then Largo Caballero and finally Juan Negrin. It was moderately socialist and anti-clerical—the two things have usually gone together in Spain. This government represented a threat to the landowning gentry, to the uncontrolled power of the great capitalists who saw the possibility of industry being forced to pay its workers a fair wage and contribute, perhaps heavily, to the cost of welfare schemes, and to the higher clergy who enjoyed more power and privileges in Spain than in any other country. The new government confirmed the fears of the Right by beginning its programme with land reform legislation which redistributed a part of the 51 per cent of all the land in Spain which was owned by fewer than one per cent of the population, to the poor peasant section who represented most of the remaining 99 per cent.

As in Italy and Germany the bourgeoisie found its salvation in Fascism,* initiated by an army officer commanding the Spanish army in Morocco, General Sanjurjo. When he was killed in September 1936 his place was taken by General Francisco Franco, military governor of the Canary Islands. By using Spain's Moorish regiments the generals were able to invade the motherland with troops only too glad of the chance to kill Spaniards, as well as with that part of the regular army which declared for the Right. They also had fifty thousand Italian troops, later increased to one hundred thousand, sent by Mussolini who also contributed armaments, and a part of the *Luftwaffe*, the Nazi airforce, Hitler and Goering having decided to seize the opportunity to try out new machines and new bomb-

---

* Here and often elsewhere I use this much-abused word in a generic rather than a specific sense. There are technical differences between *Fascismo*, *Nazism*, *Falange Española*, et alia. But all have in common their only significant attribute: they are all bourgeois-capitalist-reaction-in-arms.

ing techniques on the Spanish people in preparation for the war
to conquer the British and French empires, which they were
planning. On the government side were the people, including the
rank-and-file of the army in Spain and many junior officers, and
an International Brigade of socialist volunteers recruited, trans-
ported and trained by a communist network set up by the
Comintern. The importance of this work, the relative efficiency
of the native communists, and the leading part which they played
in the fighting, soon gave them virtual control of the Spanish
government, reinforced by the fact that the Soviet Union was
the only country that government could look to for military
specialists, provision of arms, and other supplies. The communist
dominance was to have fatal consequences for, under Comintern
orders, the communists spent a great deal of the energy which
should have been used against the rebels in trying to suppress the
anarchists, thereby alienating a very large section of the Spanish
working class and breaking the common front against fascism.

Spain thus became the battlefield for a hot war between
socialists and anti-socialists from all over the world, the place
where the hostility of many decades came to a head for the first
time since 1920.

For the British and French governments this civil-and-social
war was a source of great embarrassment: the sympathies of the
working class and the intellectuals in both countries were whole-
heartedly with the Left, of course. But those men in both
countries who wielded the real power, what the French call *la
haute banque*, and the great industrialists were with Franco
whom they saw, as they had seen Mussolini, Salazar and Hitler,
as the champions of 'law and order', that is to say of continued
middle-class dominion over the proletariat. But this, again, was
complicated by that jealous hostility of the old imperial establishments to the new fascist imperialisms. The British Conservative
government had taken the lead in condemning Mussolini's
imperialist adventure in Ethiopia and in persuading the League
of Nations to apply commercial sanctions against Italy. But it
would have been a very different matter to support a socialist
government increasingly dominated by Comintern-directed
communists, and Mussolini had covered himself in this instance
by calling the troops he sent to Franco 'volunteers'. The French

Popular Front government might conceivably have given open support to the government in Madrid but, increasingly frightened of Germany and obliged to rely on Britain to help it in the event of war with the fascist powers, it dared not act independently of the British. A solution was found in the policy of non-intervention which entailed refusing to help the Spanish government even with supplies.

The swiftness and secrecy with which Sanjurjo and then Franco, who declared himself *Caudillo* of the Spanish State, struck in the south and west of Spain, and their overwhelming military superiority in those provinces, gave them a quick and easy victory there and within a few months of the invasion the fascists' forces controlled Seville, Cadiz, Burgos and Saragossa. The government retained control of all north-east Spain including Madrid, Valencia, Barcelona and Bilbao.

Early in 1937 Franco launched an attack designed to cut the government's half of Spain into two by driving through from Teruel, which his troops captured, to the coast at Valencia. This failed: the Spanish people in arms drove the attackers back and re-took Teruel while the International Brigade inflicted a humiliating defeat on the Italians at Guadalajara. But the north-eastern drive of the fascist armies was successful and by June they had taken Bilbao, thanks largely to massive German air support: the *Luftwaffe* had already gained a singular distinction in infamy by totally destroying the Basque's 'holy' city of Guernica, which thereafter became a dual symbol of Nazi barbarism on the one hand and of the martyrdom of freedom on the other. But Franco was now fully extended, the people and their allies had fought his armies to a standstill. It looked as if neither side was strong enough to get the upper hand and in that crisis Italy doubled her expeditionary force of 'volunteers' and Germany stepped up supplies of armaments. Franco was thus enabled to resume the offensive and in a six months' campaign advanced to the Catalan coast, thus cutting government-held territory in two, and laid siege to Madrid. Meanwhile the government side was seriously weakened by the hostility which divided the communists and anarchists. Here is a passage quoted from my *The New Statesman: a History of the First 50 Years* which, while giving some idea of what was happening, will at the same time illustrate the predicament of European socialism entailed by its attitude to the USSR. George Orwell had been in Spain and had seen the damage being done to the cause of socialism and of freedom by the behaviour of Negrin's government under native communist and Russian communist pressure to suppress the anarchists. He offered Kingsley Martin, the editor of the *New Statesman*, articles exposing this scandal:

> ... Kingsley Martin himself twice went to Spain during the war; he talked with Republican leaders and he saw what one could see. Orwell, on the other hand, saw what one was not supposed to see and what most men could not see: that imperialism is imperialism whether its bosses are Russian Communists or British adventurers or American bankers. It was in Spain that he conceived his loathing for Party-line Communism. He perceived, what, by the way, any experienced British trade unionist could have told him, that if Russian Communism was at war with Fascism it was much more whole-heartedly at war with Social Democracy, with Anarchism, with Liberalism, with any kind of Leftism which did not entail toeing the Party line; above all with the pure Communism of the Trotskyist World Revolutionaries. And as the Communist Party had got control of the Spanish Government, assisted by the fact that Negrin's Government could look to no power but Russia for arms, it was able to wreak its will on its supposed allies. Orwell came back to Britain with a series of blistering articles attacking the Spanish Government and offered them to the *New Statesman*. Kingsley Martin did not disbelieve what Orwell had written, but he decided against publishing it. In Spain there was a fight between Fascism and Democracy and the latter must be supported; if neither triumphed, but Communism came out victorious over both, even that would be better than a Fascist victory. In short, the *New Statesman* had become a 'committed' paper while recognizing that, Fascism defeated, we might then have to fight for our principles against the worst elements of Communism.

It would, in short, have been heartbreaking to face the truth that, from the genuinely libertarian socialist point of view, the Russian Revolution should now be written off as a failure (its successes in other respects have nothing to do with the matter in hand).

The nature of that failure was clearly demonstrated in Spain in 1938 and 1939. Dissatisfied with Negrin's inability or unwillingness to crush the heart out of Spanish libertarianism and Catalan separatist independence; perceiving that even if he won Spain for communism he would still not have won her as a subservient colony of his empire; calculating that offering aid to Negrin's government sufficiently massive to win the war would involve him in a direct confrontation with the Nazis and fascists, which he was not ready for; foreseeing that the hostility of the British and French bourgeoisie, effective controllers of those two empires, to any alliance with the USSR would, if it came to war with Germany and Italy, leave him isolated, Stalin withdrew Soviet support and supplies. The specialists he recalled were, no doubt, dispensable—the supplies he cut off were not, and the socialist cause in Spain was fatally weakened. Madrid, having withstood a siege and bombardment lasting a year, was forced, followed by Valencia, to surrender when Franco's forces took Barcelona on 28 March 1939.

Thus by mid-1939 all over Europe excepting France and Britain, socialism, whose appeal—social justice, and a fair distribution of plenty—had threatened to persuade the working class to gather its strength and destroy the capitalist system and put an end to the power and privileges of the bourgeoisie, had been defeated by two powerful forces: the Stalinist confidence trick —a barbarous and tyrannous State Monopoly Capitalism masquerading as a socialism commanding the loyalty of all socialists; and capitalism's pre-emptive resort to armed force.

In Britain and France the business of checkmating socialism had been managed without having recourse to fascism: socialists of the kind who could be relied on not to have the courage of their socialists convictions were allowed to take office, but any attempt they might make to exceed that measure of welfare legislation which the great capitalists were willing to concede, and felt that their system could afford, was thwarted by the manipulation of the money supply.* But there was, again, another force at work to paralyse the socialists' will to take real power and use it. It was the hostility of the British and French imperialisms to the newer and more aggressive fascist imperialisms which I have already mentioned; and since fascism was the principal enemy of socialism, the socialists saw, in the bourgeoisie of France and Britain, allies against that enemy.

European socialism was finally paralysed completely by the signing of a pact between Germany and the USSR. Stalin learned the lesson of Munich, believed that the USSR might have to face an alliance of the fascist and parliamentary bourgeois powers, and took advantage of Hitler's eagerness to have peace on his Eastern frontier while he was busy conquering the French and British empires. The real nature of Stalinism was thus forced on the apprehension of the Western socialists, with the exception of the Comintern-directed European communist parties whose rationalization of the pact made them so ridiculous that they were discredited until the moment when Hitler repudiated the Soviet-Nazi pact and his armies invaded the USSR; they suddenly found themselves obliged to turn another somersault and become enthusiastic allies of their national bourgeoisie, and the implacable enemies of yesterday's ally.

* When the Labour government of 1929 was replaced by a 'National' (Conservative) government pledged to defend the pound sterling, the new government immediately went off the gold standard. The Labour economists had considered this measure but had been terrorized with 'expert' threats of the consequences into believing that this was something they must not do. Sidney Webb, a member of that Labour government, was heard to exclaim, 'Nobody told us we could do that!' I know of no more striking example of the truth that you cannot install socialism by 'Menshevik' means.

FIFTEEN

China, Korea, Vietnam:
The Triumph of Mao Tse-tung

Hitherto we have been concerned only with the Western hemisphere, but the promise of a better life and freedom implicit in the original socialist vision had been making a powerful impression on the minds and hearts of men in the Far East. To China, whose bourgeois revolution had left the country in a state of chaos facing the threat of Japanese imperialism as a house divided, the socialist vision offered a hope which nothing else could give.

Why not a liberal bourgeois government and capitalism? It was, historically, too late. An attempt to answer the question why capitalism as we understand the word developed only in Europe (and those parts of the world colonized by Europeans) will not be out of place here.

Up to a certain point in their respective histories the economies of all the great civilized cultures can fairly be compared: all are founded on agriculture, all have peasantries exploited by landlords, all build urban civilizations on the surplus wealth produced by agriculture. In short, in Europe, Western Asia, China, India and even Mexico (Inca Peru shows a completely different pattern and it is unique), urbanism is built round a class of artisans, each assisted by apprentices, who both make and sell the manufactured goods—the very word 'shop' means a workshop in one context, a point of retail sale in another. The smiths make the hardware, the spinners and weavers make the cloth, the potters pots, the cutlers cutlery, the saddlers leather-goods, etc., and each maker is his own merchant, although there is also a class of men who are not makers, but only merchants, those who carry the city's manufactured goods to remote markets. In the case of all these different cultures, the work of the artisans, the peasants and the merchants builds up a surplus of wealth represented by money-hoards. This accumulated wealth, applied to the employment of men without either land or money, that is to the exploitation of

204 The Millennium Postponed

other men's labour in the making of more goods and more wealth, is the beginning of capitalism. Now that point was reached in, for example, the Dar-al-Islam, in India, in China, long *before* it was reached in Europe. Yet only in Europe did capitalism develop.

Much has been made, in the case of the Islamic lands, of the religious objection to the receiving or paying of interest on loans and to the entering into contingent bargains (which comes under the objection to gambling) as a bar to the development of capitalism. Rodinson, in *Islam et Capitalisme*, has thoroughly demolished that argument, and one of his demonstrations of its weakness is the case of China: there were no religious objections there to the basic operations of capitalism yet it no more developed there than in the Dar-al-Islam. It looks as if there must have been some special condition in Europe which favoured the growth of capitalism.

There was, of course: the Dutch and English 'agricultural revolution'—in no previous culture was there anything quite like it.* Its chief social effect was to dispossess the peasants of land, absorbing only a minority of them into employment as wage-earning labourers; its principal economic effect was immensely to increase the yield of surplus wealth. On the one hand, then, it created a pool of unemployed labour, and on the other a pool of unemployed money. Bring the two terms together and you have the beginning of a real capitalist industry. The very existence of such industry, in for example water-driven mills for the manufacture of various goods such as paper, sawn timber, or cloth, stimulates mechanical inventiveness, that is to say the birth of industrial technology. The burgesses, once artisan-merchants and now industrialists or great traders, grow rich and aspire to a share of political power and to the replacement of the ideologies proper to absolute monarchy and aristocracy by that proper to capitalism. They make a revolution to give their class power and to act upon that liberalism—freedom of speech, of the press, of thought, of trade—which their way of life has taught them to wish for. But meanwhile their economic activity has created a new and increasingly numerous class, the proletariat of wage-

* Not literally true: the peasants of Rome and Latium were dispossessed of their land by large-scale capitalist-style ranchers; but the technological aspect was missing.

earning workers who, by serving the machines, have become, with the peasants, the sole creators of new wealth. Yet not they but the owners of the machines receive that wealth. Then, as I have described it in the first chapter, come the proto-socialists with their vision of a society both prosperous, by means of industry, and just, egalitarian and free, by means of fairly distributing both the control of industry and the product of industry. Seeing that vision, the proletariat tries to win power in parliament; or with the peasants, to rise and overthrow the bourgeoisie.

But, in the countries where a capitalist-bourgeoisie had never developed, where it had to be imported by Western enterprise, sometimes in partnership with Westernized natives aspiring to bourgeois revolution in their own country, the interval between the rise of the bourgeoisie to overthrow the old regime and that of the workers to overthrow the bourgeoisie was shortened from decades to years, unless the middle class has recourse to military dictatorship simply because the revolution of the workers, in ideas even if not yet in violent practice, was already far advanced in the lands where capitalism and the power of the bourgeoisie were already old.

The Chinese bourgeois revolution (1911) and the collapse of the authority of the worn-out Manchu dynasty left the country divided into a number of virtually autonomous territories ruled by warlords, each with his own army, battening on the peasantry and fighting each other for hegemony. The authority of the central government of the Chinese Republic founded by Sun Yat-sen hardly extended beyond Nanking and the surrounding country. At most, the Kuomintang, Dr Sun's party founded to bring to his country the benefits of capitalist liberalism, governed a province. Sun died in 1925 and was succeeded as President and Commander-in-Chief by his brother-in-law, a professional soldier, Chiang Kai-shek, who had been trained as an officer in Japan and the USSR and had deserted from the Manchu army to join the revolutionary Kuomintang army.

Another veteran of the Kuomintang revolution, Mao Tse-tung, had meanwhile, been moving Left from an originally nationalist and reformist position to a revolutionary socialist one to become one of the founders of the Chinese Communist Party in 1921.

This did not debar him from participation in Kuomintang politics; for towards the end of Sun's life, when he badly needed Soviet support in trying to assert the authority of the central government of the Republic, he had, despite the opposition of Chiang Kai-shek, altered the articles of the Kuomintang so that communists could join the Party. He had also incorporated a number of socialist measures in Kuomintang official policy, and had accepted the services of a Russian Soviet adviser, Borodin. It was possible to do this without compromising the bourgeois character of the Kuomintang revolution and policy because the Central Committee of the USSR Communist Party was rigorously doctrinaire in its Marxism, and the Marxist rule-book said that in the first stage of revolution socialists should loyally support the bourgeoisie in their struggle with absolutism, postponing the second stage, socialist revolution, until absolutism had been totally defeated. Chiang, already Sun's principal lieutenant, was obliged to accept the Party's decision and was, at a pinch, willing to make use of communist aid; but he remained suspicious of and hostile to socialism so that the next twenty years of the revolutionary struggle can be seen, by those who prefer the idea of the influence of personalities to the historical dialectic, as a long battle between Chiang, champion of the bourgeoisie, and Mao, champion of the proletariat (or, rather, of the peasants).

The son of a prosperous farmer-moneylender, Mao was born in Hunan in 1893. He was taught to read and write at seven, was repeatedly in trouble for reading romantic novels instead of working, ran away from home at ten but was brought back and at fourteen was doing a full day's work in his father's fields and had been married to a girl of seventeen whom he later repudiated on the grounds of non-consummation. At seventeen he went to school in Hsianghsiang, where he did well at history and geography, badly in the natural sciences, read the classics and became critical of Confucianism without rejecting its spirit. He also read translations of the principal Chinese and foreign social reformers and, for pleasure, poetry and the biographies of great military heroes.

When the 1911 revolution broke out Mao joined the republican (Kuomintang) army as a common soldier in the division commanded by Chao Heng-ti. But he left the army as soon as the

fighting was over for the time being, in 1912, and for a year lived
in miserable poverty while he read translations of English and
French social philosophers and economists in the Provincial
Library. In 1913 he enrolled as a student in a teachers training-
college in his home-town of Chang-sha, where the teacher who
made most impression on him, Yang Ch'ang-chi, persuaded him
to read Paulsen's *A System of Ethics*. The book made him a
politically conscious radical and he soon founded his first political
group, which he called the New Citizen's Society and which he
later used as a revolutionary instrument. He graduated in 1918
and went to work in the private library of China's leading political
economist, Professor Li Tao-chao. He read Bakunin, Kropotkin
and Tolstoy and conceived an admiration for the anarchist ideal
which remained an influence all his life. Moreover, as a result of
reading the professor's own essays on Bolshevism and the Bolsheviks, Mao became a socialist.

In 1919 he returned to Chang-sha as teacher in the Hsiu-yeh
primary school. In May of that year came the 'intellectual revolution' known as the 4 May Movement: leading intellectuals and
university students called for the breaking down of the barriers
of Confucianism, tradition and superstition to let in modern
science, modern humanism and modern technology. At the same
time they called for revolt against the acceptance of Japan's claim,
ratified by the Paris Peace Conference, to the former German
possessions in Shantung, support for which Japan had bought
by huge 'loans' to some of the Chinese warlords in control of the
country. On 4 May Peking students staged a gigantic patriotic
demonstration. It spread to the whole country and Mao used his
New Citizen's Society to form a Students' Union in Chang-sha
and then called all the students of Hunan out on strike. At the
same time he founded and edited the *Hsiang River Review* in
which he attacked the leading statesmen of the Peace Conference,
suggested that the solution for Central Europe was a Union of
Communist Republics and published (Numbers 2, 3 and 4 of the
Review) *The Great Union of the People* in which he implied
that China, too, should follow the Russian example. This led to
the suppression of the *Review* by the warlord governor of Hunan,
General Chang Ching-yao. Mao accepted the editorship of the
Students' Union weekly, *Hsin Hunan*, maintaining the same

policy and Chang promptly suppressed that too. Mao also founded a discussion group to propagate the same ideas, but was then sent as a delegate of the anti-Japanese (Chang was pro-Japanese) party to Peking to lobby for support of a campaign to get rid of Chang.

While in Peking, where his mission failed, he read Kirkupp's *History of Socialism,* the *Communist Manifesto,* Engels' *Socialism: Utopian and Scientific* and Kautsky's *Class Struggle,* and became confirmed in his communism. He went to Shanghai, selling his fur coat to pay the fare, and, working in a laundry, had his first experience as one of the proletariat. He returned to Chang-sha as teacher in his own old college in July, during the confusing struggle between rival warlords whose only good outcome was that it rid the province of General Chang. Mao took an active part in the movement to give Hunan a measure of autonomy and a democratic government and at the suggestion of Ts'ai Ho-sen he took a series of steps, beginning with the setting up of numerous socialist bookstalls, towards the foundation of a Communist Party in Hunan. This was a move towards the foundation of a Chinese Communist Party which was accomplished in July 1921 by the coming together of a number of provincial foundations similar to his own at a first congress of which Mao was elected secretary. By 1923 he had a group at work in Chang-sha, including two of his brothers, organizing industrial labour unions, another forming a provincial Central Committee of the Communist Party, a third running an association of peasants and a Communist Youth Movement with 2,000 members. In 1921 he had married an old sweetheart, Yang Kai-hui, who bore him a son and daughter.*

In 1922 the Chinese Communist Party had resolved on a revolutionary alliance of some kind with the Kuomintang, but reserved its independence of action. But a year later both Lenin and Stalin insisted on the necessity for co-operation with bourgeois nationalist parties as a first stage in the revolution and, under Soviet

* In 1930 she and her son, and Mao's sister, were arrested by the Governor of Hunan, Ho Chien and she was required to repudiate her marriage. When she refused both she and her sister-in-law were murdered by Ho's guards—the fate of the boy was uncertain, but a Mao An-yeng appears as the son of Mao and Yang Kai-hui in a Chinese work of reference of 1947, quoted by Ch'en.

pressure, the Party accepted a united front with the Kuomintang which, in practice, meant the subordination of its forces to the supreme command of Chiang Kai-shek. Mao went to Shanghai where he attended the Party's Third Congress and was elected to the Central Committee. In 1924 he attended the National Congress of the Kuomintang in Canton at which the communists and their Left allies were predominant; its Manifesto was drafted by Sun Yat-sen's Soviet adviser, Borodin. Mao was elected a member of the Central Executive Committee and sent as secretary of the organizing branch of the Chinese Communist Party in Shanghai, where his job was to co-ordinate Chinese Communist Party and Kuomintang policies. At this, partly because he was despised by the Kuomintang leaders for his humble origins, he failed; falling ill, he spent the second half of 1924 and first part of 1925 in Hunan where he concentrated on organizing revolution among the peasants, a task regarded as a confession of failure in the supposedly more important work among the urban workers and intellectuals.

Fighting between rival warlords broke out again and it became clear that their time was running out. Mao's absence from the urban centres caused him to miss the great strikes in Shanghai and Canton organized by the Chinese Communist Party when the British and Japanese used troops against the workers in those cities. This militant campaign increased the strength of the Party from only 1,000 to 10,000 in six months. A warrant for Mao's arrest was issued by the Governor, again alarmed at Mao's successes among the peasants, and he was forced to leave Hunan. He went to Canton where he was given charge of a school to train political organizers for the peasant movement and where he first made friends with Chou En-lai, who was political Commissioner to the Kuomintang First Army. Mao's own courses of lectures were 'Problems of The Chinese Peasants' and 'Village Education', while Chou lectured on 'The Peasant Movement and Military Campaigns'. In 1926 Mao became head of a new Peasant Department of the Chinese Communist Party and, after Chiang Kai-shek's reconquest of Hunan from the warlord Chao Heng-ti, he returned to work among the peasants of his native province and published the first of a great many papers on the revolutionary peasant movement, *Analysis of the Classes in Peasant Society* which he followed with *Report on an Investigation into the Peasant Movement* early in 1927, in which he listed 'Fourteen Deeds' which must be done to accomplish 'Revolution by the Peasants'. They were the blueprint for his political work during the next 22 years. Meanwhile the peasants of Hunan were already occupying and sharing the land of the rich landowners, despite the use of Kuomintang troops to prevent this expropriation. Their movement paralleled increasing proletarian unrest in the cities, although the workers' loyalty was more to the Socialist-inspired left wing of the Kuomintang than to the Chinese Communist Party whose premises and leaders several times suffered at the hands of angry anti-communist mobs.

During all this period the Chinese Communist Party, which by 1925 had nearly fifty thousand members, was taking its orders, usually but not always transmitted through Borodin, from the USSR (that is from Stalin who consistently misjudged and misunderstood Chinese conditions). Under those orders, the Party exercised extraordinary restraint in submitting to humiliation and even to persecution by the Centre and Right groups of Kuomintang. Stalin's policy was based on the orthodox Marxist dogma that socialist revolution must be made by the proletariat and could not be made by the peasants. China had only a very small proletariat and a very numerous peasantry. Therefore the situation was not ripe for a proletarian revolution and the Communist Party should accept bourgeois leadership and help to make the bourgeois revolution complete.

Trotsky, who had not yet been silenced, repeatedly pointed out Stalin's mistakes and called for a China policy which was more nearly what Mao himself envisaged in his Fourteen Deeds. But the Stalinist policy was adhered to by most of the leaders and it was with Communist help that from 1925 Chiang was able to move effectively against the warlords. In the next two years he made such progress towards bringing all China under control of the Kuomintang central government that by mid-1927 he felt able to dispense with communist support and, alarmed by the growing influence of the Communist Party and its increasing strength, turned on his allies, seized and massacred all the Party members he could lay hands on in Shanghai and forced the survivors to go underground or to fly for their lives.*

Not even Stalin could go on pretending that Communist collaboration with the Kuomintang was still possible and the Central Committee of the Soviet Communist Party now advised the Chinese Communist Party to fight back. But their advice, still revealing wilful blindness to conditions in China, was again bad: hypnotized by the dogma that only the proletariat could make a socialist revolution, the Comintern urged the Chinese comrades to concentrate their effort on seizing cities. Chu Teh, commanding the communist element of the Fourth Army, tried to carry out this policy. Chiang, who should have been fully engaged in rallying all the manhood of China regardless of party, in resistance to the Japanese who had started on their great imperialist adventure (the conquest of all east Asia), was using his strength to crush the communists, thus becoming the first of a series of 20th-century bourgeois champions to perceive that the class-war enemy was more dangerous to his caste and its privileges than the foreign enemy.

Chu Teh, the general who tried to carry out the Moscow policy of seizing cities, was, like Mao, the son of a prosperous farmer. He was born in 1886, educated at the Yunnan Military Academy, became a professional army officer and like Chiang deserted to the Kuomintang on the outbreak of the revolution. He later studied in Europe, became a Marxist and joined the Communist Party in 1922. His attempt to carry out the Moscow policy was a disaster, he was defeated by the Kuomintang forces (1927) and forced to take refuge with Mao Tse-tung in Kiangsi.

There, in the mountainous Ching-Kangshan region, Mao had retreated with the nucleus of an army. By this time he had come to the conclusion that in China the best hope of revolution lay not in the proletariat but in the peasantry. He and Chu now set about converting the peasants to socialism, setting up 'Soviets' of peasants under Communist tutelage to run the province, abolishing rent, seizing the large estates and redistributing the land and creating a Red Army, also of peasants. It was there and then, too, that Mao and Chu began to develop the theory of revolutionary

* The monument to this event, one of the great novels of our time, is Malraux's *La Condition Humaine.*

guerrilla warfare. They avoided formal, positional battles with the Kuomintang armies, left the cities severely alone and planned to 'bring the revolution from the country to the cities' as soon as they were strong enough to do so successfully. So heretical was this policy that the Comintern and the Central Committee of the Chinese Communist Party anathematized Mao and formally expelled him from the Party; it was in correspondence with the Central Committee at this time that he elaborated the theory of socialist revolution in peasant countries which was to be the inspiration of the Algerian and Cuban revolutions. As for the expulsion, Mao ignored it—for he was succeeding. The poor peasants who composed (and still compose) the majority of the Chinese population rightly identified the Kuomintang, the party of the landlords and moneylenders, as their worst enemies, and therefore Mao and his communists as their best friends. Communist influence spread wider over the countryside and by 1930 rural Soviets were governing in regions of Kiangsi, Hunan, Hupeh and Kiangtung. Moreover the communists were beginning to win over the intellectuals, the university men who, increasingly disgusted by the corruption, self-indulgence and faction-fighting in the upper ranks of the Kuomintang, were increasingly impressed by the strict honesty, personal dedication, and respect for traditional Chinese values of the communist leaders.

Still diverting forces from fighting the Japanese, Chiang who, corruption and internal dissension notwithstanding,* still commanded the big battalions and foreign aid, blockaded the entire region where the Soviets were in power and began to close in on them. The communists had neither the numbers, the armament nor, as yet, the training to fight formal battles with greatly superior forces of professional soldiers. Mao and his friends decided that the experiment in rural socialist revolution must be continued in a province beyond Chiang's reach. Then came the famous Long March in which he led the communists three thousand miles, on foot, into Shensi on the frontier of Manchuria at the same time promulgating a formal declaration of war on Japan.

* The word is there to protect me from accusations of cynicism. Subsequent history has demonstrated that corruption and internal dissension has a remarkable tropism for capital, especially US capital.

In Shensi Mao won the support of millions of Chinese of all classes by calling on them to sink class and Party differences and unite to fight the Japanese imperialists. Meanwhile Chiang had steadily lost sympathy by his obstinate dedication of the Kuomintang to the civil war. He now moved to Sian, capital of Shensi, to direct operations against the communists in person. His own, largely Manchurian, army made him their prisoner and demanded that he make an alliance with the communists against the Japanese.

The man sent by Mao to negotiate with Chiang was Chou Enlai, born in central Kiangsi in 1898 of Mandarin stock, educated at Nanking University and the Sorbonne. It was in Paris that he had become a Marxist, organizing a communist 'cell' among Chinese students at the university and other Chinese temporary exiles. Back in China by 1923, he was sent by the Party, then only two years old, to propagate socialist doctrine in south China in country firmly under the control of the Kuomintang. On his return north he was appointed political commissioner to the Whampoa Military Academy in Canton. He fought with the communists against the Kuomintang in 1927 when Chiang started the civil war; but his principal preoccupation at the time was to organize against the threat of Japanese imperialism, and to persuade Kuomintang and communists to unite against it. He was, therefore, a very suitable envoy to send to Chiang.

Chiang had not the least wish to negotiate any kind of terms with the communists: either he still did not take the Japanese threat seriously enough or, more likely, saw a place for a collaborationist Kuomintang in the Japanese 'co-prosperity sphere' which would at least ensure the preservation of capitalism and the bourgeois dominion. It was only under threat of execution at the hands of his own officers that he gave way, whereupon he was released to command a national army, in which the Red Army became the Eighth Route Army, against Japan. Thus, from 1937, while the Kuomintang armies faced the invading Japanese in positional warfare with little success, the Red Army, employing Mao's guerrilla tactics, was successfully harassing and eroding the Japanese forces. The alliance was always precarious and on at least one occasion, when a series of successes had led the Red Army to extend its field of operations beyond the agreed limits, it found itself fighting both the Japanese and the Kuomintang forces.

The long war and the long agony of the Chinese people continued. When, in December 1941, Japan blasted the United States into the war by her attack on Pearl Harbor she presented Chiang with new allies, the United States and the British Commonwealth. But since the Japanese bombers had also forced the United States to accept the USSR as an ally following the German and Italian declarations of war on her in support of Japan, Chiang was still not in a position to repudiate his communist allies once again, although deeply disturbed at the spectacle of literally millions of peasants flocking to rally round the red flag of Mao, Chou, Chu and Lin Pao. By 1945, when the atom bombs on Hiroshima and Nagasaki forced Japan to surrender to the allies, all China south of the Yangtse river was still in Kuomintang hands; but the whole countryside north of that river was in communist hands, only the cities remaining as Kuomintang enclaves. The peasants to the south of China were following their fellows of the north in turning to Mao and socialism as their best hope, while the Kuomintang administrators were regarded as enemies not much less obnoxious than the Japanese. The university men, too, were turning in ever greater numbers from Chiang to Mao, for the scandals of the Kuomintang, the now notorious fact that the Chiangs, Soongs, K'ungs, Ch'ens and other leading Kuomintang families had enormously enriched themselves out of the public pocket, became a stick to beat leaders whose real crime in bourgeois eyes was that their incompetence had led to an inflation which had ruined the currency and left the country in economic chaos.

Even the USA, Chiang's backer, was sufficiently worried by the state of affairs to try, in 1946, to persuade him to come to terms with the communists and share political power with them. More royalist than the king, Chiang refused and re-opened the civil war with the avowed intention of exterminating the communists.

From the beginning the campaign was a disaster: his armies were routed in Shantung and Manchuria where the first attacks were launched and his powerful Manchurian army was cut off and isolated in Mukden and Chingsen. Moreover, the communists now began to advance towards the river Yangtse. Mao and the communist generals had realized that the time had come to go over to the offensive.

Stalin, through his agent, Liu Shao-chi, did all in his power to dissuade Mao from this course—the last thing he wanted was a socialist China independent of and owing nothing but measures of aid in the form of armaments to the USSR. Chou En-lai led the opposition to the Russian party, Mao supported him, the Red Army seized the initiative and between July and October 1948 cleared the north of Kuomintang armies, captured Shantung and Tsianfu and continued its advance to the Yangtse. An attempt made by Chiang in November to fight his way through to the isolated Manchurian army was defeated and he was forced to remove Kuomintang HQ and the seat of government from Peking, while the Red Army was wiping out another Kuomintang army at the battle of Hsu Chou.

Chiang was still refusing to negotiate with Mao, but his party was now divided and the vice-president, General Li Tsung-jen, leader of its liberal wing, opened secret negotiations with the communists. It is said that agreement had been reached when a leak to some Western newspapers forced both sides to deny that there had been any negotiations. The plan had been to expel Chiang and the 'fascist' faction from the Kuomintang and to form a coalition government of liberal Kuomintang nationalists and communists.

In December 1948 the Red Army began the siege of Peking. Fortunately for the Chinese people neither side had aircraft. The communists, under Lin Pao, had heavy artillery but refrained from using it: Lin had no wish to alienate the citizens or damage a great city which would soon be in his hands. Artillery was not even used to breach the walls of the city at the one place where an attempt to storm it would not be too costly in lives, after the archaeologist Professor Liang Ssu-ch'ang had pointed out to Lin Pao that such a bombardment would destroy the only remaining unrestored example of Ming fortification.

On the other hand negotiation was impossible for there was a bitter personal quarrel of long standing between Lin Pao and General Fu Tso-yi, commanding the Peking garrison, an old comrade of military academy days. Lin Pao therefore resigned his command to a colleague, the brilliant guerrilla general Nieh

Jung-chen who opened negotiations with General Fu. On 22 January 1949 Peking surrendered.

The Red Army advanced south, inflicting defeat after defeat on Chiang's generals and in April Mao published the terms on which he would accept Kuomintang surrender: they were generous—the Kuomintang would retain a measure of political power and some of its leaders would be given ministerial office in the communist government, but Chiang Kai-shek and his faction must go. Chiang refused to go and, taking the rump of his army with him, retreated to Taiwan to become an American pensioner. He remained the 'legitimate' President of the Chinese Republic with the result that his representative, not Mao's occupied China's seat in the United Nations, chiefly owing to United States support and the ambiguous attitude of most of her allies, until 1972.

By mid-1949 the Jen Min Kung Ho Kwo, the Chinese People's Republic, was in being and in control of all China. Socialism had become the political creed of the world's most numerous and potentially most powerful nation one century after the publication of the *Communist Manifesto*. Was the Millennium in sight for eight hundred million Chinese?

Perhaps, perhaps not. It depends on whether the struggle which in due course developed inside the Communist Party of China was and is a struggle merely between personalities for power, or is a struggle between opposing doctrines as to what socialism should mean. Most observers treat it as a mere struggle for power, yet they may be wrong. There is a tendency to see China as necessarily following the example of the USSR, whose unhappy people made a socialist revolution only to find that they had installed a monolithic State Monopoly Capitalist tyranny and the rule of a bureaucracy, the very disaster which Lenin was crying out against, warning of, during the last three years of his life. But China is not Russia and is not obliged to make Russian mistakes. Moreover, the histories of the two revolutions have been very different and such differences should have consequences. One 'difference' we can get out of the way at once: the quarrel between the Chinese People's Republic leaders and those of the USSR, in which pots called kettles black, is a nationalist, chauvinistic row and irrelevant in our context.

* * *

It is worth looking at some of the real differences and their probable consequences. In Russia the revolution was made primarily by the urban proletariat and in theory gave power to that proletariat; in practice power was given to the Bolshevik Party which was the Party of the proletarian dictatorship. As a later consequence the revolution did not receive the support it badly needed from the peasants, and Stalin thereupon used economic force and police terror to constrain them to produce on the government's terms. The resultant famine and bitterness left a terrible mark; moreover, it was one of the 'justifications' for oppression of the people by the Central Committee, that is by the bureaucracy. In China, on the other hand, the revolution was made by the peasants: it was much more 'their' revolution than it was the proletariat's. As a result the communist government has come nearer to solving the problem of famine in China than any former government in the country's history. Consequently, from the very beginning, discipline has been more relaxed, there has been more emphasis on the local commune and measures of decentralization, less of the Stalin-type mania for heavy industry.

In the second place, the USSR had her revolutionary civil war *after* the revolution so that the young socialist State had to fight for its life against hosts of enemies for three years, further aggravating the problems of food and other supplies and of restoring the war-ruined economy. Again, the civil war and the interventionist adventures of such foreign powers as Britain and Japan justified the imposition of strict national discipline by the Central Committee of the Party and by the Council of People's Commissars. It is very easy to impose constraints on the people during a war, it is very much more difficult to remove them after the war— the habit of irresponsible power grows on the bureaucracy, the habit of requiring obedience and no questions. But China had her civil war *before* the revolution; it was in the brotherhood of arms that the peasants and workers who followed Mao and his friends forged a loyalty to the new socialist State such that there was never anything like so great a need to impose constraints in defence of the revolution. Moreover, the potential counter-revolutionaries were wiped out or converted before the revolution which, once accomplished, had no internal enemies to face. Once again, therefore, Chinese communism could probably be more 'relaxed' than Russian communism.

Finally, there is Maoism : but is there, in China, a Maoism equivalent to that kind of revolutionary socialism which bears Mao's name in the West?

If China is Maoist in the sense which the word now bears in the West and continues to be so after the Chairman's death, then there is a chance that China will be the first country to accomplish socialism. This is all speculation because we do not even know if Mao is Maoist, nor whether the struggle inside the Party in China is an ordinary struggle for personal power which politicians indulge in, or is *also* a struggle between policies—those of rigid Statism on the one hand, with its inevitable concomitant of an all-powerful faceless bureaucracy and, on the other, a reasonable measure of libertarianism.

First, according to Doctor J. Ch'en in his *Mao and the Chinese Revolution* (OUP) the term 'Mao Tse-tung chu'i', Maoism, is not used in China, or not, at least by Chinese historical writers; it is felt that the suffix *ism* affixed to a man's name should be reserved for original systematic doctrines, for example, 'Marxism'. The Maoism of Mao in China is concerned with the manner of making a socialist revolution—the waging of a People's War from the countryside, with the right, even duty, of national Communist Parties to transcend Marxist dogma in this matter and make the revolution in the manner most likely to succeed given the local conditions, and with all the implications of the dictum that a politically educated and conscious, dedicated and armed people, *cannot be defeated* whatever the weight of metal and the atrocious methods used against them. This has been vindicated in Vietnam, certainly, and in it there are philosophical implications of great importance. For one thing, it places the spirit of man above the power of machines and by implication again, therefore above the Hegelian State which is seen not as transcending the individuals who compose it, but as being a machine to be used by the workers and the people at large. In other words, this kind of Maoism is nearer than Soviet communism to the humanist point of view. It is not for nothing that Mao, a poet (and according to Doctor Ch'en a good one), a classicist despite his critical reading of the classics, a writer who has striven to perfect a simple and lucid style (again I am relying on Doctor Ch'en) so that all can understand it, has set his face, or seemed to do so when he launched the Cultural Revolution, against the growth of strength in the Party bureaucracy.

An interesting manifestation of what we call Maoism has, it seems, been the rule in another Far Eastern country in which socialist revolution was accomplished following the Chinese example, North Korea. The Koreans had been waging guerrilla war on the Japanese, who annexed their country in 1910, for 35 years. They had had a National Communist Party since 1920. In 1945 the Red Army of the USSR drove out the Japanese and established a communist government under Kim Il Sung, who had fought with the guerrillas in China, against the Japanese and Kuomintang until 1941, when he went to the USSR and became a major in the Red Army. Once Kim was in firm control of the Korean Workers' Party which conducted the war with the 'neo-colonialist' South Korean regime and the USA and her allies (1950-53), and once the war ended with Korea still divided into two at the 38th parallel, and once the Party had made North Korea economically the most successful of the smaller East Asian States, Kim purged the Party of both Chinese and Russian elements, denounced the USSR as Revisionist (i.e. as favouring peaceful means of establishing socialism by the use of, for example, parliamentary means, as against the people's-war-revolutionary means), and denounced the Chinese CP for interfering arrogance. His doctrine is a Maoist one: national communist independence combined with internationalism, manifest in the practice of *Juche* —'the principle of solving all problems of the revolution and construction independently in accordance with the actual conditions in one's own country and primarily by one's own efforts'. More to the point in the context of this discussion is the Korean Party's emphasis on the Cultural Revolution aspect of Leninism. A serious attempt to be true to this doctrine has been made by the practice of *Chongsan-ri*, designed to 'help functionaries to rid themselves of bureaucracy and acquire a revolutionary method of work by relying on the masses'. A *ri* is the lowest, the basic administrative unit: all Party officials are obliged from time to time to spend a season, which may be of months or of only some weeks working in a remote rural *ri* so that every official always has a knowledge of conditions at the grass roots. *Chongsan-ri* also spreads both knowledge and control of the Party and gives it a human face.

What, if any, means are used in China to accomplish the same purpose, I do not know: it would seem from reports of Western observers, however, that the relationship between people and officials there is a very much better one than in the USSR or any of the East European countries with the possible exception of Yugoslavia. Moreover, there is the incident of the Cultural Revolution. What, exactly, was it for? It was launched by Mao in 1965 and continued for three years, and from the West it looked like an orgy of destructive hooliganism accompanied by a nasty outburst of chauvinism. Was it a means used by Mao to get all power into the hands of his faction and destroy the opposing faction; or were the Red Guards really being used in an attempt to break the growing power of the bureaucracy and put more control into the hands of the people through their local communes, trades unions and other workers' and peasants' organizations?

In the West what is called Maoism entails preparing the revolution by a sort of *narodnik* practice. The sincere Maoist intellectual renounces his place and privileges in the bourgeois world, takes work in a factory, lives in a working-class quarter, wears the clothes and eats the food of his work-mates. He refrains from direct political evangelism but, joining in every discussion concerning industrial, economic or political—or for that matter recreational—action, he puts questions, starts discussions, gives his own opinion when asked, in such a manner as to guide the workers to discover *their own solution* to the problem. This solution will be, from the Marxist-Leninist point of view, the right one because, in the context of the times, *the workers cannot be wrong, they are the heirs of history*. They do, however, need all the discreet help they can get from the Maoist in breaking through the habits of non-thought, the blockage created by prejudices inculcated by the bourgeois press, by fears of unemployment, by the misguidance of 'revisionist' or simply 'bourgeois-collaborationist' trade-union leaders, so that they can discover what their real, their true feeling and thinking is about the problem in question. Now, if we take all this seriously (if only for the sake of argument) and at its face value, the Maoist doctrine in its Western form is ultra-democratic and strongly anti-bureaucratic.*

'While it is true,' writes J-P. Sartre, 'that morality is a super-
structure of the dominant class, it is also true that it is a bluff
because it is necessarily founded in exploitation. Now ex-
plosions of popular violence, although the economic and
political motives for them may be very clear, can only be
properly understood if those reasons have been clearly appreciated by the masses, that is if they have caused them to grasp
the supreme immorality—the exploitation of man by man.
Thus, when the bourgeois claims to be behaving according to
a "humanist" morality—work, family, motherland—he is
simply concealing his basic immorality and trying to mislead
the workers; he can never be moral. Whereas workers and
peasants, when they revolt, are wholly moral since they are
exploiting nobody.'†

What is Sartre, what are the Maoists, saying? Broadly and
crudely, this: that we cannot go to a bourgeois, however intellectually and otherwise honest he is trying to be, for guidance
concerning the way history should go; the source is necessarily
and irredeemably impure because of his bourgeois formation.
Whereas the worker as a source of guidance, once freed from any
taint of corruption by bourgeois ideas, is necessarily 'pure'.
The Western Maoist will have nothing to do with the old
Bolshevik idea of an élite vanguard of communists leading the
workers and peasants. He wants the lead to come from masses
of workers thinking together. His own role is that of the spark
which lights the fire, no more.
But does this idea obtain in China where Maoist communism,
which is not the Maoism of the West, is in power? It is very unsatisfactory to say that I don't know, but the fact is I do not
know. Let us suppose it to be so: the terrible danger remains—
Marxist states have so strong a tendency to harden into tyrannous
and faceless bureaucracies just because, despite the reservations
so conscientiously made by Marx and Lenin, the dialectic elevates

* The reader wishing to know more about this should read *Les Maos
en France* by Michele Manceaux, Paris, Gallimard.
† Foreword to *Les Maos en France*.

the State above its component individuals, makes it transcend mere function as an instrument and become a good in itself. Perhaps, if a State were to be really composed of all the people, all the workers, without the intervention of a bureaucracy, then we might not unreasonably regard it in that light, for the general weal must transcend the particular weal. But although theories for the management of the State by completely democratic means have been elaborated, they have yet to be tried in practice. Even in the trades unions only a minority of the members take an active part in their management.

The communist revolution in Vietnam is of the Chinese type; a People's War has been in progress for quarter of a century. In the first stage communists and non-communists joined together to drive out the French, that is to rid the country of the old-style imperialism. This stage was completed with the French defeat at Dien Bien Phu. The new government in the North proclaimed the Republic of Vietnam and the strongest element in that government was the communist Vietminh which had been founded by its leader, Ho-Chi-Minh in 1941. But the former 'neo-colonialist' government remained in power to the south, composed of various bourgeois parties and led until 1955 by the 'emperor' Bao-Dai and thereafter, following a referendum, by Ngo Dinh Diem. When the French quit, the continuity of the new 'imperialism' (in the Leninist sense) was ensured by the USA. Opposed to the Ngo Dinh Diem government and its successors, each given more massive American support in men, money and weapons, were the ultra-Right Hoa Hoa Buddhists and Cao Dai Catholics, both more or less ineffectual, and above all the communists of the National Liberation Front with their Viet-Cong guerrilla forces, supported and supplied by North Vietnam.

The atrocious history of the long war of imperialism against the Vietnam peasants need not be repeated here; it was for too long a part of the front-page news in the newspapers, and of peak-viewing-time documentaries on television. It was a lost war for the USA, vindicating Mao's claim that a dedicated revolutionary people cannot be beaten by machines (short of extermination). What must interest us in the context of this chapter is the nature of Vietnamese communism and whether it allows hope of a more or less libertarian socialist regime, a step towards the Millennium.

There seem to be three ideologies working on the minds and hearts of the Vietnamese people. An orthodox, Moscow-orientated group is led by Lee Duan, Secretary-General of the Communist Party. If it triumphs the Vietnamese State will be dominated by a faceless Party bureaucracy and there can be very little hope of anything approaching democracy. Then there is a Maoist Group led by the intellectuals who are responsible for the Communist Party's theoretical journal, *Hoc Tap*. And finally, there is a group led by General Giap, the victor of Dien Bien Phu and probably the mastermind behind the Viet-Cong strategy and tactics which were so successful against the greatest military power on earth for two decades, who is said to look to the Cuban-style revolution, to Castro-Guevarism, for inspiration.

The Maoists follow Mao in dismissing the threat and fear of nuclear war as a bluff and believing that men, sufficiently dedicated to their cause, will always triumph over mere hardware. They are therefore ready for a fight to the finish with the South on the grounds that it will eliminate any danger of counter-revolutionary civil war after the triumph of socialism throughout Vietnam. Conceivably, a Maoist post-revolutionary government might be much less bureaucratic than a government in the Lee Duan style. Giap and the Maoists regard the peasants as the real revolutionary strength of their country; believe that, as in China and Cuba, the country will liberate the cities; and play down the role of the urban proletariat.

The question is, has socialism a better chance of being realized in the Far East than in the West.* The answer is almost certainly —no. The reason for that pessimism will be discussed in the last chapter.

* The question of its chances in other cultures alien to its origins will be touched on elsewhere.

SIXTEEN

Half a Loaf

The time has come to review the economic, social and political changes wrought in the world by the socialist millenary vision by the end of World War Two and to see what, by the same date, had happened to the vision itself as a consequence of its achievements. At first sight those achievements appear staggeringly great; indeed, they have been. But are they what the original visionaries had expected? Far from it.

After the publication of the *Communist Manifesto* there followed a century of wars and revolutions accompanied by the killing of men on an unprecedented scale, of absolute monarchies overthrown and private-enterprise capitalism abolished in the territories of the old Russian Empire, the old Chinese Empire, the greater part of the old Austro-Hungarian Empire, a third of the old German Empire, and about half of Indo-China. Approximately one half of the population of the world is living under a regime called communism which, however, is very unlike what the first users of that word had intended.

In all the countries in question the means of production, distribution and exchange have been socialized in the sense that they have become the property of the State. Excepting where one of the imperialist powers was still waging war against the revolution, rendering ordinary life impossible, by 1972 socialist objectives in the field of welfare had been accomplished. Employment, housing, medical care and education at all levels had become the responsibility of the State and where there were shortcomings—often very great ones—they were due not to abandonment of socialist aspirations but to the State's use of resources for other purposes, for example, investment in heavy industry or armaments, and to common human failings, want of skill or sheer ineptitude. At the very least, a whole Pandora's Box full of anxieties had been eliminated from the lives of common men who now knew that a roof, work, medical care and education for the family and a pension in old age were assured, in principle and increasingly in practice.

To take the obvious example: in the USSR, although money-wages were low by American or West European standards, they were much more lightly taxed, rent was never more than 4 per cent of income, and public-utility supplies for the home were much cheaper than in the West. Standards of living were lower than in capitalist countries because the GNP was lower, but investment in capital plant was relatively higher, partly because Russia had the whole business of industrialization to accomplish in years instead of the decades it had taken in Europe and America, and partly because war devastation on an unprecedented scale had to be made good. From about 1955, however, it became possible to start increasing and improving supplies for private consumption. For the workers and peasants in all those communist countries which had not been advanced industrial capitalist countries before the war, life was better and more 'secure' than it had ever been and they could look forward to a steady improvement in material wellbeing with confidence. The worst aspects of poverty, squalor and hopelessness, were being eliminated. The Millennium had not happened; but half a loaf is better than no bread, and as for man not living by bread alone, ideological propaganda kept the millenary vision still bright.

As long as that original vision of the proto-socialists remained, then the communist countries would not, in any case, be aiming to install the 'consumer society' of the richest capitalist countries, with its private affluence, often achieved at the price of public squalor, and its ruthlessness. For the millenary vision was of a society in which every man had a good roof over his head, a decent standard of clothing and cleanliness, enough wholesome food for his needs, a fair share of the amenities—warmth, food, comfort—which civilized life affords, equal educational opportunity, the education to be the highest attainable, free medical care and provision for old age. Above all, absolute security, elimination from men's lives of the constant threat implicit in nature. In return every man would be expected to contribute work, at a reasonable level of effort, to do his best according to his capacities. Anxiety and strife were to be eliminated from life within the limits possible, given the human condition. Every man would be free to think, say and print what he believed and to act freely according to his convictions provided his conduct was not harmful to his fellow citizens—did not, in other words, constitute a breach of the peace. Some versions of the vision saw all men taking part in the management of this society in a full direct democracy; in others, the society was to be managed by an élite of administrators inspired by philosophy and benevolence.

It would, therefore, be inappropriate to reproach any society professing belief in socialism as a way of life for mankind for not offering its citizens the standard of private consumption obtaining in the American-style affluent society. To the genuine socialist such consumption is wickedly wasteful of resources at least until the progress of industrial technology enables the society to afford, for every man in it, the standard of consumption of the richest men in the affluent society: even then such a standard of consumption would probably be rejected as vulgar, debilitating to the character, and economically unjustifiable in view of the limited sources of raw material in the world.

It can be fairly said that, in the industrially advanced communist parts of the world by the 1970s, the material part of the socialist programme was, thanks to State Monopoly Capitalism, on the way to being realized. But there was not, unless China turns out to be an exception, any question of trying to realize those parts of that programme which relate to freedom of thought, speech and press, and to industrial, social and political democracy. The reason for this has been discussed but it will be as well to mention in detail some of the ways in which the communist bureaucracy, generally known as Stalinism, sins against the socialist light.

(i) The rise of the bureaucracy eliminated from the programme that direct democracy without which, as Lenin repeatedly asserted, state monopoly capitalism *cannot evolve into socialism*. To defend itself, to retain and enlarge its power, the bureaucracy sacrificed the wisdom, good sense and inventiveness of the masses which Lenin held to be so much more valuable to society and its advancement than the guidance of specialists, and which the libertarian socialist philosophers like Kropotkin had laid such stress on. With them it sacrificed the hopes and mortified the self-respect of the common man.

(*ii*) The rise of the bureaucracy sacrificed the vision of an egalitarian society: in what was to have been above all a class-less society, it re-established class. The USSR bureaucracy is a new middle class, its privilege founded not in private property in the means of production, like the old bourgeoisie, but in administrative function as managers of those means. It is true that income differentials are not as great as they are in capitalist countries: no Soviet citizen is as poor and none as rich as our own poorest and richest, there are no hopeless paupers and no millionaires, nor is the salary of the highest-paid bureaucrat anything like as much greater than the wage of the lowest-paid worker as the salary of a top 'manager' is greater than that of a man on relief or in the lowest-paid work in our society. Nor can rogues make fortunes by speculating in land or commodity values or by manipulating money. But all this is very far indeed from the vision of the most gifted men living materially on an equal footing with the least gifted, where both are giving of their best because it is just and virtuous so to do.*

(*iii*) Lenin's vision was of the workers, through their free and bold trades unions, assuming the very necessary task of reproving the errors and excesses and sternly checking the growth of the bureaucracy; the sinister partnership between the Stalinist bureaucracy and an immensely powerful and ruth-less 'security' police force has put paid to that. It never for a moment came near to being realized.

The conclusion to all this is very clear: *socialism has not been accomplished in any of the Communist countries* and, unless China turns out to be an exception, cannot be accomplished in them without resumption of the revolution which was prematurely halted at the state monopoly capitalist stage.

Why was it possible, even allowing for Joseph Stalin's lust for personal power and the interest of his chief henchmen in supporting him, for the Communist Party bureaucracy to turn into such a monster of tyranny? It is not really difficult to find the answer: the fault lies in the acceptance of the Hegelian philo-sophy of the State, as transmitted in Marxism, without regard

* In the first post-revolutionary years it is said that the leading mem-bers of the Chinese Communist Party did just that; whether they still do so I have no idea.

sophy of the State, as transmitted in Marxism, without regard to those reservations made first by Marx himself, and subsequently and more emphatically by Lenin. Wherever and whenever the State is regarded as being a transcendent entity, as being morally superior to the individual citizen just as God is regarded by the religious as being morally superior to man, the State becomes God. The Hegelian/Marxist State is a latter-day version of the Stuarts' 'Divine Right'. The bureaucrat who manages it is then automatically and inevitably invested with a power for the use of which he is not answerable to the people severally, but to the State whose will he, at the same time, interprets. The bureaucrat is in very much the same case as the priest in a society which is genuinely religious—the priest is answerable only to God and, at the same time, is the only authority on the nature and demands made by God. Now where the bureaucrat has such irresponsible power, the existence of such a national assembly of Party members as the Supreme Soviet is no safeguard of liberty, for the bureaucrat, though he may pretend to treat the assembly with respect, is not really answerable to it and his power inspires fear in its members.

Now although the anarchist philosophers are, without question, morally correct in condemning and wishing to be rid of the State as unavoidably evil because necessarily more or less oppressive, a proposition to which Marxism itself pays lip service, it is a fact that since society has to be administered, some kind of State apparatus seems essential. There remains the only remedy for bureaucratic tyranny, the management of the State apparatus and of all economic institutions by the workers themselves, as Lenin envisaged it—that is, direct democracy. This is not the place in which to discuss how this could be accomplished, but one means, again envisaged by Lenin, suggests itself: the placing of much more economic and therefore political power in the hands of the trades unions; and measures to enforce democratic management of those trades unions. Unlike a modern nation, a trade union is not of unmanageable size for the practice of democracy.

Turning now to the capitalist West, we can begin by examining the question whether parliamentary systems on the English model, democracy by representation, could provide a sufficient check on bureaucracy (by which I do not mean the present civil service, but an all-managing bureaucracy of the communist kind which, as I shall try to show, is very nearly upon us also).

The short answer is: no. It is conceivable that had extension of the franchise to more and more categories of the population to the present point at which it belongs to all members of the community over eighteen years of age not been accompanied by that evolution of the party system which has resulted in making the executive very nearly all-powerful, then the power which the House of Commons would have had to turn out governments, as it had in the past, might have had the effect of limiting bureaucratic power. On the other hand, given that every MP spoke and voted according to his conviction, as an independent and according to the interest of his constituents and was not bound to vote with his party (which, in practice, and allowing for occasional exceptions, he now is), stable government would have been impossible. I will take, from 1972, one of a hundred possible cases to show that democracy is not achieved by means of a parliament elected by universal suffrage. Opinion polls showed a majority of the British people opposed to membership of the European Economic Community. The Labour Party, in opposition, therefore modified its former approval of that membership by calling for renegotiation of the terms. A section of the Party, composed of members who put their pro-EEC conviction above party loyalty, broke away either to vote against the majority of their Party, with the Conservatives, or to refrain from voting. Meanwhile the government, with a working majority, put through the legislation to make Britain an EEC member. *A real democracy in Britain at that time would have rejected membership.*

Take another case: when Parliament abolished the death penalty for murder, it did so against the will of the majority, that is to say, undemocratically, even counter-democratically. In so doing it showed itself more enlightened than the people; and for all I know it showed itself wiser than the people in forcing through membership of the EEC. But we are not discussing wisdom and enlightenment (such absolute monarchs as Açoka Rajah, Huayna Capac Inca and Kublai Khan were a great deal wiser and more enlightened than their subjects), we are talking about democracy, government of the people by the people 'without which there is no freedom'. Many other cases in point could be advanced. An obvious one is that of Conservative governments introducing legislation which favours the high bourgeoisie against the worker-majority, or such legislation as the British Industrial Relations Act (1972) which limited the workers' freedom to use industrial action in their struggle with managements. Now, in present conditions (1970s), although parliaments have not been successful in preventing increasing erosion of freedom, it can still be said that the British, American, Italian, German, Scandinavian, and even French citizen enjoys a full measure of liberty by comparison not only with the citizens of fascist or sub-fascist countries, such as Spain, Greece, South Africa, Rhodesia, Iran, Brazil and others, but with those of the communist countries including even Yugoslavia and North Korea with their relaxed versions of communism. But I am not concerned with the state of affairs now; I am concerned with the immediate and more distant future as the growth of bureaucracy brings the capitalist countries nearer and nearer to those which are already fully monopoly capitalist, with the State as monopolist.

The socialist vision has wrought great changes in the private-enterprise, that is, 'imperialist' capitalist countries. The social result of the pressure brought to bear on the capitalist masters of Atlantic powers' economies by Social-Democratic political parties, whether in office or in powerful opposition, in partnership with strong trades unions; and of the levying of that steeply-graded income tax demanded by Marx and Engels in the *Communist Manifesto* as one means of redistributing the 'surplus value' of industry and trade, has been the Welfare State. Pioneered in New Zealand, Sweden and Denmark, it was introduced to Britain by the Labour government of Clement Attlee between 1945 and 1951. Subsequent Conservative governments have reduced its range and effectiveness but have not dared (or, perhaps, wanted) to demolish it.*

The significance of these facts in our context is this: the capitalists, great and small, the bourgeoisie, high and low, had the sense to buy off the threat of violent socialist revolution by

* The special case of the arch-capitalist USA will be discussed separately.

conceding some of the demands implicit in the socialist programme—a larger share of the product of labour to the worker
in the form of higher wages, shorter working hours, paid holidays,
municipal housing, better free education and measures of social
security.

It is even conceivable, if the pressure by Social-Democratic
parties be steadily maintained and supported by the aggressive-
ness of trades unions, that 'imperialist' capitalism can be forced
to concede to the workers their fair share of the product of their
labour, that is to say the whole 'surplus value' less the amount
required for servicing industry and for investment. The new kind
of capitalist 'manager' will no more object to this than the new
generation of communist bureaucrats provided that, as in the
case of the communist bureaucrats, a sufficiently satisfactory
measure of power and privilege be conceded to him. In both
cases the rising productivity of industry resulting from technological progress will make this concession—or at least a convincing
appearance of it—fairly painless.

In other respects also Capitalism is being socialized. The
socialist theorist Karl Kautsky argued, as we have noted, that
capitalist evolution towards monopoly must produce in the end
an economic condition in which socialist planning—the elimination of gambling from and application of scientific rationalism
to the operations of industry, commerce and credit management,
would become practicable. It will be recalled that Kautsky's
'ultra-imperialism' as this theory was called, was damned by
Lenin as treachery to the proletariat; but that was because it
was 'élitist', counter-democratic and did not allow for the dictatorship of the proletariat, the control of the economic-political
complex, the State, by the workers. We need only note here
that, apparently willy-nilly, capitalism, as Marx argued, does
indeed inevitably evolve towards monopoly: mergers and take-
overs are the stuff of our daily front-page news.

Right-wing governments still pay a sort of doctrinaire lip-
service to the value of competition in industry and trade and,
taking into account the archaic prejudices of the petty burgesses
including the most highly paid workers anxious to maintain wage
differentials, whose vote supports them, take more or less ineffec-
tive steps to check the progress of that evolution. But the

managers of industry have seen the light of economic socialism. They know very well that both lower production costs, and the growth of their own power in society, are much better served by 'rationalization', that is, socialist-style planning tending to monopolistic centralization rather than competition which, in the present state of industrial and commercial technology, is wasteful. The advance of both the social and economic sciences has made the word 'competition' a confidence trickster's locution, excepting in so far as it refers to setting off one 'team' within a general plan against another.

The most important of the socialist demands in the economic field was for the public ownership of the means of production, distribution and exchange. Social-Democratic parties in office in primarily capitalist countries have from time to time managed to nationalize certain industries; this has been tolerated by the Right in the case of industries from which it is no longer possible to make a profit (railways for example, coal mines, and public-service industries, such as those supplying energy). All this has little or nothing to do with real socialism: the worker is no better off and has no more control of his industry than under private capitalism. If all the industries in capitalist countries were to be nationalized, the result would be state monopoly capitalism, commonly and misleadingly known as 'communism', and it is very possible that its bureaucracy, using the argument that the interest of the State must transcend that of the individual worker, and therefore of all workers, would deny the worker the right to strike. Now it is in that right which, in a capitalist or mixed economy in which three parties are involved—the workers, management and the State—the workers' power to check the power of the corporation bureaucracy, which is developing into a mirror-image of the state monopoly capitalist bureaucracy in communist countries, resides.

One of the most effective and important ways in which capitalism has been influenced by socialist economic theory is by the writings of the great English economist John Maynard Keynes. Kautsky, it will be remembered, in his theory of 'ultra-imperialism', had argued that capitalism's trend to monopoly, transcending national frontiers, would ultimately produce an international, world-wide economic 'monopoly', and therefore a condition in which socialist planning would be not only possible, but inevitable. In other words, and very roughly, he argued that capitalism was evolving towards a kind of socialist economic system of its own accord. Keynes saved the capitalist nations from the bloody revolution which must ultimately have been provoked by repetitions of the catastrophic collapse of capitalism in 1929, with its hideous consequences for the workers and the bourgeoisie, by teaching the capitalists to manage the great 'imperialist' corporations on Marxist lines and the governments of primarily capitalist nations to apply socialist controls and socialist planning to the national economies.

Keynes was a civil servant working at the British Treasury, and he represented the Treasury at the Paris Peace Conference following World War One. In his *Economic Consequences of the Peace* (1919) he did his best to drive into the dogma-befogged minds of the world's credit managers and the power-drunk minds of ruling demagogues whose success in exploiting the basest feelings and fears of their constituents was mistaken for a licence to call themselves statesmen, the simple proposition that money is bus-tickets and that consequently the policy of exacting reparations from Germany would end in disaster. (It did.) In the following decades Keynes applied himself to a steady campaign of criticism of the capitalists' continued reliance on *laissez-faire* 'market' economics, the gambler's creed, and in his *General Theory of Employment, Interest and Money* (1936) he showed the way to use socialist method to save capitalism.

When Karl Marx forecast that capitalism must perish of its own internal contradictions, he did not foresee that so able a scientist would arise to teach a means of eliminating some of those contradictions without actually scrapping the whole system. President Roosevelt was the first national leader to apply Keynes' theories (if you seek Keynes' monument, look at the New Deal, and remember that the New Deal can fairly be described as a derivative of Marxism).

What does all this come to? Despite reactionary lapses from time to time into primitive capitalist freedom, both the capitalist countries and the international credit managers are being slowly but steadily forced to adopt socialist economics: the rational

planning of national economies, a juster distribution of the surplus value of production and ultimately, scientific planning and
control of the system of exchange, on a world-wide basis. In
short, economically and politically, corporation or 'imperialist'
capitalism is looking more and more like state monopoly capitalism—that is 'communism'. But that communism is nothing like
the socialism of the millenary vision. It consists in the use of the
socialist economic method to serve the power of the bureaucracy.

The United States is a special case. We have noted that she once
had her militant socialists—the anarchists, the 'Wobblies', and
a Social-Democratic Party with a full Marxist programme. But
the premature and inappropriate, though very understandable,
violence of her 19th-century socialism alienated the great
majority of Americans. The hostility between the native workers
in skilled trades, organized in 'craft' unions, and the immigrant
workers who were brutally exploited by capital before they were
organized, chiefly by socialists in the first instance, into 'industrial' unions, split the American working class into two mutually
antipathetic groups.

But there was much more to it than that. In one sense, the
'saviour' of American capitalism from socialism was Henry Ford:
his discovery that you could create a market for mass-produced
consumer durable goods by paying the workers high wages, in
other words that you could recover the cost of high wages by
winning them back into your industry, made possible that 'affluent
society' in which the vision of millenary socialism becomes
obscured. There were contributing causes to the success of that
discovery. So immensely rich *per capita* is the United States in
natural resources—every American baby is born to a heritage in
natural resources about five-hundred times that of a British baby
—that she could accomplish a very fast rate of productivity increase with a much slower rate of raw-material import increase
than any European country. Moreover, great developments in
credit management, implicit in Keynesian economics, enabled
the workers to borrow money in order to buy domestic machines,
so that the capitalists recovered a part of those high wages in
interest and bound the borrower to the system by legally enforce-
able obligations. In Marxist terms United States' industry did

not give its workers an equitable share of the wealth produced, but without going so far it could afford them a standard of living so high (relatively) that, excepting after the initial period of industrial strife during the Great Depression (1929-33), the condition of the majority of the workers was not such as to generate a 'revolutionary situation'.

When 'socialist' action did have to be taken as a means of lifting the economy out of depression, it was, then, taken from above and did not originate with the workers but with the bureaucracy. It gave the US worker a taste of social security such that, despite pressure from the reactionary Right, it has not since been possible to remove welfare legislation from political programmes. Thus, a measure of socialism has been built into the United States' economic system.

This has occurred at the industrial as well as at the national level. The American trades unions are politically as anti-socialist as the American middle class. Yet their pressure on the great corporations for a greater share of the product of industry for the workers, in the form of higher and higher wages, shorter working hours, longer paid holidays, and social security concessions, is a socialist derivative. In America, as in Europe, a more or less hypocritical lip-service has been paid to the dogma of 'competition' by means of anti-Trust legislation ('hypocritical' because the monopolistic trend of capitalism can no more be stopped, though it can be hampered, than the tide could be stopped by King Canute).

From all of this emerges a picture which is surprising only because we have been confused by the loud shouting of slogans by the dogmatists in both camps—that of corporation capitalism (imperialism) and that of state monopoly capitalism (communism). The cheerleaders on both sides do their damnedest to persuade us that the theories behind their respective dogmas are really put into practice in their respective territories. The truth is otherwise: considerable though the differences between the two social-economic systems still remain, notably in the measure of freedom of thought, speech and the press, the mutual hostility which still separates them is that of two powers struggling for supreme dominion, and not really of two conflicting ideologies, and that reality is less and less effectively masked by the use of ideological rationalization and justification. For the time being, and for historical and economic rather than ideological reasons, workers under corporation capitalism have more freedom than workers under state monopoly capitalism. But this will be corrected as the two systems continue to converge towards a common and universal system of rule by bureaucracy.

For, manifestly, the managerial society of the West is becoming the mirror-image of the bureaucratic society in the communist commonwealths. Take the managerial revolution (which makes the corporation bureaucrats masters of industry), plus the trend to monopoly, plus the increasingly wide adoption of socialist-style planning and welfare, in the West, and take, in the communist commonwealths, measures of relaxation of the rules to introduce capitalist-style incentives, rising productivity with its promise of private affluence, and the two systems will become, in all but name, identical.

Excluding, for the moment, any consideration of what is called the Third World, it would seem that in the foreseeable future the peoples of the Atlantic world and of Japan and those of the communist commonwealths will be living in super-States run on scientific socialist lines by managers/bureaucrats composing an anonymous and 'faceless' élite. Their industrial productivity will be so high, and obtained, thanks to automation, at the cost of so little labour, that they will be able to afford the workers standards of living and of working conditions such that the question whether or not they are actually receiving a fair share of the surplus produced by work will be forgotten, will be irrelevant. They probably will be, provided the bureaucracy does its work of allotting the right proportion of wealth for investment and for mankind's new adventures with a rational regard for expedient priorities.

The achievement of this state is, however, contingent on two conditions being fulfilled: success in checking population growth and stabilizing world population at a manageable level, and success in economizing in the use of natural resources and energy so as entirely to eliminate waste. Some say that these conditions can be fulfilled, others that they cannot, and no man yet knows who is right.

Supposing that the optimists are correct and that the state of affairs which I have described comes to pass: will that constitute the Millennium, will it be the realization of the socialist vision? It will not, of course. For the socialist vision honoured the humanities, and in the triumph of the socialist *method* under the corporation and state monopoly capitalist systems, men will have been sacrificed to Man, people to Mankind. I shall return to that prospect.

The Third World is a term coined to describe all those countries which are called 'emergent' in order to avoid the offensive but more accurate term 'backward', and which are not clearly committed to either the state monopoly capitalist or the imperialist doctrine. Most of them are in receipt of technical and financial aid from one or both sides. Some of them are successor states of the old European empires overseas; others, while never actually colonies of any empire, were and are exploited by capitalist imperialism.

In all the Asian and African cases, excepting those of South East Asia where states are either under communist government or where the communist and 'bourgeois' forces are at war over control of the country, the 'bourgeois' side receiving United States aid and the communist side either Chinese or Soviet Russian aid, the governments are, whether parliamentary as in India, or in the hands of military dictators as in Uganda, 'bourgeois' with a greater or lesser measure of economic socialism. In a sense, the nationalism of such administrations forces a measure of socialism on them: for example, if nationalism demands the expropriation or partial expropriation of Western capitalist concessionaires working natural resources such as oil or timber or metal ores, there is no native capitalist establishment capable of handling the work, and the government is obliged to assume the ownership of the property on behalf of the State. In some African countries the entire bourgeoisie has been expropriated and banished not because the government is socialist but because the bourgeoisie is of an alien race (Uganda is a case in point). But, in such cases, since there are no native industrial technologists or administrators capable of working the property, these states are usually forced to depend on technical aid and skilled manpower from either the Western or the communist imperialists and are, accordingly 'neo-colonialist'.

It is very likely indeed that nearly all the States in question—successor States of Asia and Africa—will become state monopoly capitalist bureaucracies. In the first place, the fact that there exists in only a few of them a native capitalist complex leaves a vacuum which only the State can fill. In the second place, since the whole evolution of industrial economy is towards monopolism, to go back and start at the 'pure' capitalist stage would be retrogressive and, as it were, against the tide. In the third place, in all these countries there are socialist parties, in some cases militant, in other gradualists, winning an increasing following. In many of these cases the parties in question are of the New Left, and it is theoretically possible to hope that they might be able to steer their countries away from both capitalisms to find appropriate native libertarian socialist solutions. But for the reasons which will be found in Chapter Nineteen, I believe that this hope is illusory. In the Third World, as in the two great blocks, the trend is towards the establishment of bureaucratic administration of the economy of the kind which confers political power on that bureaucracy. The wars being waged at the time of writing against 'imperialism' in Indo-China and Portuguese Africa (by the Viet-Cong and by Frelimo and the MPLA respectively), the war of the same kind which ZAPU and ZANU and other revolutionary groups are trying to wage in South Africa and Rhodesia, the sporadic guerrilla war, again of the same kind, being waged in all the Latin American republics excepting Cuba where communism is established and Chile which had a Social-Democratic government, which was overthrown by the bourgeoisie in arms, and the cold war of the East European peoples against the other 'imperialism'—all these are actually or potentially people's wars, are ideologically libertarian in spirit and purpose. Could victory in any one of them lead to the installation of a libertarian socialist society? It is depressingly difficult to believe that it could.

SEVENTEEN

The Vision Resurgent

The failure of the communist parties in power and the Social-Democratic parties in parliaments to accomplish the socialism of the great vision, the noble vision of a just and democratic society, and a number of new terms in the social equation to be solved, have together given rise to a world-wide movement called the New Left. It has many and diverse elements: in the so-called Third World it is possessed by the idea that the revolutionary poor peasants must, as they did in China, bring the Marxist-Leninist revolution to the cities, but keep their evolution completely democratic and anti-bureaucratic; in the world of the two imperialisms, it is libertarian socialist, often anarcho-communist, seeing little to choose between corporation monopolist capitalist imperialism and state monopoly capitalist imperialism. But everywhere and at all levels the men and women of the New Left share one thing in common: a resurgent vision of the just society.

The new terms of the equation which must be taken into account are, broadly, as follows: the threat to the human environment produced by the swift progress and enormous growth of industry has made it impossible to look forward to industrial expansion under control of the workers as a means of universal enrichment; it is no longer a matter of replacing capitalism by socialism, but of bridling materialism itself. Moreover, it is not merely a question of revolting against material squalor, against the fouling of land, air and water; there is a moral pollution, the subtler squalor incident to the state of mind of the acquisitive consumer society, of demoralization by vulgarity.

Marxism, like capitalism, unconsciously assumed that the earth's raw material and energy sources were, for all practical purposes, inexhaustible: all it had to accomplish was control of those sources by the class which, by its labour, turned them into useful artefacts. We know better now—raw material and energy sources are exhaustible and some of them are probably not far from being exhausted. So there is a new reason, an urgent one, for establishing socialist economic planning. Add one more factor, the dangerously high rate of rise in world population, and it becomes clear that equitable distribution of wealth must entail a very considerable reduction in consumption by the rich nations. A triumphant socialism would not have the pleasant task of sharing out riches justly, but the unpleasant one of sharply checking wasteful consumption and sharing out necessities justly.

Thus the New Left visionary regards both imperialisms, capitalist and communist, not only as enemies of the workers because both exploit and oppress them, but enemies of the human race on earth, whose military-industrial complexes ruin the quality of life and irresponsibly waste irreplaceable resources. A distinction is made—the sins in this field of corporation imperialism are far greater than those of communist imperialism, but for how long will that be so? The state monopoly capitalists who call themselves communists aspire to make theirs, too, an acquisitive, consumer society.

On the lunatic fringes of the New Left are the votaries of the Counter culture or Alternative Society—the Hippies, the Flower Children, the *communards* among the Student Power quietists, the Dropouts. Eremitical, monasticist or nomadic, the Alternativists preach salvation by love; and the use of hallucinogenic drugs to enlarge the spirit from the body. Their 'Alternative' is without form and void. It is, as I have said elsewhere, no new thing. In economic, social or demographic crises of every great society in history, some men have escaped the stress by turning in upon themselves or outward to some god or other. There have been ancient Chinese and Japanese, Hindu, Zoroastrian, Buddhist, Jewish, Moslem and Christian Alternativists; no doubt ancient Egypt had them. A few Alternativists have been saints, but none that I ever heard of have been economists. If the European monastic movement saved something of the past for the future, it did so under stern discipline and the rule of a hierarchy. Our business is not with mystics, real or bogus, but with practical men.

It will be as well to discover how the practical socialists of the

New Left propose to give substance to their vision of a just society.

By and large they are Marxist-Leninists: the means of production must become public property and their use be scientifically planned, and the product must be shared equally by all. But also, the whole economy and all political activity whatsoever must be managed democratically; the representative and bureaucratic roles and the role of the executive must be reduced to a minimum and rigorously controlled by the workers, the producers of wealth, *directly,* for representative assemblies cannot be democratic. Thus the New Socialists follow Marx in his *Critique of Hegel's Philosophy of the State,* and Lenin in his writings on Cultural Revolution and so many of the works of his last three years. They identify parliamentary democracy as a dangerous fraud, and bureaucracy as the arch-enemy of the good.

Some have been led into an anarcho-communist position and, like Kropotkin, seek to dispense with the State entirely. Some have come to a virtually Proudhonian solution and see society as a fabric of agricultural and industrial communes run by the workers through their trades unions and similar organizations. Others allow a State apparatus to be necessary but insist that it should be operated by the workers themselves and not by paid bureaucrats, excepting at a very low level; for bureaucrats cannot but treat men as the objects instead of the subjects of history.

The particular attitude of African socialists of the New Left, both in Africa and America, has been modified, and some would say deformed, by their reaction to white racialism. For a great many of them the Marxist 'bourgeois' means white, and the Marxist 'proletariat' means black. There is, of course, good reason for this: in America colour bar and denial of civil rights, in Africa dominion of the 'colonist' over the 'native', of the master-race over the servile race, have, until very recently, 'proletarianized' the majority of the black and brown peoples of the world. Thus, for the black New Leftist, the class war and the race war tend to be one and the same; or a concession to a better sense is made by claiming that the blacks must be the spearhead of the revolutionary working class if only because they are 'ultra-exploited'. Wiser black revolutionaries have seen the problem more rationally: a glance at the work of one of them, Frantz Fanon, will be in place here.

A Black Martiniquian born in 1925, Fanon took a medical degree at Lyons University and then fought against the Nazis in World War Two, under De Lattre de Tassigny. In 1952 he was working as staff psychiatrist in the Blida Hospital, Algeria, where among his patients were men whose minds had broken down as a result of having been tortured by French officers, and men whose minds had broken under the strain of inflicting the tortures. He concluded that the real cause of the trouble lay not in the men but in the colonial system, in colonialism, in that imperialism which, alienating man from man, the worker from his society, the citizen from his State, produces intolerable strains. He therefore espoused the Algerian cause in the struggle to shake off the French yoke, and became a violent anti-French militant. In 1960 Fanon, realizing that he was suffering from leukaemia and had not long to live, sat down to get his ideas onto paper before he died. The book he wrote—not his first but by far his most important—is called *The Wretched of the Earth*. In it he sees the whole world as a pyramid of exploitation: at the top are the imperialists and at the very bottom not the industrial working class, but the poor peasants who, therefore, must be the revolutionary class since they alone have 'nothing to lose but their chains'. In short, let the peoples of Africa, Asia and Latin America rise and destroy imperialism, economic, military, colonialist or neo-colonialist. The justification for this violence is that violence is used against them, the violence of miserable poverty, starvation, disease and illiteracy. As a psychiatrist, Fanon found in such just violence another justification: that, and only that, could cure the apathy of despair and restore self-respect to people who had been deprived of it.

This promotion of the Third World poor peasant to the honourable place of the proletariat, heirs to the earth and the fulness thereof in the old Marxism, is typical of the New Left and has two very obvious justifications. Most of the Third World countries, the countries of New Left militancy, have very small proletariats with Communist Parties bound hand and foot by the dogma that only the proletariat can make a socialist revolution; and large populations of miserably poor and oppressed peasants.

Secondly, the industrial workers in the advanced industrial countries, the imperialist countries, having been conceded wages and conditions which to the poor of the Third World represent fabulous wealth, those workers are identified with their national bourgeoisies and are therefore accessories to the crime of imperialist exploitation.

Like Fanon, Nelson Mandela, of the originally reformist African National Congress, was driven to the advocacy and use of violence by the imperialists' use of violence—specifically, the Sharpeville Massacre of peaceful demonstrators by the South African police in 1960. He was a founder and active leader of the *Umkhonto we sizwe* (Spear of the nation), the militant wing of the ANC responsible for numerous acts of sabotage against government installations and establishments. How was this gentle and intelligent lawyer brought to such a pass? At his Rivonia Trial in 1963 he said that, after the long and patient trial of peaceful means which was a matter of history, the South African blacks were faced by two alternatives: acquiescence in a permanent and hopeless condition of subservience, or recourse to violence. 'I have cherished the ideal of a free and democratic society in which all persons live together in harmony. It is an ideal which I hope to live for and to achieve. But if need be it is an ideal for which I am prepared to die.'

Transfer of political power from a white to a black bourgeoisie, of economic power from white to black capitalists, is no longer enough: for such thinkers have realized that the exploitation of man by man must go, that an exploiter is still an exploiter though his skin be black.

Amilcar Cabral, born in the Cape Verde Islands in 1921, an agronomist by profession, was one of the founders of PAIGG (African Independence Party of Guinea and Cape Verde). He saw the peasants and black petty burgesses of Portuguese Africa, rather than the proletariat, as the effective revolutionary socialist force. And he has been vindicated: the Popular Front for the Liberation of Angola now controls about one third of that province while Frelimo, the Mozambique Liberation Front, originally led by Eduardo Mondlane who was killed in action in 1968, pins down sixty thousand Portuguese troops with only twelve thousand rebels and controls about a quarter of the colony. Much the same kind of success was achieved by Cabral and his men in Guinea. Agostino Neto and Spartacus Monimambu, the leaders in Mozambique, published as their aim not simply the defeat of the Portuguese imperialists, but 'the basic transformation of society'. A vague formula, but Cabral made himself clearer: 'If we wage this war just to drive out the Portuguese, the struggle is not worth it. We fight for that, yes ... *But also that no man shall ever again be able to exploit any other man, black or white ...*'

It is the New Left creed in eighteen words. Don't shrug it off; they are doing more and better than we are.

The New Left socialists have, of course, no more use for USSR communism, stigmatized by Daniel Cohn-Bendit, leader of the May Revolution in Paris (1968), as 'Stalinist filth', than for the other and more obvious imperialism. They may look to the Chinese revolution if only because it was made by peasants, albeit suspicious of the bureaucracy's power in the Chinese Communist Party. They are Maoist, but only so long as it is the Maoism of the Cultural Revolution. They look, too, to the Cuban revolution and, although his image begins to pale and his myth to sound distant, to the New Left proto-martyr, Ché Guevara (ché means 'chum' or 'mate' in colloquial Italian).

This Argentine aristocrat who turned physician in the hope of understanding his own asthma only to find himself more interested in the disease of the most wretched of mankind, leprosy, was brought up by a clever, liberal mother, Celia de la Serna, on an intellectual diet which included Marx, Engels and Freud, in a household where the demagogue Peron was despised and the antics of his regime deplored, and which was frequented by refugee socialists from Franco's Spain. He early learned an equal contempt for the brutal ineptitudes of military politicians and the fraudulent hypocrisy of parliamentary democracy, and something more than contempt—passionate hatred is more like it—for United States' imperialism in Latin America, with its support of corrupt oligarchies and its exploitation of cheap native labour. As a student with his finals still before him he travelled, chiefly by bicycle, all over his country and beyond, meeting Salvador Allende, the man who was to give Chile a Social-Democratic government,* visiting Venezuela, Florida and Colombia when guerrilla bands were plunging that country into the revolutionary turmoil called *La Violencia*. It was doubtless during those journeys (1949-51) that he concluded that he had been studying a disease even more worthy than leprosy of engaging a dedicated healer's attention—the terrible and hopeless poverty of the people whom Fanon was describing as the wretched of the earth and identifying as its potential revolutionaries.

Qualified in medicine and specializing in dermatology, Guevara found himself too involved in plans to cure the ultimate disease, exploited misery, to stick to his medical work. He was in Bolivia to watch the abortive attempt to shake off the imperialist yoke, and dismissed it as 'opportunist'. He was in Guatemala during the Presidency of the socialist Arbenz; but he had been reading Lenin, he knew a sterile party bureaucracy when he saw one and lost a valuable and important medical appointment by refusing to join the Communist Party. He saw CIA agents at work to break Arbenz and his party, learned that the poor must emulate the rich and take to violence, took refuge in Mexico when the American-backed counter-revolution succeeded, and there met two Cuban political exiles, Raul and Fidel Castro. In Fidel he recognized the man Latin America needed, a dedicated revolutionary leader. He had already found the right man to train himself and his brother and their handful of friends in guerrilla warfare, Alberto Bayo, an exiled officer of the Spanish Republican army and author of *Ciento-cincuenta Preguntas a un Guerrillero* in which he had drawn on the teachings of Mao Tse-tung. Bayo found his most brilliant pupil in Ché.

There is no need to repeat here the history of the Cuban revolution: the point is that it was won by peasants, the pattern was the same as the Chinese, the Vietnamese and the Algerian. In charge of the Cuban economy after their revolution, Ché ignored the advice of Soviet economists and 'socialized' it without compromise. The Cuban cash-crop which put her economy at the mercy of the United States was sugar, so Ché began a programme of crop diversification and sold the sugar to the USSR. Out of one imperialism into the other; the fact is that he and Castro could

* His government was overthrown and Allende murdered by a military *junta* in 1973.

not quickly extract the Cuban people from the exploitation trap. But at least they, and especially Ché, had no illusions—it was not the old pattern of communist bureaucratic rule he wanted. The text of his 'Socialism and Man in Cuba' (*Marcha*, 12 March 1965), was this: 'Man only attains the state of complete humanity when he produces without being forced to sell himself as a commodity.' In his speeches in various parts of the New Left world he attacked the USSR as well as the USA as squalidly imperialist.

It was at least as much for his vision of an end for ever to the exploitation of man by man and of a society run on goodwill by its workers and not on law backed by force, as for his flamboyantly romantic way of making revolution, that he became an object of a New Left cult and the supreme martyr of the new socialism.

Thus it was with Ché's vision of a new and libertarian socialism before their eyes and his assurance that you do not have to sit, like the Communist Party, waiting for a 'revolutionary situation' but can make one by provoking insurrection, ringing in their ears, that young men like the Peruvian poet Javier Heraud and his comrades Hugo Blanco Galdos and Luis de la Puente died fighting the infamous thing. It was because he, too, saw that vision and heard those words that the Moroccan El Mehdi Ben Barka was murdered by the Moroccan police with the help of their French colleagues. The same vision of a just society, albeit clouded by racialism, inspired Eldridge Cleaver's *Soul on Ice* and inspires the Sozialistischer Deutscher Studentbund and French, British, American student socialism. The same vision, of a society in which men would not have to sacrifice freedom and self-respect as individuals to material well-being gave spirit and courage of the highest order to Marquetalia, the little anarcho-communist peasant republic founded by the writer Jacobo Frias Alape, *nom de guerre* Charro Negro, and Pedro Marin, in Colombia, that spirit and courage which required sixteen thousand regular troops provided with American aircraft and tanks to overcome.*

The same noble vision was the inspiration of Régis Debray's *Revolution in the Revolution* (1966) in which, for the first time in print, Moscow communism was identified as that state mono-

* Marquetalia was wiped out, with CIA help, in 1963-64.

poly capitalism which Lenin had shown to be the product of socialist revolution without democracy. It is the Grail sought by such French Maoists as Alain Geismar. It moved Yon Sosa and Turcios Lima to wage war on the American puppet governments of Guatemala after the CIA had destroyed Arbenz.

Perhaps it is not too much to claim that a very similar libertarian vision roused the communist Imre Nagy and the Hungarian people to revolution in 1959, and possessed Dubcek and other leading communists nine years later in their attempt, swiftly crushed by Soviet imperialism, to establish socialism in Czechoslovakia. Dubcek's purpose was, in his own words, to give communism 'a human face'—the bureaucracy, it will be recalled is faceless. Risings against the USSR communism are interpreted in the West as pro-capitalist; in fact they are libertarian-socialist when they are not simply undirected revolts against bureaucratic tyranny.

It was the power of the vision of a just society, no doubt, which led Rohan Wijeweera and the *guerrilleros* of his Janatha Vimukthi Peramina in their hopeless attack on the squalid government of Ceylon in 1966. For, like the vision of the proto-socialists, the vision of the New Socialism is world-wide. Men everywhere aspire to a measure of seemliness in their daily lives, achieved without the sacrifice of freedom which the state monopoly capitalist demands, or the sacrifice of self-respect demanded by the corporation capitalists. It is doubtless very odd but certainly very true that they believe that there must be a viable economic and political system which is neither comfortable wage-slavery nor comfortable prostitution.

The New Left, then, is internationalist, despises frontiers, patriotism—wasn't it that sensible man Samuel Johnson who called patriotism the last refuge of a scoundrel?—flags and chauvinistic religions. Its leaders have called for Afro–Asian–Latin-American revolution: to accomplish which Guevara and Castro held the tricontinental congress in Havana, to found OLAS, the Latin American Solidarity Organization to co-ordinate the activities of all the Latin American New Left militants. North American, Asian and African groups were affiliated to it in OSPAAAL, the Organization of Solidarity of the Peoples of Africa, Asia and Latin America.

There are New Left 'guerrillas' inside the factories in most of the advanced industrial countries. The League of Black Revolutionary Workers, founded by the barrister Ken Cockerel and the automobile fitter John Watson, made a film, *Finally got the News*, of their own operations in the US automobile industry; it was shown to sympathetic and similar but white groups as far away as Italy. The League is Marxist-Leninist, advocates co-operation with like-minded white organizations and gives its objective as '... A society free from all oppression, whether racial, sexual, class or nationalist, based on the principle "to each according to his needs".'

The broad and general doctrine of the New Left everywhere, for the 'alienated' even within the two great imperialisms regard themselves as a part of the Third World, was originally put into words by the Chinese communist leader Lin Pao, who was killed in an aeroplane crash when escaping from China after being implicated in a plot to overthrow Mao Tse-tung:

> The countryside and only the countryside can provide the revolutionary base from which the revolution can go forward to final victory. Taking the entire globe, if North America and Western Europe be called the cities of the world, then Asia, Africa and Latin America constitute the countryside ...*

The real New Left socialist would add the USSR to the 'cities', and would regard the slums of towns from which urban guerrillas operate as part of the 'countryside'. These 'countryside' and 'peasant' themes can no longer be taken too literally. Movements wholly in the spirit of the New Left, like the Jordanian–Palestinian Popular Democratic Front, the Puerto Rican Armed Commandos of the Liberation, the Uruguayan Tupamaros and the Argentinian Montoneros have operated chiefly in cities if only because the right 'targets' are to be found there.

In some cases rural guerrilla movements have expanded to take in the town and deal with specifically urban problems: the 'Chicano' (Mexican–American) Tierra y Libertad is a case in point. For them, as for the Negroes of some of the Black Power movements, for example, the Black Panthers, the imperialist ex-

* *People's Daily*, Peking, September 1963.

ploiter is very easily identified, for he is any white American. Rural-based, the Chicago movement invaded the cities of the south-western States, organized Chicano boycotts of 'Anglo' businesses, setting up exclusively Chicano co-operative enterprises and dealing out 'revolutionary justice' to collaborationists, that is Chicanos continuing to work within the 'Anglo' rules and accepting Chicano subservience.

Although the New Left is most closely associated with the Third World, at least at the level of militancy and violence, most revolutionary libertarian socialists, living and working inside imperialist territory and being both anti-capitalist and anti-communist, identify with the New Left and some take Herbert Marcuse, Professor of Philosophy at Brandeis University, with his theory of the alienation of modern American-style man from his society, as their prophet. In Britain and most of Europe very few of these new socialist groups have made use of violence and those that have done so, like the German anarchists and the United States' Weathermen, have come off badly in their war with the police. The violent Weathermen group, composed chiefly, like the Tupamaros, of middle-class young men and women of good education, emerged as the militant faction of the forty-thousand-strong 'Students for a Democratic Society'. They, and the students of the May revolution in Paris in 1968, made a cult figure of Ché Guevara and were with the Third World New Left against both the great imperialisms.

Enough has been said to establish that the younger generation, for whom the libertarian socialist vision is resurgent, has clearly learned the bitter lesson implicit in the failure of Social-Democratic parties to accomplish socialism and in the catastrophe of the Russian Revolution betrayed by the bureaucracy. These lessons have taught these new socialists that not even the economic part of the Marxist programme can be achieved by parliamentary means; that economic imperialism cannot be wiped out and socialism accomplished merely by socialization of the means of production; that the greatest obstacle to that achievement is the rise of a party bureaucracy, and that direct democracy is a *sine qua non* of socialism.

The remaining question is what, if anything, they can do with this knowledge.

EIGHTEEN

A Possible World?

After some seconds of silence they saw a kind of fog rising dramatically above the city, at a distance of about three kilometres, beyond the river in the richest quarter. A moment later the sound of the explosion reached them, and a great tree of smoke grew and climbed towards the clear sky. Then little by little the air round them became alive with an inarticulate humming sound; it was the clamour of many thousands of voices. And they heard loud cries from quite close, coming from the square:

'What was that explosion?'

Great was the amazement, for although such catastrophes were now frequent, an explosion of such violence had never been seen and it was clear to all that this was something new.

People were trying to locate the disaster; quarters of the city, streets, particular buildings, clubs, theatre, shops, all were suggested. Topographical information became more exact, the location was fixed:

'It's the Steel Trust that's been blown up.'

Clair returned his watch to his pocket.

Caroline looked at him attentively and her eyes filled with astonishment and then she whispered:

'You knew it? You were expecting it? ... It was you who ...?'

Very calmly he answered her:

'This city must perish.'

And softly, thoughtfully, she rejoined, 'I think so too.'

The reader should have little difficulty in identifying this passage from the last chapter of Anatole France's *Penguin Island*. The book was published in 1908, by which time men like France could see that the society created by imperialist capitalism was becoming intolerable. Clair and Caroline are, clearly, dedicated

New Leftists. Let us, for a few minutes, assume that the impossible has happened, that the New Left all over the world has grown in strength and ruthlessness, that black, white and brown men have joined hands across oceans and frontiers to *écraser l'infame*; that by strikes and sabotage and some measures of violence both corporation and state imperialism have been overthrown and the way cleared for the installation of a world-wide society designed to realize the millenary vision of pure socialism. A brief indulgence in fantasy will do no harm.

With the history of the first seven decades of the 20th century before them, the socialist designers have two priorities in mind: all power to the people themselves; no power for the bureaucracy. Is it possible to imagine a modern, industrial society *which is also free?* It is, at all events, amusing to try.

First, with all the natural resources of the earth and all the means of production owned by mankind collectively, and with all economic and political frontiers abolished, political nationalism and nationality disappear and with them the armies, navies and air forces, with a resultant colossal saving in resources.

The basis of the political fabric of the bad old world had been geographical: a nation was, above all, a certain piece of territory. But also, for example, in Britain, parliamentary constituencies were residential, that is to say were geographical neighbourhoods. The reason was that the franchise was originally based on property in real estate. But the 'franchise' is now to be based on the workers, on society's producers of wealth, on being a worker, not on being a landowner: so the warp of the political fabric becomes industry. As for the concept 'nation', it has, for economic and political purposes, been scrapped as pernicious.*

The 'constituency', then, now becomes 'industrial' and every

* There is not and never need be any reason why the pleasing diversity of culture and custom associated with nationality should disappear with economic and political nationalism. The idea of a single 'global' culture belongs to the last phase of all great societies (*cf.* the Hellenization of all Europe, West Asia and North Africa under the Romans). Hitherto mankind has been saved from this sterile universalism by the destruction of great empires by barbarians. The New Left will have to be our barbarians: for the idea of a global culture is as absurd and repulsive an anomaly as economic and political nationalism are absurdly and repulsively archaic. Their defenders, the chauvinist minority in all

industry is to be run by the workers themselves. The trade union becomes the management; but the trade union is composed of and is run democratically by the workers, all of whom have a duty to be fully involved. Here, harking back to an earlier chapter of this book, we are borrowing from the syndicalists.

If the workers are to manage their own industries democratically in this way, surely they will waste a great deal of time which should be devoted to production? First, it is as much every man's business to involve himself in the management of society, i.e. of the economy and social policy of the community, as to do his share of productive labour. There is, in any case, another consideration : it has lately become clear that the problem of modern industry is redundancy of workers and that the great social problem a few years from now will be not that of employment but that of leisure. Working days will become shorter and shorter and the hours of idleness will, to many men and women, be intolerably tedious. Now note this : in the conditions briefly sketched above, this problem would solve itself. For, in any really democratic socialist society, every worker, whether with hand or brain must have three jobs to do : (*i*) production; (*ii*) the management of his trade union which is now, also, the management of his industry; (*iii*) a certain amount of public service, for example, policing duty, attendance at the law-making Assembly of the People, service on co-ordinating committees, etc.

The management of his union by the worker would entail hearing and studying the plans, projects, and business arrangements suggested by the professional organizers of the work, debating them, and voting on them. It will be objected at once that this way of running industry would be intolerably slow, laborious and inefficient. It would probably not work out nearly as badly

nations, have tried to frighten us with the idea that, with those troublesome and dangerous anachronisms will vanish national language, literature, art forms and terms, customs and ways of life. There is a very real danger of that happening under imperialist capitalism, corporation or state, because conformity of behaviour is essential to the maintenance of discipline by the bureaucracy and standardization of the product essential to the making of large profits. But, as we shall see, the millenary socialist is prepared to sacrifice a measure of order, and part of the GNP, in the name of freedom and a decent way of life.

as those with an interest at stake pretend; but let it be so. The libertarian, democratic socialist is not trying, as the capitalist must be, constantly to force up consumption and then drive the productive machine faster and faster to supply the demand. His object is to design a society of free men, self-respecting men, men to whom no man can give orders, men who know that the earth is their own. In short, a genuine democracy of equals. Some sacrifice of production, a considerable reduction of the level of consumption (desirable in any case on purely economic grounds) are well worth tolerating for such a cause.

In that same cause other sacrifices of a measure of efficiency (which in any case tends to turn men into machines), would become necessary. Direct democracy cannot work in bodies of men above a certain order of magnitude, even if we make use of advanced systems of electronic intercommunication to enlarge our senses. Probably nobody knows what the maximum number at which real mutual understanding and effective co-operation is possible should be but I believe that we have a fair guide here in the case of ancient Athens. During the lifetime of, for example, Pericles and Themistocles, the citizen roll numbered seventy thousand, all of whom were entitled to attend the law-making, policy-making, decision-taking Assembly of the People. This Assembly *was* the government of the city; there was no formal executive and men like Pericles or Themistocles were simply citizens whose talents and whose eloquence in debate persuaded their fellow citizens to follow the courses they suggested, vote for the Bills they introduced. As Dr A. R. Burn puts it, they had influence but not power. Would not such an Assembly be at the mercy of demagogues? One can only point to the fact that the Athenian Assembly did support the leadership of Pericles, one of the ablest and most upright of statesmen in all history, throughout his career and often against strong opposition, although he was, on one occasion, forced to plead with tears for his mistress, Aspasia, on trial on a trumped-up, politically motivated charge of impiety. And even Cleon was not such an unscrupulous ruffian as Aristophanes would have us believe, nor Demos such a clownish fool as that arch-Tory made him out to be.

If, then, we take a group of seventy thousand, for argument's sake, as workable by direct democracy, then obviously the govern-

ment of the industrial socialist democracy cannot be on an in-
dustry-wide level or even on the old national level—it will have
to be at plant level. One can envisage each industry as a federation
of self-governing plants closely linked by co-ordinating committees of experienced workers who might, perhaps, be men over
fifty, the industry's 'elders', chaired by professional industrial
organizers. So, more work for those short-day workers: clearly
redundancy will not be a problem. What must at all costs
(literally at all costs) be avoided—it cannot be repeated too often
—is the rise of a bureaucracy which, by taking the real responsibility and the real power of decision from the workers, leaves
them with nothing to do but wield a rubber stamp. That is what
happened to the Soviets and prevented the introduction of
socialism into the USSR: in theory the workers' councils (factory
Soviets) were supposed to play an important part in the management of their plant, in practice they carried out the party bureaucracy's orders.

The system envisaged would be laborious, clumsy and inefficient. We accept that, though with reservations (it may work
better than we imagine). The point is the gain in freedom, self-
respect and responsibility for the workers. What we are after here
is a more human and humane life for all men, not consumption for
consumption's sake.

The co-ordination of each industry, each federation of self-
governing plants, would be world-wide. Here, the great international industrial corporations and the organization of international consortia have shown the way.* The links would consist
of committees of workers steered and chaired by professional
administrators who would be, to the committee, what a magis-
trate's clerk is to a bench of magistrates, that is, without responsibility—that remains the privilege of the workers themselves. Such
committees would be ignorant, obstructive and contentious.
Good: again I emphasize that the socialist humanist is interested
primarily in making a society to fit people, not forcing people to
fit a society designed to produce and consume as much as possible.
Let it be said yet again: if economic inefficiency (short of real
economic disaster, of course) is the price to be paid for keeping

* So, of course, have some other and older supra-national institutions,
for example, the Roman Catholic Church.

the concept *men* above the concept Man, and the concept *people* above the concept Mankind, let us pay it willingly. And I also repeat that Aristophanes notwithstanding, Demos is not a bloody fool: given our world-wide federated industries using sophisticated methods and equipment, effective planning of production, to provide for need and avoid waste, should be possible.

No industry is an island. The world's producing and distributing industries would have to be linked by co-ordinating agencies composed of professional steering-committees of workers—very suitable work for men between the age of retirement from the productive part of their labour, say fifty-five, and the age of full retirement, say sixty-five. In other words, the last decade of the worker's working life would be given over to industrial government. So it would be 'conservative' and cautious? Again, good; we have here a nice balance, for there would be plenty of pressure from the young men serving on the administrative and planning boards of the industries.

What about pay? In millenary socialist theory equality of reward is axiomatic. It would be damaging to any democratic socialist society not to make equality of income an important aim, and almost equally so to begin with it, for that would necessitate sacrifices on the part of higher-paid workers, especially the brain-workers, which it would be foolish to expect even at the dawn of a golden age and in the initial euphoria of being allowed to be virtuous and generous without being ruined.

The GWP (Gross World Product) being known—for the barriers of childish secrecy are down and a sensible candour is the mood, and we are using sophisticated computing gear—then so is the level of possible consumption. And in some respects, despite the inefficiencies incident to ensuring that the management of society is democratic, we find ourselves much richer than we used to be: we are no longer paying out about twenty or thirty per cent of the GWP on armies and armaments; we are rid of the burden of interest paid to moneylenders at a rate grossly in excess of the proper rate for the job of managing credit. It is probable that we shall make the happy discovery that it is possible, by endowing every human being from birth with a fair share of the GWP, to provide (in the form of money pay or payment in kind whichever is appropriate) all men with a decent basic minimum in housing, food, clothing, medical care, education and recreation. Either this is true, in which case from the socialist point of view it should be done, or it is not true, in which case the socialist demands that we make it so by a planned and deliberate industrial shift in favour of mankind's real necessities and by planned stabilization of world population by making it socially disgraceful for any couple to have more than two children.

For, even in this vitally important matter of population control, we cannot, if we are not to damage the integrity of our own respect for freedom and for democracy, afford to use force, for example, economic sanctions, against those persons who are irresponsible only in their unthinking obedience to natural instincts not directly and obviously harmful to their fellow men; and we are therefore left with only two means, education and social disapproval. It has been objected by very respectable libertarian philosophers, among them George Orwell, that the use of social disapproval against those who demand absolute freedom and who reject even the gentlest of necessary rules, produces in the society an intolerable and perhaps dangerous holier-than-thou attitude which breeds a socially undesirable hypocrisy. All one can say of this is that the consequences of oppression are far worse; that the good results we know we can get from an adequate expenditure of resources on both pre-school and school education, something which has not yet been tried,* should reduce the incidence of social irresponsibility in free societies; and that Orwell and others probably had in mind the evil consequences of the holier-than-thou attitude among 'patriots' in post-revolutionary France and among the 'saints' in the theocracy of the New England colonies rather earlier, both cases in which a rising bourgeoisie was using every means, fair or foul, to establish its dominion.

It is permissible to believe that it would be possible, then, to fix a basic 'dividend' (the word 'wage' is avoided because of its exploiter–exploited association) which would represent a decent, human standard of living for all men. Remember, when doing

* The (British) Plowden Report called for the allocation of £16m. on the pre-school education of 'deprived' children. The sum allocated was £4m., and this in one of the world's richest countries. In the world's richest country the situation is even worse.

your critical mental arithmetic, that, under the present dispensation, such resources as oil which should have enriched the peoples of the Middle East and North Africa are squandered on air forces and armies; the, as it were, tax levied on the world's resources by the military will have been remitted.* If all the material and labour wasted in military expenditure were shifted to food-growing and constructive work, we might have every human being alive fed, clad and housed to a decent human standard, an object which would be given first priority all the more easily in that wasteful production, for example, in the manufacture of a gross excess of motor-cars and domestic machines—a car or a refrigerator should be good for at least twenty years' service before scrapping—would also be eliminated.

All very fine and large, but surely Orwell disposed of such pretty illusions about socialism decades ago? Have I never read *Animal Farm?* I have indeed, several times. Orwell was not, if one accepts Lenin's definition, writing about socialism, for I have identified the pigs as the bureaucrats. *Where there is a bureaucracy with effective power there is no socialism.* And we are here taking very great pains, and if really necessary sacrificing a measure of the GWP, to prevent the pigs from getting the kind of power which makes the realization of the millenary vision impossible.

We now have every man, woman and child in receipt of a basic minimum income from birth to death in return for a basic minimum contribution of work in school, university or polytechnic, field or workshop or office, and in public service. In the new beginning we should, of course, have to make payment above the basic and universal share of the GWP for the higher orders of skill and higher ranges of responsibility; and it would be desirable as well as necessary to build houses and manufacture goods to meet the noble human demand for diversity and beauty; let us with good heart sacrifice, where we must, the shibboleth efficiency for freedom and democracy. But it would be madness to sacrifice the consolation of seemliness and beauty in the objects of daily use to instant egalitarianism, for few things are more depressing and therefore socially demoralizing and therefore inimical to our purpose, than drab uniformity. It is not only pleasanter and more

* The total saved is not calculable exactly but it can hardly be less than 25 per cent of the GWP.

stimulating to have beautiful and well-made articles of daily use; it is also much more satisfying to be making them than to be making ugly and shoddy ones. Man is a maker or he is an animal, and perish the thought that a socialist society should ever make the kind of rubbish churned out by *Lumpenkapital* because, and only because, in a society indifferent to economic justice, there is a profit to be made out of it.

Nevertheless, it would be understood that in the long run differentials in reward must go, for they are unjust: a man is no more responsible for being born with less 'capacity' than his neighbour than he is responsible for being born with a smaller inheritance in wealth under the present dispensation. No man can contribute more than his best, his wholehearted goodwill. The phasing out of the differentials in reward might well be managed fairly painlessly over a long term by sharing that part of the increase in the GWP available for distribution in increased personal incomes in inverse proportion to the worker's share before the rise: the smaller the income, the larger the percentage increment.

How, under libertarian, democratic socialism, do you 'popularize' the administration of justice? For something of the kind is very clearly necessary if the judiciary is to be purged of the taint of bureaucracy, of being a closed corporation guilty of the sin of pride and lamentably wanting in a decent humility towards its employers, the people.

It will here be worth while looking at the juridical system in the Athenian democracy;* it was as democratic as the system of government and the following short introduction will first establish just how democratic that was. The business of government was prepared by a council of five hundred citizens *chosen by lot*, so that every citizen had a good chance (about one in three) of serving on the council for a year at some time in his life. Business was then debated by the Assembly of the People of which every citizen was automatically a member. Thus the people made the laws, and when a decision taken by the Assembly called for

---

* The fact that Athens had slaves and also sub-citizens, the *perioikoi*, is beside our point, since in the society we are designing every human being alive would have full civic rights.

executive action, the Assembly appointed executive officers—generals, ambassadors, etc.—for that specific task. There was no executive branch, no ministers, no such thing as an official leader. And, of course, no bureaucracy. This rigorously democratic system extended to the law courts. The courts were presided over by the archons, but as mere chairmen whose job was to maintain order, not as judges.* All cases were tried by juries who listened to the pleading, gave the verdict and pronounced judgement by voting. Those juries numbered not fewer than 501 citizens and might be as numerous as 2,501 in very important cases such as treason trials. The Athenian law courts really were People's Courts.

Our law code, although it will be weeded out and simplified by socialist jurists with the task of making it possible for citizens to know and understand the law, is bound to be more complex than that of Athens, and much larger. We should doubtless have to retain professional judges learned in the law. A greater measure of democracy in justice could be obtained by empanelling much more numerous juries, say 101 citizens. So, more public work to fill that automation-engendered leisure we are so afraid of. And there are certain vicious practices which would, of course, have to be abolished: the practice of forcing citizens to buy justice—the payment of solicitors and of costs, and the use of paid pleaders. Criminal cases would be 'instructed' by examining magistrates, pleaded on both sides by barristers who were public servants before a judge who was a public servant and decided by juries which, as I have suggested, should be much larger than is now the case. Civil cases would be 'instructed' by technically competent boards, and then pleaded and decided in the same manner. There are very sound objections to the judging of highly technical cases by lay juries—then let the juries in such cases be taken from the appropriate section of society, for there are very much stronger objections to allowing any part of the administration of justice to be taken out of the hands of the democracy. As for legal advice and action, they would be provided by public law offices just as medical advice and treatment would be provided by public clinics.

* This refers to the period when the archonship had become a merely ceremonial office like the British monarchy.

The question of the policing of a democratic society is a difficult one. Again applying the rule that no bureaucracy must be allowed to acquire power unchecked (a rule of even greater importance when it comes to police forces), it is obvious that a wholly professional police force is very undesirable. Such an institution is a bureaucracy of the most dangerous kind since it disposes of force which it is sanctioned to use by the society it serves and, too often, virtually rules. In parliamentary party oligarchies, such as the United States, it is apt to become corrupt, a mere tool of the rich. In state monopoly capitalist countries it is simply the tool of the oppressive bureaucracy. On the other hand, policing a populous modern society, albeit purged of some of the most potent causes of crime by the abolition of private petty commerce, want and gross inequality, is probably no job for unaided amateurs. The anarchist philosophers thought that police forces would not be necessary in a really free society—they were surely too optimistic. The problem then is to democratize the police force. It might be done by having a force composed of professional cadres assisted by a much more numerous body of special constables serving for one year at most: citizens doing their stint of public service.

Politics: well, what does it consist of? Law-making, foreign affairs, the business of the armed forces, the business of the public services, and, in a greater or smaller measure, the management of the economy. Let us see what is left of all this in the kind of socialist society envisaged in this fantasy.

Law-making: there can be no question of a world assembly—it would be unmanageably large or else merely representative and therefore certain to give rise to party and therefore to oligarchy. Moreover, there can be no question of a central world government—nothing could be more contrary to the spirit of the New Socialism and in any case such a government would turn into a tyranny. What about assemblies based on the old, pre-revolutionary national territories? These would be undesirable on several counts. The heirs of national and chauvinistic bourgeois parliaments and neo-bourgeois Supreme Soviets, they would tend to revive nationalism and to be even moderately democratic would have to be unwieldly. There is another consideration: *centralized*

law-making is not compatible with our anti-bureaucratic rule.
This would not be the case if political units were about the size
of our existing local government territories. They might well be
modelled on the Athenian system: a council to prepare the
business of the day, and an assembly, as large as possible, say
of 2,000 citizens, serving each for six months by rota—if the
term were longer there would be a serious danger of parties and
caucuses emerging.

As a basic uniformity in the most important laws is desirable,*
there should be a central council of professional legislators, who
would have to have legal and educational qualifications, to prepare
'projected legislation', under control of an international assembly
of workers chosen by lot. Projects which passed would be printed
and distributed to all local assembly offices and presented to the
assemblies. The results of their voting on the projects would then
be returned to the central office and collated. And the decision
to make the project law, or throw it out, would be dependent
on the voting figures, a substantial majority, say 75/25 being
necessary for acceptance of any project as a universal law.

Foreign affairs: they have disappeared with the national frontiers
and the union of all men in a free society or, in so far as anything
of the kind remains, they are managed within the industrial
federations.

Military affairs: there are none. The armies have vanished with
the economic and political frontiers. At long last the workers of
the world have united and thrown off their chains.†

* Desirable but *not* essential. It would be a great pity to lose the
advantage inherent in the good example set by the gentler and more
enlightened in, for example, the matter of punishment for murder.

† There is no real evidence that the animal man is any more inclined
to make war on his own kind than tigers or voles. There is a great deal of
evidence that war is a by-product of the institution of property, above all
in territorial property. Archaeologists do not find weapons among the
artefacts at the lower levels. In other words, war, at its origin, is simply
robbery with violence. The emergence of the leader who sees the
acquisition of property by the men he leads as personal aggrandizement,
establishes warfare as a way of life. The most ill-educated journalist has
such a pure instinct for this truth, that the popular press represented, for example, World War Two as a struggle between a superman
called Hitler and a superman called Churchill and a superman called
Stalin. But supposing there are no led, no dupes? Were the 'chains' of
the *Communist Manifesto* those which bind men to 'leaders'?

Public services: these are either industrial or professional. In so far as they are industrial—generation and distribution of energy and collection and distribution of water, and collection, processing and recycling or disposal of wastes—they would be managed by the respective industries and would cease to be the business of government at any level. In so far as they are professional—medical, legal and educational services, for example—they should be managed at local assembly level so that they can be controlled democratically.

Finally, management of the economy has also ceased to be the business of 'government' excepting in so far as all industries would be subject to the laws passed in the assemblies. What, in fact, we have now achieved is a very high degree of decentralization and we have taken some very long strides in the direction of that 'withering away of the state' predicted by Marx as the ultimate aim.

Would the system we have sketched work smoothly? Would the assemblies be calm and collected, and deliberate in a dignified manner? Would order be well maintained and law universally respected with only a minimum of recourse to the use of police? No, certainly not. There would, from time to time, be much disorder, breakdowns, dangerous disputes between different interests resulting in hardship and suffering and bitterness. In short, men would remain men, although better fed, less unequal, better educated and therefore more reasonable. But we accept all this; for, quite certainly, the highest possible measure of freedom and genuine democracy are not, never have been, and never will be compatible with seemly order permanently maintained.

NINETEEN

The Millennium
Has Been Cancelled

I wrote the last chapter from the heart. I shall write this one from the head.

Two conditions for the installation of the socialist Millennium are freedom and democracy: the conditions in which freedom and democracy could be realized no longer exist and it is now very unlikely that they ever will. It follows that the Millennium will not happen.

Perhaps it does not matter: those large and generous concepts —freedom, democracy, equality of reward, economic justice— were ever those of a minority of men. The majority will be satisfied with physical comfort; perhaps the coming all-powerful bureaucracy will have the sense to avoid educating all men to the point at which they become aware of the cruel joke of the human condition and, unable to revolt against that and deprived by their intellects of the consolations of religion, revolt against order out of pure bloodymindedness. 'The boys stone the frogs in fun; but the frogs die in earnest,' no doubt, but men can be anaesthetized against the stones until the moment of truth, which is the death agony.

Even supposing the said noble and generous concepts to have become those of the majority, they are now irrelevant to the human condition on this earth, archaic. For they need elbow-room, and we have very little and shall have less and ultimately none. The sooner we give up pretending that they might yet be the moral foundations of a possible world, the better prepared shall we be for the truth of our state—unless, of course, enough of us are really prepared, like Anatole France's New Leftists, to blow up the whole bag of tricks and make a fresh start.

Here is the text: as must once have happened in the cases of the other successful social species—the ants, the bees and the termites—the species *Homo sapiens* has now reached the point at which survival of the species depends on sacrificing the individual's joy in living free.

These are sweeping and dogmatic statements. An attempt must be made to justify them.

That freedom depends on elbow-room should be obvious. Go back a way in time: a hunter in sparsely populated country rich in game and not under a rule of law is as near to freedom as any man could be without exploiting his fellows. He can kill what game he needs, range where he likes, take what materials he may need from whatever the country affords, beat or caress his wife and children as he feels inclined without any danger of interference, praise or curse God according to his mood. But the moment that his country fills up with other hunters attracted by the wealth of game, his freedom is restricted. He cannot range at will but must keep to his own territory or risk his life. He can no longer express his ideas and passions without constraint: the neighbours, having their own ideas and passions, may interfere. Even his freedom to loaf is now restricted, for, the demand for game having risen steeply, he must work harder to get a living. Finally, since neither he nor his neighbours have read Max Stirner and wouldn't think much of him if they did, the clash of personal interests within a limited space makes law necessary. As the anarchist philosophers made so clear, when law comes in at the door, absolute freedom flies out of the window.

Move forward a little in time: there is a way for a man, or a small class of men, to attain even greater freedom than the hunter without neighbours—a certain kind of civilization. Books and the power to read and understand them confer on the reader the freedom of other men's minds; painting and sculpture and music and the power to experience them at will confer on the civilized man the freedom of other men's feelings and insights; sophisticated means of travelling at will confer a freedom on those who can afford them beyond anything the old hunter, confined to his own feet, ever knew. Scientific instruments confer the freedom to penetrate remote space or probe into the nucleus of the atom or the lives of micro-organisms. To support those freedoms our man needs a subservient class to do his hunting-equivalent for him, and to turn raw materials into the articles he needs. Hence the institutions of slavery and wage-slavery. But, in the long run, the slaves and wage-slaves want their freedoms too. And, as they get them, the freedom of the rich man is restricted. The more people there are in a given territory, the less freedom each can enjoy, for every man's freedom in such conditions is restricted by the next man's. Out of this comes a social law: the measure of freedom available to the individual is in inverse proportion to population density.

One of the promises of scientific progress, the application of advanced technology to industry, was that it would liberate man from both drudgery and hunger and squalor. It would restore the primal freedom but with an immensely broader range both physical and intellectual. It would enable him to get more reward for less work. It might have done so effectively under some such regime as I imagined in Chapter Eighteen. It has failed to do so excepting on a limited scale and locally, in the advanced parts of the world, largely because the same kind of scientific progress as that which worked to our advantage in raising production worked against us by removing the two most effective controls of population growth, famine and a high infant mortality rate. Under neither corporation capitalism, state capitalism nor socialism can science save us from the same miseries which afflicted our ancestors, given that the hundreds of millions of people in the world who now go short are no longer willing to do so, unless we solve the problem of population control. The technical problem has been solved; there are several effective means of contraception. The psychological problem has not been solved. Women want children—so do many men. We can stabilize the world population by restricting births to two children per couple. We can only do so by the imposition of laws or the use of economic sanctions. Such imposition is a denial of liberty of the most serious kind. Without liberty there can be no socialism: under socialism the people would have to impose the discipline of restricted fecundity on themselves, voluntarily and effectively. I cannot contrive to believe that they would do so. As I have said, the conditions for liberty, and therefore for socialism, millenary socialism, no longer exist. For suppose we recoil from imposing restrictions on fecundity, then our increasing numbers will entail progressive contraction of 'freedom'. Hell, as Baudelaire said, is other people.

I will try to demonstrate the proposition that freedom necessarily declines as population rises with two cases in point, one social, the other political.

When the motor-car was invented it conferred on the men who could afford it an unprecedented measure of freedom of movement. As motor-cars were cheapened and salaries and wages rose and more and more people could afford to buy cars and did so, it became necessary to restrict that freedom. Speed limits had to be imposed, parking restrictions introduced, highway codes made a part of the law. The freedom of movement of the pedestrian was more and more restricted, with death or mutilation as the penalty for disobedience to the regulations. Taxes had to be levied to build new roads, restricting our freedom to spend money on what we wanted, and the townsman was denied the freedom to breathe clean air and the freedom to enjoy peace and quiet. In the extreme case we are even denied the freedom to build our cities as we should like them—they must be built to satisfy the motor-car. Meanwhile even the original extra freedom of movement was being eroded away and is now much reduced, as a glance at any traffic jam, or any overcrowded motorway will prove.

Now the political case in point. As I have tried to show, millenary socialism is not compatible with any political regime short of absolute, direct and universal democracy. Direct democracy is unworkable where the number of people in the group in question —community, municipality, society or industrial plant—exceeds a few tens of thousands. Could the population of London or Moscow or Tokyo, let alone that of whole great nations, all participate effectively in a political assembly, each man having his say if he wanted it, before recording his vote? The alternative is decentralization down to political units of a manageable size. Does anyone believe that that is really on the cards? The second best is representative assemblies; but not only were they always incompatible with the real democracy, they must be increasingly so as the technological bureaucracy, the only kind capable of managing modern societies with their enormous numbers, grows

stronger and stronger in proportion to the magnitude and growing complexity of its task.

Demographically we are faced by three alternative prospects:
(*i*) We fail to control population growth and are exterminated by
a combination of starvation and war over food supplies. (*ii*) We
fail to control population growth and, after the war over food
supplies, there are victorious survivors not too numerous to make
it worth while trying to live under some such rational system as
I described in the last chapter, numerous enough to make such
a system economically workable. They might have a chance if
the food war had not destroyed earth's viability as a home for
mankind and their own capacity to behave like civilized men
and not like fear-and-hate-crazed savages. (*iii*) We succeed in
stabilizing the world's population at a figure which the planet
can support.

I am going to dismiss the first alternative because it is an
insupportable prospect which, if realized, leaves nothing to say
except that man will have lived in vain, and the second because
it is in the highest degree improbable. The third alternative is
the prospect before us.

It would be foolish optimism to suppose that we shall be able
to check population growth short of the maximum figure which
the planet can support. Nobody knows what that figure will be,
but certainly not below ten thousand millions. To sustain such
a population, fed, housed, clad and at peace, will certainly require
the most rigorous management and austere rationing of resources,
very strict rules touching the nature, qualities and quantities of
production, and very firm police control of conduct. There is
only one conceivable kind of government which could manage
such a world: government by a highly trained technological
bureaucracy. Such a government is not only utterly incompatible
with socialism—though it will, of course, be applying the socialist economic method since no other could possibly work—but
even with any considerable measure of freedom, of the kind we
still have for the time being, under the representative systems of
parliamentarianism.

The bureaucrats, the managers, the *apparatchiki* who will manage that populous world are already with us, of course, creating the managerial society under corporation capitalism and trying to improve its yield under state monopoly capitalism, laughingly known as 'communism'. They are already in control of the communist half of the world, and if their performance, from the point of view of the workers, the people, has not been brilliant, it will improve as productivity rises and as the education of the next generation of bureaucrats trained in the sophisticated techniques of economic prediction and management comes into power.

Corporation monopoly capitalism has still to obtain a sufficient measure of social and political control to make itself as efficient as it could be. The four hundred great corporations which are effectively international will grow fewer and larger. They have already contrived means to transcend those absurd anachronisms, national frontiers; but they still have some way to go before they can prevent national parliamentary governments from making a nuisance of themselves and obstructing the way to that full adoption of the crypto-socialist economic method which will make their empire indistinguishable from that of the state monopoly capitalist bureaucrats. But they will have a powerful ally in the trade union movement, which is also a bureaucracy.

For some time the party game which gives the illusion of democracy in the parliamentary government countries has been a game of snap between a Tweedleheath and a Tweedlewilson, a Tweedlenixon and a Tweedlemcgovern. This will become increasingly so; meanwhile the important decisions will be taken by the managers of the greater and greater/fewer and fewer corporations—whether 'owned' by shareholders or states is entirely beside any possible point—in association with the managers of greater and greater/fewer and fewer trades unions. I do not for a moment suggest that the allied (ultimately united?) corporation and trade union bureaucracies will formally take over the apparatus of the State and that voting for representatives, parliaments, executives, presidents and, as the kids would say, all that jazz, will disappear. When parliament became the real holder of power in England, the monarchy did not vanish; the Crown remained as the symbol of national authority. Even in Athens, the democracy did not dispense with the kings; they had their uses. The Roman imperial bureaucracy which, created by Augustus, successfully ran the enormous Roman empire for five centuries, was careful to retain the Senate as a 'front'. The forms will still be respected under the coming bureaucracy. It will be supranational, but the old, formal, national government apparatus will still have its uses: it will pass those laws, for example, dictated as necessary by the economic bosses, like the law to impose family limitation, and it will be the agency responsible for the distribution of social security charity to those outside the economic system and impoverished by its operations.

There will be no *Nineteen Eighty-Four*: it will no more come to pass than the Millennium will come to pass. Under both state monopoly capitalism and corporation monopoly capitalism, economies scientifically managed with the aid of increasingly sophisticated electronic gear by bureaucrats more and more precisely trained for their work should make it possible to give the people, kept out of mischief by sport, television entertainment, gambling, religion, drugs and the illusion of democratic government through national assemblies, a sufficiently high level of consumption in return for their labour and their obedience. The bureaucrat is not a fool: why should he bring about the conditions of drab hardship most likely to provoke revolt against his rule? He is not malignant, he is a man of goodwill, so why should he want to do so? An all-powerful tyrant may be mentally sick and enjoy inflicting suffering on the greatest possible number of people. Did not Caligula wish that the Romans had but one throat? Elias Canetti has suggested that the subconscious aim of the classical 'Leader' is to be the sole surviving male triumphant upon a heap of corpses—all the other males.* But large committees of the most highly educated and trained men in the community are hardly likely to go mad *en masse*.

The Third World will be no problem: the worst aspects and consequences of its exploitation, the looting of its wealth in resources by private capital backed by national military force, are disappearing as nationalist governments either expropriate or come to terms with the imperialists on one side or the other. The same 'laws' which promote bureaucratic rule in the two imperialist blocks must operate also in the Third World and it is

* *Crowds v. Power.*

of no great importance whether the peoples of Latin America, Africa and Asia opt for state monopoly capitalism or corporation monopoly capitalism; like us they will be born, fed, taught, married, clad, housed, medicated, entertained and at last buried by the bureaucracy.

In short, Aldous Huxley's *Brave New World* is a truer vision than George Orwell's *Nineteen Eighty-Four*. But his biologically contrived caste system will not be necessary. The lesson of the first three quarters of the 20th century is that we are no longer interested in noble visions: we are interested in physical well-being which a competent bureaucracy should be able to provide. It is not necessary to deform men physically and mentally to prevent them revolting—it is only necessary to make them comfortable and keep them amused. The use by the bureaucracies of socialist economics to ensure that the worker's share of the surplus product is a fair one and the avoidance of ostentation of wealth by the bureaucracy, will together remove the most serious of the greed-provoking irritants; and a reasonable measure of superiority of reward for superior services rendered to the community will be tolerated provided that popular representative assemblies be maintained to sustain the illusion of democracy.

Is there, in all this, even a gleam of hope for the noble vision of a world of free and equal men managing their own society by virtue, free from the oppression of authority and of formal law? The bureaucracy will be massively stable and provocation to destroy its power will be absent. There is, perhaps, one thing. Some Frenchman once said that the most alarming words which those responsible for law and order in his country could hear during a period of peace and plenty are *La France s'ennuie*. It would be odd indeed if we, having failed to install the socialist Millennium under the provocations of theft of what is our own, of hunger, squalor, humiliation and the fear of war, did it to save ourselves from boredom.

But it is not very likely.

Index

Russia—*cont.*
munist Party, 178, 179, 206; Council of People's Commissars, 74, 171; cultural revolution, 181, 241; Duma, 160, 162; economic situation, 225, 227; February revolution, 162; Five Year Plans, 184; Imperial Fleet, 158; land and liberty, 156; Mensheviks, 160, 161, 163, 167, 168, 170, 171; Military Revolutionary Committee, 170, 171; Narodniki, 155, 156; new economic policy, 174, 184; October Manifesto, 158; October revolution, 131, 148, 150, 167, 171, 183; People's Will, 156; Populist movements, 59, 73, 155; Red Army, 136, 176; revolution, 146, 217, 249; revolution 1905, 158, 159, revolutionaries, 133; Revolutionary Insurrectionary Army, 136, 137; Social-Democratic Party, 114, 119, 133, 175; socialism, 154; Socialist-Revolutionary Party, 135, 156, 157, 160, 163, 167-171, 177; South Russia Workers' Union, 165; syndicalism, 148; terrorism, 156; Tsar Alexander II, 59, 156; Tsar Nicholas II, 114, 157-163; Tsarism, 59, 62, 89, 135; Tshushima battle, 158; White Guard, 173; Workers' Councils, 254
Rutenberg, 46

Sagra, Ramon de la, 126
Saint-Simon, Claude de, 20-23, 27, 29, 31, 36, 43, 60
Salazar, Dr, 193, 198
Saltpetre, 14
Salt industry, 15
Sanjuro, General, 197, 199
Sartre, Jean-Paul, 221
Scandinavia, 230
Sergei, Grand Duke, 157
Service industries, 15
Shaw, 106
Shelley, Percy Bysshe, 82
Shipbuilding, 14, 16
Silver, 18
Sismondi, 31
Social-Democracy, 107, 109, 112, 116-122, 153, 192, 200, 230, 231, 239, 249, 251-254

Social Democracy, International Alliance of, 91
Social-Democratic Federation, 113
Social philosophers, 17, 18
Socialism, 3, 5, 10, 11, 13, 19, 21, 27, 31, 33, 35-37, 41, 66, 80, 93, 107, 129, 173, 189, 201, 224, 232, 240; *see also* under Countries; economic, 231; Guild, 150; Libertarian, 89, 178, 246, 258; Parliamentary, 94; scientific, 20
Socialist League, 114
Socialist planning, 78
Socialist thought, 9
Sorel, Georges, 145
Sosa, Yon, 246
South Africa, 230, 238; and Sharpeville, 243
Spain, 230; Alfonso XII, 129; anarchism, 92, 122, 125, 126, 130, 131; anarcho-syndicalism, 147; civil war, 197-201; Communist Party, 132, 198, 200; Confederacion Nacional del Trabajo, 131, 148; Fascism, 197; federalists, 126, 127, 128; general strike 1902, 147; Popular Front, 196; Prince Amadeus, 127; Queen Isabella, 127; Social-Democrats, 115; Solidaridad obrera, 148
Spence, Thomas, 9
Spinning, 15
Spinoza, 3
Staël, Madame de, 20
Stalin, 12, 17, 21, 40, 68, 135, 173, 176-184, 190, 192, 201, 202, 209-211, 215, 226, 227
State education, 78
Steam-engine, 16
Steam-power, 16
Steel-mills, 15
Stendhal, 29
Stirner, Max, 96, 105
Strauss, 49
Strikes, 62
Sugar refining, 14
Sun Yat-sen 205, 206, 209
Supply, theory of, 104
Sweden: Social Democracy, 112, 120, 195; Sveriges Arbetares Central, 151; syndicalism, 151; trades unions, 151
Switzerland, 57, 71, 92; Social-